THE LIFE OF

EDWARD FITZGERALD

'THE PHILOSOPHER' PORTRAIT

'THE STATESMAN' PORTRAIT

EDWARD FITZGERALD

THE LIFE OF
EDWARD FITZGERALD

BY

THOMAS WRIGHT

AUTHOR OF 'THE LIFE OF WILLIAM COWPER,' ETC.

WITH FIFTY-SIX PLATES

TWO VOLUMES

VOL. I.

LONDON
GRANT RICHARDS
1904

Republished 1971
Scholarly Press, Inc., 22929 Industrial Drive East
St. Clair Shores, Michigan 48080

Library of Congress Catalog Card Number: 70-108556
ISBN 0-403-00254-0

4/72

THIS WORK

IS DEDICATED, BY KIND PERMISSION,

TO

THE REV. E. KENWORTHY BROWNE

RECTOR OF NORTH STONEHAM, HANTS,

SON OF EDWARD FITZGERALD'S

GREATEST FRIEND

PREFACE

Whatever may be the merits or demerits of the following biography, I should like to draw special attention to the fact that it contains a very large amount of new information about FitzGerald, his particular friends and his works. There is, indeed, something new on almost every page.

By many, no doubt, my discovery of the origin of 'Euphranor,' and the circumstances in which it was written, will be regarded as one of the most interesting revelations of the work.

Then the numerous extracts from the large number of unpublished letters placed in my hands throw all sorts of unexpected lights on FitzGerald and his circle. These letters are as follows:—

(1) About fifty written by FitzGerald to Mrs. W. Kenworthy Browne. They cover a period extending from 1840 to 1875, and are important because they contain many references to the relations between FitzGerald and his wife.

(2) About fifty written by FitzGerald to Joseph Fletcher ('Posh'), of which many are in my own possession. Of the hundred letters above referred to not a word has hitherto been published.

(3) Several letters written by FitzGerald to Horace Basham.

(4) A letter (18th June 1852) in the British Museum.

(5) *Some unpublished letters written to Mr. Herman Biddell.*

I have also been able to use a large number of unpublished letters written to FitzGerald and others by Thackeray, Mrs. FitzGerald, W. Kenworthy Browne, Spedding, Captain Addington, Rev. George Crabbe, Miss Crabbe, and other friends of FitzGerald.

Of intense interest is the unpublished manuscript, containing, in FitzGerald's handwriting, word-pictures of his principal friends—Alfred Tennyson, Thackeray, W. Kenworthy Browne, Edgeworth, Morton, Malkin, and Bernard Barton among them. From this I have quoted largely.

I have also set down some thirty hitherto unrecorded anecdotes of FitzGerald, and a number of notes written by him in books, the most important being those in copies of 'Godefridus,' 'Euphranor,' and Baedeker's 'Manual of Conversation,' the last containing a reference to a hitherto unrecorded visit of FitzGerald's to Germany.

It is a curious fact that the great central circumstance of FitzGerald's life, his friendship for W. Kenworthy Browne, one of the most remarkable friendships in the history of literature, has hitherto been hardly mentioned. Take up any work you will relating to FitzGerald, and there will be found nothing about it beyond the few references in the published letters. I have laid bare the whole story. The close connection between FitzGerald and his brother John and the Bedford evangelist, the Rev. T. R. Matthews, has also hitherto been unsuspected. That story I have also completely unfolded.

Other hitherto unknown facts relating to FitzGerald here recorded are:—(1) Scores of interesting particulars relating to the friendships of FitzGerald with Squire Jenny, Major Moor, Rev. W. Monkhouse, Harry Dyott Boulton, Captain Addington, Miss Maude, Miss Lynn, 'Mademoiselle,' Horace Basham, Joseph Fletcher ('Posh'), and Newson. (2) Many interesting particulars about the 'Meum and Tuum' (FitzGerald's lugger), 'The Scandal' (FitzGerald's yacht), and 'The Bethel' at Lowestoft. (3) The incident of the drive with Dickens. (4) The Bredfield School episode. (5) FitzGerald's courtship of Miss Crabbe. (6) Facts relating to his connection with Naseby, and his favourite Bedfordshire villages. (7) His opinions on cremation and other subjects. (8) The identification of 'The Three Tuns' at Chesterton, which was the scene of 'Euphranor.' (9) The identification of W. K. Browne as Pendennis.

Then, too, I have rescued from a forgotten annual, 'The Keepsake,' FitzGerald's two poems 'The Old Beau' and 'The Merchant's Daughter.'

In short, I have been successful beyond my utmost expectations, and for the simple reason that nobody before had taken the trouble to make exhaustive investigations.

As it is now twenty years since the death of Edward FitzGerald, I do not think an apology need be made for recording any of the facts here given. His foibles and faults, as well as his virtues, are faithfully put before the reader, and to objectors (and no biography was ever written without displeasing somebody) I would offer a remark made to me by one of FitzGerald's most intimate friends, 'We have a right,' said he, 'to enjoy the memory of great men.'

Very soon after commencing the study of Edward FitzGerald, I discovered the very great resemblance in character between him and his brother John, and that, their *lives being much mixed up, some account of John FitzGerald would be necessary to a complete understanding of Edward. In some respects the brothers were even ridiculously alike. John was a public character, and well known in every village of Suffolk and in many parts of Bedfordshire and Northamptonshire twenty years before Edward's name was heard of, and his eccentricities were common talk in religious circles. Then he has been dead nearly thirty years. I do not think there is—I trust there is not—anything in these pages that could give pain to any living person.*

Of very great value, too, are the illustrations—fifty-six in number. Many of these are reproductions from rare prints and photographs, and hitherto inaccessible oil paintings. Of particular interest, for example, are the various portraits of W. Kenworthy Browne, including one by Thackeray and one by Lawrence; the pictures of Boulge Hall with the volunteers, and Naseby Woolleys; the silhouette of the Rev. T. R. Matthews; the pictures of 'The Scandal' and the 'Meum and Tuum,' and the portraits of Squire Jenny, Major Moor, John FitzGerald, and Miss Lynn. Of these fifty-six pictures only nine or ten have previously been seen by the public.

The origin of this work is as follows:—

Edward FitzGerald, as everybody knows who has studied the published letters, was associated intimately with two, and only two, English districts, namely the Suffolk sea-board and Bedfordshire—or, to be more accurate, that belt of country extending from Baldock (in Herts) and Luton to Naseby and Kettering, and including Bedfordshire, the northern tip of Bucks and Northants.

Living in the latter district, having all my life been

connected with Bedford, having spent as much time as FitzGerald himself rambling among his Bedfordshire and Northamptonshire villages, it was very natural that I should be interested in him.

Perhaps fewer facts have been recorded about Edward FitzGerald than of any other great modern English writer. It has hitherto been understood that the reason for this scarcity of biographical matter was that there were no materials. In view of the circumstance that FitzGerald was born so recently as 1809, and died so recently as 1883, I came to the conclusion that while those biographical materials had not been made public, they must somewhere exist, and accordingly I set about the collection of them, though without any definite idea as to the use I should put them to.

In my researches I had the advantage of assistance from the late Mr. George Hurst of Bedford, and several other gentlemen who had information to impart and anecdotes to tell respecting FitzGerald, FitzGerald's brother John, Matthews the preacher, and other personages.

In the spring of 1901, when visiting a friend, I happened in the course of conversation to observe that, my edition of 'Cowper's Letters' being ready for the press, I had nothing literary in hand. A few minutes later, the talk having turned to Bedford and my FitzGerald collection, my friend said, 'Why not write "The Life of Edward Fitz-Gerald"? You ought to be very much obliged to me for the suggestion.'

I at once resolved to attempt the task, provided only that I could enlist the sympathies of three persons, namely Mr. Aldis Wright, FitzGerald's literary executor; Professor E. B. Cowell; and the Rev. E. Kenworthy Browne, son of

FitzGerald's greatest friend. I presently wrote to Mr. Wright and Professor Cowell regarding my project, and both replied in terms of extreme kindness. A little later I called on Mr. Wright at Cambridge. He showed me all his FitzGerald treasures, including the famous 'small tin box'[1] and its contents, allowed me to take what notes I liked, permitted me to copy some letters from FitzGerald's friends, and one from Mrs. FitzGerald, and gave me a number of useful hints. He then introduced me to Professor Cowell, who furnished me with much valuable information, most of which I have been able to use in these pages. Both he and Professor Cowell helped me subsequently by letter.

In response to the invitation of the Rev. E. Kenworthy Browne, I then went to spend a few days at North Stoneham Rectory, in Hants. Mr. Browne placed in my hands a large number of unpublished letters written by FitzGerald, several other valuable manuscripts connected with the subject, and a number of interesting pictures that had never previously been used. The manuscripts which I had not time to copy he courteously allowed me to bring away.

To Mr. Browne's sister, Mrs. Staunton-Wing of FitzHead Court, Taunton, I am indebted for the loan of the copy of 'Godefridus' presented to her father by FitzGerald (see chapter vi.); and to his brother, Captain Gerald E. Kenworthy Browne, FitzGerald's godson, for the portrait of 'The Bloody Warrior' at Aldershot.

Besides the visits to North Stoneham and Cambridge, I made four other journeys in order to converse with persons who had known FitzGerald, going three times into Suffolk and Norfolk (March, July, and October 1902), and once to

---

[1] See Mr. Wright's preface to *FitzGerald's Letters*.

PREFACE

Naseby. From first to last I must have interviewed two hundred persons, but to the following I am most indebted:—

Miss Mary Lynn of Aldeburgh, playmate of FitzGerald's boyhood, and friend of his declining years. She gave me various information, told me several anecdotes, and allowed me to take from her book of water-colour paintings two views to illustrate this work.

Mrs. White of Boulge Hall. To Mrs. White, whose guest I was for two days in August 1902, Miss Margaret White and Miss Agnes White, I am indebted not only for hospitality at Boulge Hall, but in many other ways; and I have to thank Mr. Eaton White for a number of the photographs used in this work.

Mrs. White, Bredfield House. Mrs. White of Bredfield House, where FitzGerald was born, showed me much kindness when I called on her, and assisted me with reminiscences and anecdotes.

Mr. Alfred Smith of Rendlesham, with whom I spent two days at Lowestoft, had stories to tell me of a friendship with FitzGerald that had lasted forty years.

Mr. Herman Biddell, who showed me many original letters written by FitzGerald, and some FitzGerald relics.

Joseph Fletcher, 'Posh,' FitzGerald's 'great man,' ideal sailor, and hero. I had many conversations with him at Lowestoft.

Miss Sarah Thornton, the blind lady to whom John FitzGerald was so kind, and who was also well acquainted with Edward FitzGerald.

I should also like to tender my sincere thanks to the following:—

Rev. Basil Airy, Vicar of St. John's, Torquay (son of FitzGerald's friend).
Mrs. Agutter, Goldington, Beds.
Mr. Oliver Aldis, Beccles.
Rev. H. B. Allen, Colmworth, Beds.
Mrs. Thomas Allen.
Mr. George Barker, Wickham Market.
Mrs. Barlow, Hasketon.
Mrs. Isaac Berry, Woodbridge.
Miss Anna Biddell, Ipswich.
Mr. Cable, Aldeburgh.
Mrs. Callis, Grammar School, Bury St. Edmunds.
Miss Ellen Churchyard, Woodbridge (daughter of FitzGerald's friend).
Mr. J. L. Clemence, J.P., 14 Marine Parade, Lowestoft.
Mr. William Colby, 'Dickymilk,' who knew FitzGerald for fifty years. He lived at Lowestoft, and was alive in 1902.
Major Doughty, Aldeburgh.
Mr. Elijah Edwards, 62 Carlton Road, Lowestoft.
Mrs. FitzGerald, widow of FitzGerald's nephew Maurice.
Mr. Fosdyke, Woodbridge.
Mr. V. Galloway, Bookseller, Cambridge.
Mr. Charles Ganz, Aldeburgh.
Mr. John Green, Aldeburgh.
Mrs. R. M. Grier (Grace Allen), daughter of Archdeacon Allen, FitzGerald's friend.
Mr. Edward Haines, Naseby.
Mr. Halford, Naseby.
Mr. W. M. Harvey, Goldington Hall, Beds.
Mrs. Hogben, The High School for Girls, Bury St. Edmunds, formerly King Edward VI.'s Grammar School.
Mr. Isaac Joyce, 59 Bower Road, Bedford.
Rev. John Kerrich, FitzGerald's nephew.
Miss Sarah Linnet, Naseby.
Mr. John Loder, Woodbridge.
Mr. William Marjoram, Woodbridge.

PREFACE

Mr. Marjoram, Lowestoft.
Rev. R. A. L. Nunns, Wherstead.
Mr. Henry Ogle, The Library, Ipswich.
Rev. J. H. Orpen, Rector of Burton-in-Rhos, Pembrokeshire.
Mrs. Pytches, 'Little Grange,' Woodbridge.
Mr. J. A. Reid, Cutcliff Grove, Bedford.
Mrs. Jane Ringrose, Naseby.
Mrs. Rogers, Woodbridge.
Mrs. John Rolls, Bedford.
Mr. Gerald Smith, Great Bealings.
Miss Spalding, daughter of FitzGerald's friend, Mr. Frederick Spalding.
Mr. A. Stebbings, Lowestoft.
Mr. W. Tams, 18 Priory Street, Huntingdon Road, Cambridge.
Rev. R. C. Thursfield, Naseby Vicarage.
Mr. and Mrs. Vincent Redstone, Woodbridge.
Mr. K. H. Watts, King Edward VI.'s Grammar School, Bury St. Edmunds.
Mr. William Woodward Welton, Farlingay Hall, Woodbridge.
Mr. Welton, Photographer, Woodbridge.

While the 'Life' is in the main founded on unpublished material, I have not neglected to make full use of all the published works relating to the subject, and the more important magazine articles. My principal indebtedness is to the various works, relative to FitzGerald, published by Messrs. Macmillan; and, thanks to the kindness of Mr. Aldis Wright and the generous permission of Messrs. Macmillan, I have been able to make a number of extracts of considerable length. Then I have to thank Mrs. R. M. Grier for the use of the portrait of her father, Archdeacon Allen, which appeared originally in Mr. Grier's work, 'The Life of Archdeacon Allen.' The following is a fairly complete list of the books and magazine articles that have been laid under contribution :—

Allen (*Archdeacon*), *Life of.* By R. M. Grier (*Rivingtons*).
Arbuthnot (*F. F.*). *Persian Portraits* (*Quaritch*).
Barton (*Lucy*). *Bible Letters*, 1831.
Barton (*Bernard*). *Household Verses*, 1845.
Blackwood's Edinburgh Magazine, November 1889.
Colvin (*Sidney*). *Magazine of Art*, 1885—'East Suffolk Memories.'
Contemporary Review, March 1876. Article by H. Schutz Wilson.
Carlyle's Works (*Ashburton Edition*).
Dutt, W. A. *Highways and Byeways in East Anglia.*
Fraser's Magazine, June 1870.
    „   „   May 1879—'The True Omar Khayyam.' By Jessie E. Cadell.
FitzGerald, *The Letters and Literary Remains of.* 3 vols. Edited by Mr. Aldis Wright. (*Macmillan.*)
    „   *Letters of.* 2 vols. 1894. (*Macmillan.*)
    „   *Letters to Fanny Kemble.* 1895. (*Bentley.*)
    „   *More Letters of Edward FitzGerald.* 1901. (*Macmillan.*)
    „   *Sea Words and Phrases*, 1869 and 1870. (*Samuel Tymms, Lowestoft.*)
    „   *Miscellanies.* (*Macmillan.*)
Gentleman's Magazine, 1830 to 1850.
Glyde (*John*). *The Life of Edward FitzGerald.* (*Pearson.*)
Groome (*Francis Hindes*). *Two Suffolk Friends.* (*Blackwood.*)
Heron-Allen's edition of the *Rubaiyat.* (*H. S. Nichols.*)
Houghton (*Life of Lord*). By Sir Wemyss Reid.
Idler, The, July 1900. 'The Suffolk Homes of Edward FitzGerald.'
James (*Henry*). 'Frances Anne Kemble.' *Temple Bar*, April 1893.
Kemble (*Frances A.*)—
    Record of a Girlhood (1809-1834). 3 vols. 1878.
    Records of Later Life (1834-1848). 3 vols. 1882.
    Further Records (1848-1883). 2 vols. 1890.
Lady's Magazine, The, 1822. 'Dramatic Intelligence.'
Layard. *Life of Charles Keene.* (*S. Low and Co.*)

'*Letters of a Man of Leisure.*' *Temple Bar, January* 1893.
Literature, 28*th September* 1901.
London Society, May 1866. '*The London Opera Directors.*'
Macmillan's Magazine, November 1887. *Article by H. G. Keene.*
Monckton Milnes (Lord Houghton). Temple Bar, vol. xcii.
Moor (Major). Suffolk Words.
Pollock (Sir Frederick). Personal Reminiscences. (Macmillan.)
Prideaux (Colonel W. F.). Notes for a Bibliography of Edward FitzGerald. (Frank Hollings.)
Shorter, Clement. Article on '*The Omar Khayyam Club*' *in Great Thoughts.*
Thackeray. Biographical Edition of the Works of W. M. Thackeray, with Introductions by his daughter, Anne Ritchie. 13 *vols.*
Temple Bar, 1889, *May.* '*The Prototypes of Thackeray's Characters.*'
  ,,   ,, 1893, *January.* '*Letters of a Man of Leisure.*'
  ,,   ,, 1893, *April.* '*Frances Anne Kemble.*'
Tennyson (Lord). Life of Lord Tennyson.
Two Suffolk Friends (with corrections made in margin by Mr. J. Loder).
Wright (Mr. Aldis). See FitzGerald.
Zincke (Rev. F. Barham), '*Wherstead.*'

THOMAS WRIGHT.

b

CONTENTS OF VOLUME I

BOOK I: BREDFIELD AND BURY SCHOOL

Sixteen Years (31st March 1809-1825).

CHAPTER I

THE WHITE HOUSE AND THE RED HOUSE

31st March 1809—1825

	PAGE
1. The White House and the Little Owl,	29
2. FitzGerald's Parents and the Kembles,	30
3. The Red House,	37
4. Naseby Woolleys,	41
5. Major Moor,	44
6. Woodbridge,	48
7. In France. The Rodez Murder,	50
8. Aldeburgh. Mary Lynn,	52
9. The Poet Crabbe,	53
10. The Haymarket Theatre,	56
11. At Bury, 1821. Peter's Escapade,	59
12. The Naseby Obelisk,	65
13. Bernard Barton,	65
14. The Maple's Head,	67

BOOK II: WHERSTEAD

Ten Years (1825-1835).

CHAPTER II

WHERSTEAD LODGE

1825—November 1830.

15. Wherstead and Ipswich,	71
16. At Cambridge, 1826-1830,	75
17. The 'Three Tuns' at Chesterton,	82
18. The Two Antipholuses,	85
19. Mrs. Kerrich, Dr. Crowfoot, Le Bon Pasteur, Torrijos,	86

CHAPTER III

NASEBY AND TENBY

November 1830—May 1834.

20. At Naseby. The Meadows in Spring,	92
21. Lines on Will Thackeray,	95
22. Perry Nursey and Newton Shawe,	96

	PAGE
23. Matthews and his Trumpet,	96
24. Tenby and the Allens, 1832,	100
25. William Kenworthy Browne,	104
26. 'Paradise-making,'	107
27. At Lowestoft, 1831,	108
28. Death of the poet Crabbe, 3rd February 1832,	111
29. Canst thou, my Clora,	111
30. W. B. Donne. Castle Irwell,	113
31. Word Portraits,	114
32. Vegetarianism, October 1833,	115
33. The Museum Book, 15th October 1833,	116
34. Death of Anne Allen,	117

CHAPTER IV

HARP AND LUTE

May 1834—July 1835.

35. Genius for concentrating,	119
36. Cauldwell House, Bedford. Frank Edgeworth,	120
37. 'The Old Beau,' 1834,	124
38. In the Lake Country,	126
39. Farewell to Wherstead,	129

BOOK III: BOULGE

Eighteen Years (July 1835-1853).

CHAPTER V

BOULGE HALL

July 1835—August 1838

40. Boulge Hall,	133
41. George Crabbe the Second,	138
42. Newton and Cowper,	139
43. The Cottage at Boulge, April 1837,	142
44. Bernard Barton and his daughter Lucy,	147

CHAPTER VI

CHIEFLY BEDFORD

August 1838—June 1841.

45. 'Flowing Rivers full of Fishes.' 'The Falcon' at Bletsoe, August 1838,	152
46. *Godefridus* and Keysoe,	154
47. At Lowestoft with Browne,	161
48. Samuel Lawrence and Geldestone,	162
49. In Love with Miss Caroline Crabbe. 'Bredfield Hall,' 1839,	163
50. In Ireland with W. K. Browne, October 1839,	165
51. At Geldestone. J. H. Newman, April 1840,	166
52. 'Chronomoros,'	167

CONTENTS

CHAPTER VII

NASEBY EXCAVATIONS

July 1841—July 1844.

	PAGE
53. In Ireland again, July 1841. The Edgeworths,	169
54. Strada del Obelisco. A Drive with Dickens,	170
55. Frederick Tennyson; Pierce Morton; and Carlyle's *Hero-Worship*,	173
56. In London, Spring 1842,	174
57. At Bedford, Yardley Hastings, and Castle Ashby, August 1842,	175
58. Carlyle in a 'Branglemess.' Naseby Excavations,	176
59. In Ireland again,	182

CHAPTER VIII

REV. T. R. MATTHEWS

April 1844—September 1845.

60. The Bromham Road Chapel,	187
61. Browne's Marriage, 30th July 1844,	188
62. Goldington Hall. 'The Bloody Warrior,'	193
63. Andalusia's Marriage, August 1844,	202
64. Bernard Barton's eighth volume. 'Le petit Churchyard,'	205
65. Death of Matthews, 4th September 1845,	206

CHAPTER IX

E. B. COWELL

October 1845—1853.

66. A Peep at the Hall Farm, 1846,	214
67. The Wits of Woodbridge,	215
68. E. B. Cowell,	217
69. Death of Edgeworth, 12th October 1846,	219
70. The 'Squire' Papers. Kemble at Cassiobury,	220
71. Cowell's Marriage,	222
72. FitzGerald as a Teacher of the Bible,	222
73. Death of Major Moor and Bernard Barton,	224
74. The Cottage at Bramford. Spedding's Forehead,	230
75. Cowell goes to Oxford,	236
76. *Euphranor*,	237
77. Alfred Smith, Boulge Reader,	240
78. Bankruptcy of FitzGerald's father,	241
79. Death of Squire Jenny, 1851,	243
80. Fanny Kemble at Woodbridge. Miss Maude,	244
81. A Visit to Archdeacon Allen, February 1852,	246
82. Death of FitzGerald's father, 18th March 1852,	247
83. *Polonius*, 1852,	248
84. At Goldington Hall. On Song-Making,	250
85. Six Plays of Calderon published, 1853,	252

BOOK IV: FARLINGAY

Seven Years (December 1853—November 1860).

CHAPTER X

PERSIAN STUDIES

1853—1855.

	PAGE
86. Farlingay,	259
87. Persian Studies,	260
88. *Salaman and Absal* published, 1856,	266
89. With the Cowells at Oxford. Death of FitzGerald's mother, January 30, 1855,	269
90. Carlyle at Farlingay, 8th to 18th August 1855,	271

CHAPTER XI

OMAR KHAYYAM

91. Omar Khayyam,	276
92. The two Theories,	277
93. Omar's Poem,	281
94. Omar's Personality,	281
95. 'Heart's Desire,'	283
96. The Inconsistencies of Omar,	285
97. Omar's attitude towards God,	285
98. Goldington Hall. FitzGerald in Germany, June 1856,	288
99. Cowell goes to India, Aug. 1856. Reminiscences of Bramford,	291

CHAPTER XII

SIX MONTHS OF WEDDED LIFE

(4th November 1856—May 1857).

100. A Week at Donne's. George Borrow,	296
101. FitzGerald's Marriage, 4th November 1856,	297
102. The Birds' 'Pilgrim's Progress,'	302
103. The Paddock at Goldington Hall. Baldock 'Black Horse.' The Separation,	305
104. The 'Far niente' life again,	312

CHAPTER XIII

GOLDINGTON

(May 1857—March 1859).

105. Death of George Crabbe the Second	315
106. Goldington Bury, 23rd September 1858,	319
107. Death of W. Kenworthy Browne, 30th March 1859,	320

LIST OF PLATES IN VOLUME I

PLATE

I.	EDWARD FITZGERALD,	*Frontispiece*
II.	BREDFIELD HOUSE AND NASEBY WOOLLEYS,	27
III.	FITZGERALD'S MOTHER,	31
IV.	THE RED HOUSE,	35
V.	SQUIRE JENNY OF HASKETON,	39
VI.	MAJOR MOOR, WITH STICK FROM 'ROYAL GEORGE,'	45
VII.	KING EDWARD THE SIXTH'S SCHOOL, BURY ST. EDMUNDS,	57
VIII.	THE OBELISK, NASEBY,	63
IX.	WHERSTEAD LODGE AND THE FERRY, CHESTERTON,	73
X.	FITZGERALD'S LODGINGS, CAMBRIDGE,	77
XI.	CAMBRIDGE HOUSE, CHESTERTON, AND GELDESTONE HALL,	83
XII.	REV. T. R. MATTHEWS OF BEDFORD,	97
XIII.	THE TRUMPET BLOWN BY THE REV. T. R. MATTHEWS,	101
XIV.	W. KENWORTHY BROWNE,	105
XV.	CAULDWELL HOUSE, BEDFORD,	121
XVI.	BOULGE HALL AND BOULGE CHURCH,	135

PLATE		
XVII.	BOULGE COTTAGE,	143
XVIII.	'THE FALCON,' BLETSOE,	155
XIX.	'THE ROSE AND CROWN,' YARDLEY HASTINGS,	177
XX.	JOHN ALLEN (1844),	185
XXI.	TURNPIKE COTTAGE AND GOLDINGTON HALL,	191
XXII.	GOLDINGTON VICARAGE,	195
XXIII.	THE REV. W. MONKHOUSE AND THE REV. W. AIRY,	199
XXIV.	W. KENWORTHY BROWNE,	203
XXV.	THOMAS CHURCHYARD,	207
XXVI.	MATTHEWS'S CHAPEL, BEDFORD,	211
XXVII.	BERNARD BARTON,	227
XXVIII.	THE COTTAGE AT BRAMFORD,	231
XXIX.	FARLINGAY HALL,	261
XXX.	COPY OF PHOTOGRAPH PRESENTED BY CARLYLE TO ALFRED SMITH	273
XXXI.	TOMB OF OMAR KHAYYAM,	279
XXXII.	'THE BLOODY WARRIOR,'	289
XXXIII.	PROFESSOR COWELL,	293
XXXIV.	GOLDINGTON HALL FROM 'THE PADDOCK,'	307
XXXV.	GOLDINGTON BURY,	317
XXXVI.	W. KENWORTHY BROWNE,	321
XXXVII.	GOLDINGTON CHURCH,	325

BOOK I

Bredfield and Bury School
Sixteen Years (31st March 1809-1825)

BREDFIELD HOUSE (FITZGERALD'S BIRTHPLACE)

NASEBY WOOLLEYS
THE NORTHAMPTONSHIRE HOME OF THE FITZGERALDS

THE LIFE OF EDWARD FITZGERALD

CHAPTER I

THE WHITE HOUSE AND THE RED HOUSE

31 MARCH 1809—1825

EDWARD FITZGERALD, the famous letter-writer and adapter of Omar Khayyam, was born, 'hither hurried,' 'without asking,' and 'with a silver spoon in his mouth,' at the White House, Bredfield (now called Bredfield House[1]), a quaint yet stately brick-built, plaster-coated Jacobean mansion, about a mile and a half to the north of Woodbridge, on the 31st of March 1809. He was the third son of John and Mary Frances Purcell, who were first cousins and of Irish descent; and in this corner of Suffolk—the country of level wheatfields, noble estuaries, and dwindled towns—FitzGerald spent the greater portion of his life—a life of brilliant lights and dense shadows. Mr. Purcell's father, John Purcell, M.D., who prided himself on his descent from Cromwell, was of Richmond Hill, Dublin; Mrs. Purcell's father, John FitzGerald (sixteenth in lineal descent from Maurice, fourth Earl of Kildare), married his first cousin, Mary, daughter of Keane FitzGerald. John Fitz-Gerald, who is described as of Little Island, Waterford,

1. The White House and the Little Owl.

---

[1] The 'Bredfield Hall' of FitzGerald's poem.

was a man of great wealth, being the owner of vast estates in Ireland, Northants, Suffolk, and elsewhere. The repeated intermarrying in the family may in some measure account for what Edward called the 'FitzGerald madness.' Of his maternal grandfather—a handsome, powdered gentleman—Edward has preserved the following anecdote: 'My grandfather had several parrots of different sorts and talents. One of them (Billy, I think) could only huff up his feathers in what my grandfather called an owl fashion; so when company were praising the more gifted parrots, he would say—"You will hurt poor Billy's feelings. Come! do your little owl, my dear!"'[1] This story, which Mrs. Purcell used to tell her children, much impressed Edward, who often applied it; and sixty or more years after, when his selections from Crabbe were printing, we find him speaking of having 'done his little owl.'

The other children of John and Mary Frances Purcell were *Mary Frances* [1802-1820], *John* [1803-1879], *Andalusia* (Mrs. De Soyres) [?—1879], *Mary Eleanor* (Mrs. Kerrich) [1805-1863], *Jane* (Mrs. Wilkinson) [1806—?], *Peter* [1807-1875], *Isabella* (Mrs. Vignati) [1810-1864].[2]

Mr. John Purcell, who upon the death of his wife's father[3] in 1818 took the FitzGerald name and arms, and whom we shall henceforth call Mr. John FitzGerald, was a big-built, ruddy-faced, kindly man, but of no account (or not much) beside his wife. He was merely Mrs. FitzGerald's husband. He hunted, shot, served as High Sheriff of the county, and sat in Parliament as member for Seaford, near Brighton, where he had an estate; living, in short, the life of an

2. FitzGerald's Parents and the Kembles.

---

[1] *Letters to Fanny Kemble*, p. 142 (Bentley).
[2] Parish Registers of Bredfield.
[3] He is buried at old St. Pancras, London.

FITZGERALD'S MOTHER

ordinary country gentleman. For doing nothing he was peculiarly adapted (he was born to it), and had he only recognised this fact, instead of putting his mediocre talents to use—instead, for example, of indulging in colliery developments on his estate at Pendleton, near Manchester, he might have continued life as he began it, a rich, successful, and happy man. Of the gardens, the well-timbered lawn, the lofty, extensive, and umbrageous coverts (now vanished), 'haunt of hare and pheasant,' the pleasaunces 'dashed by the scarlet-coated hunter, horse, and dappled hound,' and the 'hospitable fires' of Bredfield Hall, there are deathless memories in FitzGerald's graphic poem of that title. From the road in front of the lawn, glimpses could be caught of men-of-war lying in Hollesley Bay.

The boy derived his force of character not from 'papa,' but from 'mamma,'[1] who was exceptionally handsome (her beauty dazed kings), gifted, well educated (she knew four languages), a lover of poetry, especially of Crabbe, imperial, as became a daughter of the FitzGeralds of Kildare, and eccentric; but, better than any description, are the two speaking portraits of her by Sir Thomas Lawrence. One of them was considered by her son to bear a striking resemblance to the Duke of Wellington. In the other, which we reproduce, her pride of race is as much in evidence as her beauty, which consisted chiefly in her perfect features and dark, luxuriant hair. From her ears and at her breast hang pendants—apparently pearls—and we are told that she used to wear a bracelet of her husband's hair, with a massive clasp inscribed with the words 'Stesso sangue, stessa sorte.'[2] Her children felt towards her awe rather than love, and when she came to

[1] FitzGerald invariably used these words in speaking of his parents.
[2] *Fanny Kemble: Records of a Girlhood*, i. 136.

the nursery 'they were not much comforted by her visit.' Her Junonian beauty brightened, her violent temper devastated, the home; but she did not neglect the religious training of her children, and the prayer at night, which each, in little white surplice, repeated at her knee, sank into their memories; which was well, for of spiritual advantages out of the house they had few, the pastor of Bredfield being of the old sort, with vermilion nose, caused by good cheer, who used to lay his hat and whip on the Communion table, gabble over the prayers, work his way perfunctorily through a sermon of some one else's composition, and run down the pulpit stairs, with a view to being invited to dinner at the Hall.

The White House is little changed from the days when FitzGerald and his brothers and sisters lived in it. One apartment, indeed, 'the stone room,' is the same even to the wall-paper, with its pattern of great squares and flowers. Another, 'the magistrates' room,' where Edward 'used to be whipped,' is also pointed out; and one may mount to the nursery in one of the gables, the doorway of which still exhibits on each side the grooves made to receive the imprisoning-board, or look out from its small window on to the lawn, and listen to the bells of St. Mary's, Woodbridge, as Edward and his brothers and sisters so often did. Their mother, who was frequently from home —for the FitzGeralds had a handsome town residence in Portland Place, where they usually passed the season— sometimes saw her children only once a fortnight, and in after years Edward would point to the shrubs in front of the house, behind which he used to hide in order to see her coach, 'of a good full yellow colour,' and four black horses come magnificently up the drive. Though he stood in awe of his mother, however, he was both proud and fond of her. In *Euphranor*, surely, are preserved

THE RED HOUSE (SQUIRE JENNY'S)

THE WHITE HOUSE AND THE RED HOUSE

some reminiscences of his childhood. In idea we see him and his brothers playing in the garden 'wet or dry, regardless of aunt's screaming from the window' for them to come in when a cloud appeared threatening; we are 'shut up with them for two hours' morning service in the pew without being allowed to go to sleep there,' with nothing provided for our amusement except that finely coloured nose of the vicar's, and teased about text and sermon afterwards; we 'climb up the poplar in our garden by way of beanstalk,' and get whipped for chasing the sheep about in the neighbouring field. The wealth of the FitzGeralds—derived chiefly from Mrs. FitzGerald's father—enabled them to make at dinners and on other occasions a display which dazzled the eyes of the less favoured; and we are told particularly of the magnificence of the gold dessert and table ornaments, and their successors in favour, a set of ground glass and burnished silver, 'so exquisite that the splendid gold service was pronounced infinitely less tasteful and beautiful.'

At the Red House in the neighbouring village of Hasketon lived Squire Jenny, a friend of Edward's father. The name Red House was probably bestowed upon Squire Jenny's mansion to distinguish it from the White or Bredfield House, when the latter was first coated with plaster. Squire Jenny was of a short stature, with long, yellowish face, shaggy eyebrows, and enormous ears—the last quite a monstrosity. An ardent, jovial sportsman of the kind Randolph Caldecott delighted to draw, carrying, when he visited London, a delightful breath of the country into street and house, he shared with FitzGerald's father the cost of keeping a pack of harriers, and adorned his walls with pictures of racehorses, puppies, and jockeys. One picture (painted by a Miss Page, afterwards Mrs. Phillips),

3. **The Red House.**

is here reproduced. It represents the squire in blue coat, whip in hand, 'Going to see sick Betty,' though whether mare, puppy, or woman we are left to imagine. An extremist in the matter of sanitation, he wisely took care that his windows should, whenever possible, be open—a great wonder in those days. If the snow came in he simply had it shovelled out, and would have no carpets—in fact 'nothing comfortable in his house': he didn't want to be stifled, he said. On a Sunday he always attended church in the morning, and spent the rest of the day reading *Bell's Life*, which, with its big eye, might be seen lying on a great oak table cut from one of his own trees. In the attics, it was understood, were great hampers which nobody ever opened, filled with old china of fabulous value. With Squire Jenny lived his sister Anne—keen housewife, oddity, miser. He liked the smell of the stables, she the colour of current coin, which, however, on reaching her immediately ceased to be current—there it remained.

The families of FitzGerald and Jenny were extremely intimate, and frequently exchanged visits, dining at 'The White House' like emperors, seated on gilded chairs upholstered with satin, among ancestral portraits and sconces reflecting multitudes of candles, their feet on luxurious carpets. The table groaned with plate, rich foods, choice wines, every dainty to tempt the appetite. These banquets gave the bluff, outspoken squire the occasion for an oft-repeated coarse jest. At 'The Red House' they fared frugally (Miss Jenny, careful soul, seeing to that), and the homeliness of the meal harmonised with the cold, hard, shiny, uncomfortable chairs and the naked floors. There was no stint, however, of fresh air. The breezy, good-natured, horsy squire and little Edward soon became the best of friends, and many were

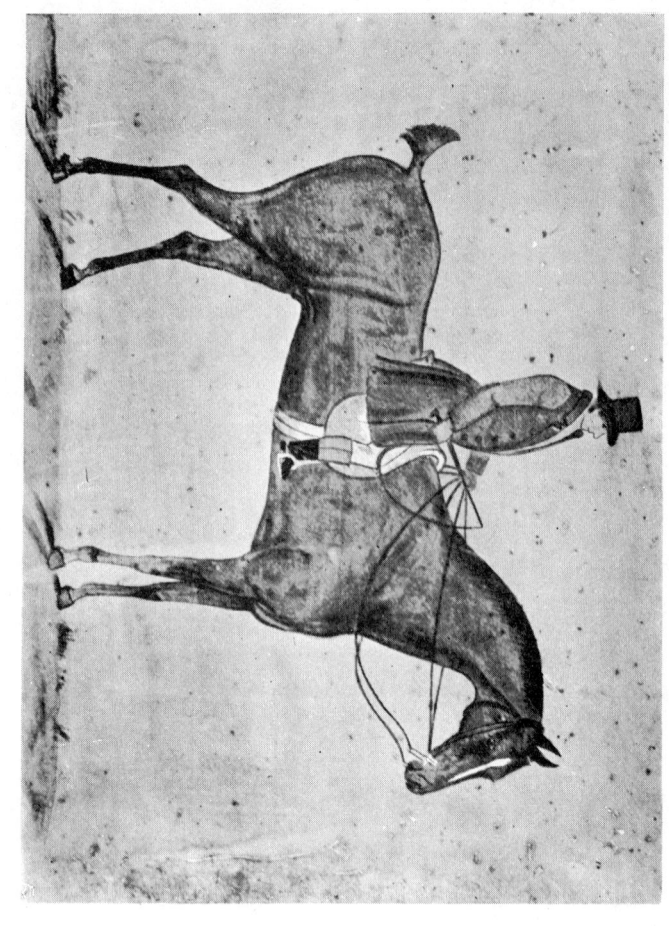

SQUIRE JENNY OF HASKETON
'GOING TO SEE SICK BETTY'

the happy hours spent at Hasketon. But the getting there! The path pierced a dense and dismal wood. FitzGerald told Mrs. Barlow of Hasketon that he never passed through this wood without trembling, even when he held his mother's hand. He fancied sheeted ghosts. Every tree and hedge-clump seemed a shelter for fiery snake, dragon with tusks, hobgoblin with puffy and quilt-like body, or other clammy terrors. In after years, however, that wood was his perpetual delight.

Among the homes of the FitzGeralds—and they seem to have had as many as six[1] at a time—one of them, Naseby Woolleys, has been entirely overlooked by previous writers. Yet it was here that FitzGerald spent a great part of his early life, and next to Bredfield, this house had most attraction for the FitzGerald family.

4. Naseby Woolleys.

On the map Naseby village looks just like a big butterfly with dwindled thorax, exaggerated head, and inordinately long feelers, the body being inclined to the north-east, whilst the configuration of the neighbouring fields makes well-defined wings. The church is the left eye, the vicarage is in the left wing; on the right feeler is an 'ass of an obelisk' (of the erection of which we shall presently speak, and which will loom rather large in these pages); the left feeler stretches over Mill Hill and the battlefield. Naseby Woolleys is out of the butterfly altogether, far away on the left. Naseby, 'the navel of England,' is 630 feet above the sea level, and gives origin to two of our rivers—the Avon, flowing west, and the Nen, east. In the time of the Rev. John Mastin, vicar, who in 1792 wrote on its history and antiquities, and during Edward FitzGerald's boyhood, the houses were built

---

[1] Naseby Woolleys, Little Island, Castle Irwell, and the house at Seaford were their own property.

'mostly of kealy earth,' and Mastin, a facetious and pleasing chronicler, could not imagine what more any man could wish for who lived in one of these human swallow's nests. Aged people were plentiful. 'They are proverbial, being called "Naseby children," frequently becoming a second time so by age.' A tale is told of one old fellow who cut at seventy 'an entire new and regular set of teeth, which grew to a proper size, and continued firm and good to the time of his death,' at the age of ninety-five—'so good that he would quarrel with his family for crusts.' The garrulous vicar also observes that, brought up on high ground amid storms and winds, the folk 'vociferate loudly' in order to be heard above the forces of nature; and he speaks of three marvellous wells, one of blue water, 'Warren's'; one of yellow water, the chalybeate Scrough Hill Spring; and one of icy coldness, 'St. Dennis's,' now filled up. The church, which is in the middle of the village, displayed in FitzGerald's childhood above its tower a great copper ball. 'The FitzGerald Arms,' opposite the church, still reminds of the family, though in name only, for the contemporary edifice has disappeared; and the stump of the old Market Cross,[1] and the ancient Tithe Barn, refer us to the days of monk and missal and payment in kind. Another but less entertaining account of the parish was furnished in 1830 by Henry Lockinge, one of its curates, who dedicated his book to FitzGerald's father and mother, 'the Lord and Lady of the Manor.'

For some time Mr. and Mrs. FitzGerald lived at Naseby Woolleys, and subsequently, when it was untenanted, would go there for the summer. The house, which had a verandah in front, and was surrounded by flower gardens, is now much altered. To the east extends Broad Moor,

[1] Now at the end of the village. Another cross occupies its old site.

the scene of the famous battle of Naseby, and on the west runs the Avon, coaxed at this spot to broaden out into a picturesque artificial lake, the haunt of swan, wild duck, and water-hen. To Mr. FitzGerald's descent, or supposed descent, from Cromwell we have referred, and in the house, which contained many objects of antiquarian interest, might have been seen a wooden figure of his reputed ancestor in steel armour, with his actual sword. Cromwell's gold watch, and coins, bullets, and other relics picked up on the battlefield were displayed in glass cases; and there was a musical clock—the wonder of the neighbourhood—which played eight tunes and set a number of quaint little figures in motion. The Cromwell in armour was too lifelike to be pleasant, especially at dusk. 'It used to frighten folk so; it's been dreadful to hear the FitzGerald children scream if they happened to be left alone with it'; and we may be sure that Edward, who trembled so in Hasketon Wood, screamed as loudly as the others. Oliver's sword, however, which maintained its virtue, once came in handy, for John Linnet, the gardener, a hardy, vigorous man (no linnet either in heart or person), who was left in charge of the house when the FitzGeralds were away, being once disturbed by burglars, snatched this weapon from Oliver's gauntleted hand, and, causing history to repeat itself, sent his foes in full flight across Naseby Field. The number of precious objects in the house was, nevertheless, a source of constant anxiety to poor Linnet, who had frequent need of his intrepidity. Then, too, there were horse-stealers and sheep-stealers—dainty rogues who carried off the prime joints only, leaving contemptuously for the FitzGeralds the mangled carcass with the skin.

Mrs. FitzGerald dearly loved Naseby—every inch of it —delighted to visit it, and to call on, and send or carry presents to, her old servants, especially her footman and her nurse (Watchams and his wife), who lived close to the stump of the old cross, in the house at which Edward used afterwards to stay. Well it had been for the Fitz-Geralds had all their dependants been as faithful as doughty John Linnet and the Watchams; but they had enemies against whom neither Cromwell's well-tried sword nor the indefatigable vigilance of the shepherd could defend them—namely, their own stewards. One of these gentry went off with £7000, whereupon Mr. FitzGerald provided himself with another steward, who turned out honester, for though he too, by and by, also disappeared suddenly, it was with only £3000. And what was Mr. FitzGerald doing all this time? He was busy, when not hunting and electioneering, in revolving schemes for making at his Manchester estate untold wealth by coal-mining, but in reality laying foundations for untold anxiety and trouble to himself and all his connections. He was digging a pit for himself and his houses, and his friends and their houses all to tumble into —that was to swallow him and them up as neatly as the gulph in Bible story swallowed up Korah and Dathan and all their belongings.

Of the friendship between Edward and Mr. Jenny we have already spoken. The boy was also devotedly attached to another friend of his father, Major Edward Moor, a meditative and erudite Anglo-Indian and linguist settled at Great Bealings,[1] a portly man in stiff, white, broad-brimmed hat, considerably too large for his head and constantly threatening to eclipse his eyes, frilled shirt-front, and cut-away coat. When a cadet of thirteen, on board the transport that was to carry him to India, he had seen the *Royal*

5. Major Moor.

---

[1] Bealings House.

MAJOR MOOR, WITH STICK FROM 'ROYAL GEORGE'

THE WHITE HOUSE AND THE RED HOUSE 47

George go down—an incident in connection with Moor that FitzGerald often alludes to. This was in 1782. Years after, managing to secure a piece of wood from the sunken vessel, he had made from it a walking-stick, which, out of doors, became his constant companion. One of his first actions on arriving at Madras was, though to him then a rupee was a rupee, to buy an imperfect copy of Shakespeare, whose pages never ceased to delight him. Promotion and opulence followed in due time, and while yet in India he published several works on Hindu subjects, the one that evidently gave him most pleasure to write being the *Hindu Pantheon*. 'Gods' were the Major's weakness. He collected them as one might collect fossils or postage stamps—rendered them even a sort of reverence as the objects of other men's worship, and brought home a posse to Great Bealings—little gods, big gods, squatting gods, and many-armed gods. And at length, wearying of his hobby, he buried the whole collection above-ground in a pyramidal sarcophagus, close to the drive leading to his house. Here, under stone and cement and in Egyptian darkness, they grin to this day. A lover of Tusser and other antique Suffolk writers, and of archaic words and folklore in general, he collected the provincialisms of his native county, and embodied the results of his study in a work called *Suffolk Words* (1823). The Major and his *Royal George* walking-stick and young Edward FitzGerald had many an expedition together. A glorious man for a boy to companion with, he it was who first gave to the future adapter of Omar Khayyam, trotting at his foot, on road or in field, a taste for philology and expressive words, and first interested him in the glittering, odorous, fascinating East. Alas! the Major, like other folk, had his faults; but FitzGerald never heard him 'charged with any except one,' and 'that was by a very humane friend and fellow-magistrate of his,' who complained that, though the Major discountenanced poaching, he 'sometimes hindered judicial business at the weekly bench,' inasmuch as 'you could scarce persuade him of a poor man's guilt.'[1]

FitzGerald's education began at a private school at Woodbridge, one of his schoolfellows being Anne Carthew, who became the wife of his future near neighbour, Major Pytches[2] ('Pytches and Westminster Abbey!'). Even the derivation of the word Woodbridge is interesting to us in the light of Carlyle's lectures on Hero Worship,[3] which, as we shall show, exercised no little influence on FitzGerald. 'Woden's Bridge,' ventures the philologist; and if it be urged that there is no bridge over the Deben just there, Imagination must step up to help him. The gaunt, one-eyed god, after stalking disconsolately on the river wall, and eyeing wistfully the opposite and alluring fields of Sutton and Shottisham, suddenly recollects his divinity, puts one leg across the flood, draws the other after it, and the thing is done. He is his own bridge. Those, however, who have not Woden's legs, can still cross the river by taking the ferry, just as nothing can debar the really determined—the Speddings, Carlyles, and FitzGeralds, for example, of these pages—from arriving at the Suttons and Shottishams of their dreams. That FitzGerald was without ambition is, as we shall show, a myth, and a very foolish one. Of those ample and lordly 'salt rivers' which form the most striking characteristic of this corner of Suffolk, the Deben is the most picturesque, and many a poet, though none more persistently than

6. Woodbridge.

---

[1] *Sea Words and Phrases*, No. 1.
[2] It was of Major Pytches that FitzGerald in 1864 bought 'Little Grange.'
[3] Odin, or Woden, is the first of Carlyle's heroes.

THE WHITE HOUSE AND THE RED HOUSE 49

Mitford,[1] has sung its broad and sinuous flood, its islets 'green with waving samphire,' its pinnaces, barges, and fishers' skiffs, the 'silvery pennons' of its sea mews, and the majestic woods that embosom it and creep down to its margin.

Woodbridge, which, to FitzGerald's mind, was merely the foil for the Deben's renown, is a quaint old market town with a somnolent and obsolete air, save on market days, when for a few hours the inflocking country-folk give it brogue, spirit, and vivacity. Its shipping-trade, formerly considerable, is now almost extinct, but the town keeps up its population level of five thousand, and presents—the old-world market-place excepted—a far smarter appearance than it did in FitzGerald's boyhood, which, considering the number of shrunken towns in the vicinity, is a distinction. Proceeding from the station to the market-place, one threads Quay Street and Church Street, crossing on the way the London Road (called on the left Cumberland Street, and on the right The Thoroughfare) and passing, a little further on, the winding lane that leads to the Friends' Meeting-House—sacred to the memory of Woodbridge's once popular poet, Bernard Barton. In the middle of the market-place, which is wedge-shaped, widening as you proceed from Church Street, stands the Shire Hall, a red-bricked building with exterior flights of steps. At the thin end of the wedge is the Bull Hotel, and from the thick end proceeds Seckford Street, in which are the Seckford Almshouses (rebuilt in 1840), a notable pile, the outcome of the munificence of Thomas Seckford, Woodbridge's Elizabethan philanthropist. Another thoroughfare, extending from the broad end of the

---

[1] Rector of Benhall, near Saxmundham, editor of Gray, and for many years editor of the *Gentleman's Magazine*. Arboriculture his hobby, he made his vicarage famous throughout Suffolk by the great number of ornamental trees which he planted round it.

market-place, is Theatre Street, which leads past the Grammar School (also Seckfordian), erected in 1865, towards Farlingay;[1] while branching from Theatre Street is Bredfield Road, leading to Bredfield and Boulge. As you stand in the market-place and face 'The Bull,' you have on your right St. Mary's church, and on your left the gunsmith's shop, which, on account of its FitzGerald associations, will have much prominence later in this history. North of the market-place and its western tributary New Street, the ground rises gently and forms Mill Hill, the view from which, looking towards the river and Sutton, is cut by the intervening spire of St. John's church,[2] and hard by is 'Little Grange,' of which we shall shortly have so much to say. To the south-west of the town lies Martlesham, lighting up the county with its red and gold Lion ('red as Martlesham Lion' being a Suffolk saying), an object that must have satisfied even a colour-loving FitzGerald; to the north-east is Ufford, the home of Captain Brooke.

Owing to the recent widening of the river wall, the erection of a bandstand and shelters, and the creation of an artificial beach, Woodbridge and its river, studded with the white sails of pleasure-craft, have taken on the habit of a seaside resort. When the tide is up, indeed, it is impossible to disabuse yourself of the idea that you are at Aldeburgh or Felixstowe. A few yellow sea-poppies would quite complete the illusion.

When Edward was five the family went to reside in France, first at St. Germains and afterwards in Paris, where they took a house that had been Robespierre's. For several years they fluctuated between Paris and Bredfield, residing a few months in France and a few months in England

7. In France. The Rodez murder.

---

[1] For some years FitzGerald's home.   [2] Erected in 1842.

THE WHITE HOUSE AND THE RED HOUSE 51

by turns. If Edward was at Bredfield in the middle of 1815, he probably saw 'the long strings of tumbrils laden with Waterloo wounded passing through Woodbridge on their way from Yarmouth to London.' He was certainly at Bredfield in the middle of the following year, for he speaks of the anniversary of the battle being celebrated throughout the country with feasting and sports. Among the places in gala was a village adjoining Bredfield, and the people borrowed of FitzGerald's father a pair of Wellington boots for the legs of a stuffed effigy of Buonaparte, at which they discharged guns and pistols, while the quality, including the parson of the parish and Edward, sat in a tent eating beef and plum-pudding and drinking loyal toasts.[1]

In 1817, when the boy was again in Paris, occurred in France an event that ate itself deeply into his memory—the assassination of M. Fualdès, a magistrate of Rodez—'the great murder,' and 'one of the most interesting events in all history to him,' he is sorry to say. It was not only the murder itself that impressed him, 'but the scene it was enacted in; the ancient, half Spanish city of Rodez, with its river Aveyron, its lonely boulevards, its great cathedral, under which the deed was done.'[2] Murders whose incidents were picturesque or suggestive of chiaroscuro, or which exposed the bed and secret recesses of the soul, whether of the assailer or the victim, excited his deep and perennial interest; whereas a brutal common murder, unaccompanied by startling psychological accessories, only disgusted him. Thus early did the artist and the philosopher reveal themselves; but we are not to forget, while chronicling this, that FitzGerald was the milk of human kindness—boy or man, lovable and beloved.

[1] *Life of Lord Houghton*, by Wemyss Reid, ii. 406.
[2] *Letters to Fanny Kemble* (Bentley), pp. 85 and 90.

Next year he was taken to the Ambigu Comique to see a play, the *Château de Paluzzi*, which was said to be founded on the Rodez murder; and he remembered 'a closet, from which came some guilty personage.'

On 19th June 1820 there was a death in the family—that of FitzGerald's eldest sister, Mary Frances, at the age of eighteen. She was buried by the side of Mrs. FitzGerald's father, in the family vault in old St. Pancras church. Another trouble was the defective eyesight of his sister Isabella. It is agreeable, however, to be able to record that the poor girl (who was an accomplished pianist), after suffering blindness for nine years, partially recovered her sight.

The FitzGeralds often made excursions to the quaint and attractive, if rather moist and woebegone, watering-place of Aldeburgh; with its fens and meres, habitat of the sallow, the septfoil, and the 'soft, slimy mallow'; and its level fields, in which leisurely oxen, that might have just stepped out of the Bible, still drag harrow and plough; with its time-old, brick-noggined, picturesque moot-house, pleasant sands, and miles of shifting, rattling shingle. Edward's playmate during these visits was a pretty, fun-loving little girl named Mary Lynn, niece of his good friend Major Moor of Bealings. Sixty years later he renewed his acquaintance with Miss Lynn in the same town, and spoke of her pleasantly as one of his 'old friends—and flames—Mary Lynn—(pretty name).' Here, too, he underwent the terrible experience of being 'ruthlessly ducked into the wave that came like a devouring monster' under the awning of a bathing-machine—a structure whose inside he detested to his dying day. He was much struck by the melancholy and desolation of the neighbouring Slaughden, with its sloops sticking sidelong in the mud,

margin: 8. Aldeburgh: Mary Lynn.

THE WHITE HOUSE AND THE RED HOUSE 53

its wilderness of shingle, its soppy, clammy banks, and its ferry that takes you—if the eye is to be relied upon—to nowhere.

About George Crabbe, Aldeburgh's poet, FitzGerald at this time probably thought little enough, paddling in the sea or romping in the sands with his merry playmate. Still, he thought something, for, thanks to his mother's partiality for that poet, Crabbe was his horn-book. He picked up lines from 'The Village' and 'The Parish Register' with his A B C and the Lord's Prayer. The poet Crabbe (and he looms so large in FitzGerald's life that it is better to set down at once the cardinal events of his career) was born in 1754 at Aldeburgh, the son of a saltmaster or collector of salt dues at Slaughden Quay. In 1771 he was apprenticed to a Mr. Page,[1] surgeon at Woodbridge, where he wrote his first lengthy poem, 'Inebriety,' in 1775. Four years later he returned to Aldeburgh, where for a time he practised, though with small success, as a surgeon; and in 1780, at the age of twenty-six, he went up to London in the *Unity* sloop, as FitzGerald so often impresses upon us, to try his fortune—in literature above all things. Strange to say, after a brief struggle with poverty he succeeded; but the story of his trials and success should be read in that entrancing fairy tale, which has the additional charm of being true, *The Life of the Rev. George Crabbe*, by his son. In 1781 he entered the church, and was appointed curate of his native town. In 1783 appeared his first important poem, 'The Village,' and in 1785 'The Newspaper.' As regards his writings, there now ensued a huge gap of twenty-two years. Then came 'The Parish Register' (1807), 'The Borough' (1810), 'Tales' (1812),

9. The Poet Crabbe.

---

[1] Mr. Page's daughter was the mother of FitzGerald's friend, Lord Hatherley.

and 'Tales of the Hall' (1819). After holding livings in various parts of Suffolk, and spending seven years in Leicestershire, Crabbe settled at Trowbridge (1812); and in 1821, when FitzGerald and Mary Lynn were romping together on Aldeburgh sands, he had still some ten years to live.

Even the most venturesome and intrepid lover of literature might hesitate before entering that vast jungle which is Crabbe; and the poet's sad habit of enclosing a tale or tales within a tale—his love for centric and eccentric wheels—adds confusion to confusion. The adventurer, however, would be well repaid for his trouble; for the poems contain many words of wisdom, very many striking, and not a few humorous passages, and here and there a complete tale excellently told.

The chief attraction of 'The Parish Register' is 'Roger Cuff';[1] of 'The Tales' none are more beseeching than 'The Frank Courtship'[2] (VI.), and 'The Widow's Tale'[3] (VII.), whilst of 'The Tales of the Hall' the best are the inner stories of 'The Maid's Story' and 'Sir Owen Dale.' Abundant, too, is the debt we owe to Crabbe for setting before us, with Cuyp-like, or even photographic exactness, picture after picture of the long, low Suffolk sea-board, and of Aldeburgh in particular—that Andromeda of the East Anglian coast, around whom, for centuries, the great sea dragon has shown, and now and again savagely used,

---

[1] 'Now to his grave was Roger Cuff conveyed.'

[2] Of the girl whose parents were afraid she would refuse the man of their choice. In reality, however, her ideas coincided with theirs, and it ends:

'Dear child! in three plain words thy mind express—
"Wilt thou have this good youth?"—"Dear father! Yes."'

[3] Of a boarding-school miss, who had despised household duties and repulsed a worthy farmer suitor, but afterwards got rid of her pettish humours, and prettily gave the young man encouragement.

'To useful arts she turned her hand and eye,
And by her manners told him—"You may try."'

his terrible teeth. In Crabbe, indeed, you ever hear the sough, the plash, and the moan of the sea, and ever look upon fretted sands and far-extending sea banks, viridescent with samphire and many-branched saltwort; whilst seeing or hearing, you are never allowed to get away from a moral—

> 'Still as I gaze upon the sea, I find
> Its waves an image of my restless mind;
> *Here* thought on thought: *there* wave on wave succeeds;
> Their produce—idle thoughts and idle weeds.'[1]

Slaughden has fallen even from the humble importance it had in FitzGerald's early days. Its shipping-trade has much decreased, and little remains of the village save a few houses, some half-buried in shingle, a woebegone inn —FitzGerald's favourite 'Three Mariners'—and a lonely, useless, trefoil-shaped, gigantic tea-cake called the 'Martello Tower,' which lords it over the shifting and rattling shingle. A more weird or desolate scene could not be imagined. Cheerless indeed must it be on a wild day in winter when there are no sea-poppies with their glorious yellow to transform the pebbly wilderness into a garden of the Lord; and when the soft, purring, tumbling sea, transformed into a demon, precipitates itself in unpropitiable fury upon the devoted and disappearing village. Winter after winter has the 'Three Mariners' stood the shock. Often and often has the sea rushed in at one door and out at the other; but, courageously as the onslaught has been met, the conflict cannot go on for ever. There will come a day when the mop of the good wife of the 'Three Mariners' will trundle out the German Ocean for the last time, and all that will be left of one of FitzGerald's most frequented haunts will be the site where it stood— if even that.

[1] Fragment written at Aldeburgh, 1779.

The boy loved to mingle with the sailors, and to hear their creepy tales of smugglers and vaulted caves stocked with tea and tobacco and tubs of spirits. Every fishy little village and inlet of the Suffolk coast, from Kirkley to Sizewell Gap, had its story of daring adventure. There was the tale of the funeral in Kirkley churchyard, said to be of somebody who died at sea, though as a matter of fact the coffin was full of silks—the sham mourners wearing cloaks and hatbands, and the duped parson solemnly reading the burial-service at the grave. The boy heard also of kegs of Hollands being found under the altar-cloth of Theberton church, dreamt of 'chopped hay' (contraband tobacco) and 'run tea,' and looked with awe on the revenue cutters which passed Aldeburgh, especially remembering one that went down with all hands—the *Ranger*.

Mrs. FitzGerald, as we said, was frequently in London, and no woman in society dressed better or looked more queenly. Her superb beauty, heightened by her rare taste in dress, expected, and everywhere received, adulation. She delighted in the theatre, had a box 'on the third tier' at the Haymarket, and numbered among her friends Mrs. Charles Kemble, one of the wittiest and most agreeable women of the time; and Mrs. Kemble's children, John Mitchell, now remembered as a distinguished Anglo-Saxon scholar; Fanny (afterwards the 'divine Fanny'), a troublesome and unmanageable child, often crowned with a fool's cap; and Adelaide (who became Mrs. Sartoris), were occasionally Edward's playmates. A miniature of Mrs. Charles Kemble 'in a white dress and blue scarf, looking with extended arms upward in a blaze of light,' was among Mrs. FitzGerald's treasures. The boy Edward, whose affection for the stage, to use his own expression, was inherited, often accompanied his mother to the theatre (the

10. The Haymarket Theatre.

KING EDWARD THE SIXTH'S SCHOOL, BURY ST. EDMUNDS

THE WHITE HOUSE AND THE RED HOUSE

very pillars of the old Haymarket were dear to him), heard Madame Vestris,[1] in her Pamela hat with a red feather, sing 'Cherry Ripe'; Miss Stephens, 'We're a' Noddin''; Rubini,[2] Braham,[3] and Vaughan; and saw and retailed anecdotes about Madame Pasta[4] the actress, and Mlle. Taglioni[5] the danseuse—'a dream, a vision, floating, literally *floating*, before one's eyes as the "Sylphide."'

John, FitzGerald's elder brother, had been for some years at King Edward the Sixth's School at Bury St. Edmunds under Dr. Malkin;[6] and in 1821, the year he left, Edward and his brother Peter were sent there. The King Edward's School of those days[7] was the long building in Northgate Street, now used as a High School for girls. Over the schoolroom door was a bust of the founder with a Latin inscription,[8] and from the dining-room, which was on the south side, extended a passage which led to the pupils' studies, situated in the garden. Dr. Malkin, troubled with lameness, was a portly, intellectual-looking, handsome man, brimming with energy—hearty, genial, humorous; Mrs. Malkin, a woman of much strength of character, was dignified, vivacious, and kind. Many years

11. At Bury, 1821. Peter's Escapade.

---

[1] Madame Vestris (1797-1856), actress. She appeared at Drury Lane in 1820, and became famous in *The Haunted Tower* and *Paul Pry*.

[2] Giambattista Rubini (1795-1854), great tenor singer.

[3] John Braham (1774-1856), tenor singer. His first great success was at Drury Lane in 1796.

[4] Guidetta Pasta (1798-1865), actress and opera singer. Her most splendid triumphs were won in London and Paris from 1825 to 1833.

[5] Maria Taglioni (1804-1884), celebrated danseuse. Made her début in Paris in 1827, where she caused a perfect furore. Her success was equally great in London.

[6] There is a monument to him in St. James's Church, Bury. Sir Benjamin Heath Malkin, friend of Macaulay, was his eldest son. Another son, Frederick, wrote a History of Greece.

[7] The present school, finished in 1883, is in the vineyard of the old abbey.

[8] The bust is gone, the inscription remains.

after, when Adelaide Kemble remarked to Edward FitzGerald, 'How charming Mrs. Malkin appears to be!' he replied enthusiastically, 'Oh, you can never know how charming she was; you were never a schoolboy under her care.'[1] The school has always had a high reputation, its pupils having carried off numbers of the Cambridge classical prizes, and many have risen to eminence. One of its features was the unusual amount of attention devoted to English literature, and the pains Dr. Malkin took to make his pupils good English as well as good classical scholars. There was much essay-writing, and the essays that gained approbation were honoured with a place in a series of large volumes entitled *Musae Burienses*. The year that Edward entered (1821), the subjects were 'Mr. Hogarth's compliments to Mr. King, and requests the honour of his company to dinner on Thursday next to Eta Beta Pi,' and

'At her feet he bowed' (*Judges* v. 27);

and among the essays honoured were those of John FitzGerald, who treated the first theme as though its meaning was equivocal, and considered the second as a warranty for comparing the poetry of the Hebrews with that of Pindar and other Greek lyrists. A more suitable school for the particular genius of Edward FitzGerald—for the incipient poet and letter-writer—could not have been found in all England. Among his schoolfellows were his old playmate J. M. Kemble (destined to be 'Anglo-Saxon Kemble'), Tom and James Spedding, Arthur Malkin—a stutterer, 'always very kind' to FitzGerald—W. Bodham Donne and William Airy (some day to be Vicar of Keysoe), all of whom became his lifelong friends. Donne was of the same stock as the poet

[1] *Further Records* (Fanny Kemble), ii. 179.

THE WHITE HOUSE AND THE RED HOUSE 61

Cowper, whose mother was great-aunt to both Donne's parents, while Donne's own great-aunt was the Mrs. Anne Bodham who presented Cowper with the portrait which led to the writing of 'The Lines on the Receipt of my Mother's Picture.'

Few towns are historically more interesting than Bury, with its monastic ruins, the great Abbey Gate, the noble Norman Tower, the quaint Jews' House, Moyses Hall (now a museum), Cupola House, the reputed residence of Daniel Defoe, and the fine churches, St. Mary's and St. James's—the latter with the pilgrim's staff and scrip, and the dragon sprawling on a chalice over the great entrance. St. James's was the church which the pupils of the school attended in their caps and gowns, certain seats having time out of mind been set apart for them. There seem to have been about sixty pupils, half of whom were day scholars or 'royalists,' the rest boarders or 'foreigners.' The schoolroom, with great oak beams in the ceiling and a platform at one end, presents the same appearance as it did in FitzGerald's boyhood; and one may still see, though not there, for they are now in the new school, the old desks—massive, ink-stained, and knife-hacked. Before me lie one of the school exercise-books, with the white printed label, 'Gulielm. Airy, Reg. Schol. Buriensis,' and the date 1st September 1823, and the speech-day programmes and prize-lists for 24th June 1824, and 28th June 1825. In 1824 Airy recites 'Catarach,' from Beaumont and Fletcher's play; Spedding minor (James), Gray's 'Bard'; J. M. Kemble, who had himself 'the profile of Alexander as seen on medals'—straight nose, parted lips, ample hair—'Alexander's Feast'; whilst to FitzGerald minor (our FitzGerald) was allotted 'Mr. Bickerstaff,'—Swift. On another occasion Kemble recited Hotspur's speech, beginning, 'My liege, I did deny no prisoners'—the best piece of declamation FitzGerald ever listened to.

FitzGerald major (Peter), a rather innocent boy, though original enough out of school, was very much of a dullard. He was invariably beaten, and badly, by FitzGerald minor, who always had one of the speeches on speech-day. Owing, however, to his ingenuity and originality, Peter obtained honours among his companions in the playground and out of bounds. Accustomed at home to driving his mother's four-in-hand, that noticeable equipage 'of a good full yellow colour' with black horses, he used at Bury to make up for the loss of this diversion by walking out to meet the London coach, the ribbons of which he was permitted to handle. But his reckless driving frightened the passengers, and they complained to Dr. Malkin, who put a stop to the proceeding. Subsequently complaint was made to the doctor that Peter had been seen dressed as a mute 'driving a hearse with four horses carrying plumes,' to which the doctor replied drily, 'I don't see that I need interfere unless the passenger complained.'[1]

FitzGerald looked back with pleasure to the days spent at Bury, and often revisited his old haunts. He would talk of the ruins, the noble and massy towered gateways, St. James's church, with its sun-dial motto, 'Go about your business,'[2] and the 'good old Angel.' Thus Bury, which had coloured the lives of Defoe and Goldsmith,[3] entered also, and for good, into the being of Edward FitzGerald.

In 1823 FitzGerald's father and mother, who describe themselves as 'Lord and Lady of the Manor of Naseby,' erected, a little to the north-east of Naseby village, an

[1] Glyde's *Life of Edward FitzGerald*.   [2] See Preface to *Polonius*.
[3] Associated with Barton Hall.

THE OBELISK, NASEBY

ERECTED BY FITZGERALD'S FATHER AND MOTHER

THE WHITE HOUSE AND THE RED HOUSE 65

obelisk to commemorate the famous battle. Owing to the fact that it stands not on the battlefield but a good mile away, Carlyle has hurled at this obelisk a perfect dictionary of abusive epithets. To this 'foolish Naseby monument,' erected by 'a blundering Irishman,' 'obstacle rather than obelisk,' 'this deluding obelisk,' this 'ass of a column,' 'blockhead obelisk,' that 'might as well stand at Charing Cross, the blockhead that it is!' we shall often in these pages have occasion to refer. It will be quite a landmark for us.

12. The Naseby Obelisk.

Of Bernard Barton, the Quaker poet of Woodbridge, Charles Lamb's 'B. B.' and 'Busy Bee,' FitzGerald must have heard at an early age, for his mother was one of Barton's admirers and staunchest friends, but how soon the two became personally acquainted we do not know. Barton, who had first come to Woodbridge in 1806, married a Woodbridge girl, who died the following year after giving birth to their only child, Lucy. He then removed to Liverpool, where he stayed twelve months, and finally settled at Woodbridge as clerk in Messrs. Alexander and Co.'s bank. Had he only remained at Liverpool—he and that baby daughter of his—how many heartaches, how much poignant sorrow, how many tears would have been spared Edward FitzGerald! Inspired chiefly by the verses of the elder Quaker poet, John Scott of Amwell,[1] Barton began himself to rhyme, and between 1822 and 1828 he published five volumes of poetry. His work has some prettinesses, and much wholesome and Christianly advice, but little polish; indeed, whilst he liked to set down what issued spontaneously, he abhorred, and could not be got to see the necessity of, revision. He corresponded with Southey,

13. Bernard Barton.

---

[1] John Scott, 1730-1783.

Byron, and Charles Lamb, and would possibly have abandoned the bank in favour of literature but for the strenuous urgings of the last two. Byron said, 'If you have a profession, retain it'; Lamb: 'Throw yourself rather, my dear sir, from the steep Tarpeian rock, slap-dash headlong upon iron spikes. . . . Trust not to the public. . . . I bless every star that Providence, not seeing good to make me independent, has seen it next good to settle me upon the stable foundation of Leadenhall. Sit down, good B. B., in the banking office. What! is there not from 6 to 11 P.M. six days in the week, and is there not all Sunday? Fie, what a superfluity of man's time, if you could think so! Enough for relaxation, mirth, converse, poetry, good thoughts, quiet thoughts. Oh the corroding, torturing, tormenting thoughts that disturb the brain of the unlucky wight who must draw upon it for daily sustenance! Henceforth I retract all my fond complaints of mercantile employment — look upon them as lovers' quarrels. I was but half in earnest. Welcome, dead timber of a desk that gives me life.'[1]

So Barton clung to his bank, and he and his daughter, destined to become FitzGerald's wife, remained at Woodbridge. He rarely leaves the town, except to see his friends Mr. and Mrs. Arthur Biddell, at Playford, or to visit Benhall, where Mitford seats him under a chestnut and listens to his oracular sayings. Like his sister the nightingale, he has a grievous defect. 'She devours glow-worms, he takes snuff.'[2] He loves art, of which he knows nothing, and becomes the easy prey of wily and unscrupulous picture-dealers.

In 1823 occurred the second 'great murder' of FitzGerald's recollection—that done on Mr. William Weare

[1] 9th January 1823. [2] Mitford.

by the notorious John Thurtell. Charles Lamb, Lord Lytton,[1] Theodore Hook, and Carlyle, with his gigmanity,[2] have taken care that this tragic event shall not escape our memory. Thurtell was executed at Hertford on 9th January 1824. ''Tis twelve o'clock,' observes Lamb to Bernard Barton, 'and Thurtell is just now coming out upon the new drop.' The attraction to FitzGerald of murders presenting startling psychological features has already been noticed, and this one—he was now a lad of fourteen—made an impression on him only less vivid than that of the Rodez murder; and more than fifty years after we find him dwelling upon one moving—he calls it 'sublime'—circumstance: that of Thurtell sending for his accomplice Hunt, who had saved himself by turning King's evidence, and, after shaking hands with him, saying 'God bless you—God bless you; you couldn't help it—I hope you'll live to be a good man.'[3] An additional prominence was given to this tragic event by the publication of the lines entitled 'The Owl,' by the Rev. John Mitford, the weirdness and picturesqueness of the first stanza of which appealed forcibly to many—

14. The Maple's Head.

> 'The maple's head
> Was glowing red,
> And red were the wings of the autumn sky,
> But a redder gleam
> Rose from the stream
> That dabbled my feet as I glided by.'[4]

---

[1] He utilised the circumstances in the incident of the murder of Sir John Tyrrell by Thornton and Dawson in *Pelham*.

[2] Weare was driving in a gig from London to Gill's Hill. *Q*. What sort of person was Mr. Weare?—*A*. He was always a respectable person. *Q*. What do you mean by respectable?—*A*. He kept a gig.—Report of Thurtell's Trial. See Carlyle's essay on 'Richter' (*Essays*, vol. iii. p. 537. Ashburton Ed.).

[3] See *Letters to Fanny Kemble* (Bentley), p. 152.

[4] These lines, according to Mrs. FitzGerald, who was herself much struck with them, first appeared in Raw's *Pocket-Book*; they may also be seen in the *Gentleman's Magazine* for October 1837.

For Mr. Mitford's writings FitzGerald had considerable admiration, and late in life he took the trouble to collect them.

In 1825, when FitzGerald was sixteen and about to leave Bury School, his father and mother moved from Bredfield to Wherstead.

BOOK II

WHERSTEAD

TEN YEARS (1825-1835)

CHAPTER II

WHERSTEAD LODGE

1825—NOVEMBER 1830

WHERSTEAD is situated about two miles to the south of Ipswich, from which it is approached by a practically straight road commanding fine views of the Orwell. On the right is Stoke Park, and on the left an inn showing on its signboard a figure of an ostrich and the legend *Prudens qui patiens*, derived from the crest of the Earls of Leicester who formerly had property in the parish. Thence one mounts Bourn Hill, enters its red sand-gorge, fantastic with pendulous boughs and bright with yellow of broom and silver of stellaria, passes the lodge at the entrance of Wherstead Park, and follows a drive which, winding through a covert thick with ornamental shrubs, brings one at last to the house— 'Wherstead Lodge'—a loftily and pleasantly situated eighteenth century residence of white brick, covered with climbing plants and surrounded by magnificent ornamental trees. Wherstead Lodge boasts an imposing hall and staircase, and in FitzGerald's time it possessed a valuable collection of pictures, including canvases by Canaletto, Lely, and Reynolds, brought together by the builder of the house, Sir Robert Harland. It was at Wherstead Park in 1823, just before the FitzGeralds' arrival, that the Duke of Wellington accidentally discharged his gun in the face

15. Wherstead and Ipswich.

of Lord Granville. FitzGerald interested himself in the villagers of Wherstead, particularly in the old women, one of whom, Mrs. Chaplin,[1] was his pensioner. Wherstead church has a beautifully carved Norman doorway, and displays above its striking embattled tower a huge black ball, formerly a sailing-mark for vessels navigating the Orwell. FitzGerald's friend, Dr. Merivale, Dean of Ely, once asked what the ball was for, and, on being told, remarked drily that he was glad to find that any use could be made of a church. From the churchyard and its vicinage glorious views are seen of the Orwell, which, just there trending eastward, presents the appearance of an extensive lake fringed by picturesque woodlands and verdurous commons. The ghost of Gainsborough haunts these levels, and the heron (there are cormorants no longer) stands with shrugged shoulders fishing in the ooze, or rises in flight, his long legs slanting behind him, while the passing boatman rests his oars and lustily cries 'Frank!'

If FitzGerald drew little spiritual nutriment from the vicar of Bredfield, it is to be feared that he got even less from the vicar of Wherstead. This gentleman, the Rev. George Capper, though an improvement on the generality of the clergy of his time, was not only a pluralist (having three livings) and a mighty fox-hunter, but spent the greater part of the summer on his yacht, and was therefore to all intents and purposes an absentee. In 'the sport divine' his congregation were no less interested than himself. It is recorded that one Sunday morning during service a villager who had elected to sleep in the porch instead of inside the church, noticed, just as he was settling himself comfortably, a vixen stealing along in the grass among the tombs. Forgetting all about time

[1] She died March 1844, aged eighty-four.

WHERSTEAD LODGE

THE HOME OF THE FITZGERALDS FOR TEN YEARS (1825-1835)

THE FERRY, CHESTERTON

and place, he jumped up and cried vociferously 'Tally-ho! Tally-ho! There she goes!' and the congregation, to a man, rushed pell-mell out of the church. One piously hopes that the vicar only looked out of the window.

Ipswich, lying so near to Wherstead, was naturally a frequent haunt of FitzGerald, and he had there several friends, including the Rev. J. T. Nottige.[1] The town is of course rich in mediæval and ecclesiastical associations. But it was its book-shops and not its churches that endeared it to FitzGerald. The establishment which he most favoured was that of a Mr. James Reed. Here he browsed continually. The novel was just then beginning to shoulder the biography and the history out of the shelves. *The Talisman*, successor of so many other fine stories, had but lately appeared, and in the words of a rhyme then going the round, 'Nothing drew but Sir Walter Scott.' Scott had no greater admirer than FitzGerald, who read and re-read him.

On 6th February 1826 FitzGerald was entered at Trinity College, Cambridge. He went into residence in the following October, lodging at Mrs. Perry's, subsequently Oakley's, No. 19 King's Parade, with the imposing chapel of King's College to meet his eyes when he looked out of window in the morning. Trinity College consists mainly of three great courts. The first and largest is entered by a noble Tudor gateway ornamented with a statue of Henry VIII., of meek and celibate memory. Entering the great court you notice in the middle the conduit, on your right are the chapel and King Edward's tower, and on your left Queen's tower—the rest of the quadrangle being mainly occupied by the apartments of fellows and students. A semi-circular flight of steps on the west side brings you to a passage,

16. At Cambridge, 1826-1830.

---

[1] He died 21st January 1847.

'The Screens' (with the hall on the right and the kitchen on the left), leading into the cloistered or Neville's court, the west side of which is occupied by the library, designed by Wren. Thence one can reach the third large quadrangle, the New Court, and approach the river by an avenue of limes. The master of Trinity in FitzGerald's time was Christopher Wordsworth, youngest brother of the poet, and 'like all the Wordsworths, pompous and priggish.' He recommended everybody to read Aristophanes.[1] His drawling out of the chapel responses led the undergraduates to call him the 'meeserable sinner,' and naturally it occurred to them to call his brother 'the meeserable poet.' Among the tutors were the future Dean Peacock and Connop Thirlwall (afterwards Bishop of St. David's). Just as FitzGerald entered Cambridge there left it, and in ill odour, an Edward Marlborough FitzGerald, a fact which, combined with other reasons not given, caused FitzGerald to dislike heartily his own name, and led him on most occasions to use as a signature merely the initials E. F. G. Among his fellow-students was John Allen, who became Archdeacon of Salop, and for his few sins stood to Thackeray for the portrait of the tender-hearted gaby Captain Dobbin.[2] Allen was a tall, thin, dark youth with black hair and a plaintive voice. He occupied rooms in Queen Elizabeth's tower at the top of a treble flight of steps, which his crane legs mounted three at a time.[3] Chief of FitzGerald's friends, however, was William Makepeace Thackeray, who went into residence in 1829. His rooms were on the ground-floor of the great court, one set of chambers removed from the chapel.

---

[1] See *Gentleman's Magazine*, vol. xxiii. p. 459.
[2] In *Vanity Fair*.
[3] Mr. W. Aldis Wright writes to me: 'John Allen, afterwards Archdeacon, went into the rooms at the top of the Queen's Gateway on the south side of the old court in the Lent term of 1829. This would be his second term of residence.'

FITZGERALD'S LODGINGS (MRS. PERRY'S)
19 KING'S PARADE, CAMBRIDGE (NOW DEMOLISHED)

To Thackeray, FitzGerald was by turns Ned, Neddibus, Neddikins, and Yedward. Other friends of this period were Francis Duncan (who became Rector of West Chelborough, Somerset), W. H. Thompson (who rose to be Master of Trinity); Frank B. Edgeworth, brother of 'the great Maria'; Charles Buller, who had been the pupil of Carlyle, and was to obtain distinction in parliament; Frederick Maurice; Richard Trench; FitzGerald's fellow-Burians John M. Kemble and James Spedding; and Richard Monckton Milnes. Charles, Frederic, and Alfred Tennyson were contemporaries at Cambridge, but FitzGerald did not become acquainted with them till after he had left Trinity. King Henry on the gateway, the learned centuries and the shades of Bacon, Barrow, Newton, and Dryden, whole platoons of men of genius, cast interested eyes on the new undergraduate as he passes among those grey walls and towers and admonish him to high labours. At first FitzGerald is disposed to listen to them, but gradually he becomes indolent and devotes more attention to desultory reading, music, and painting than to systematic study; and when King Henry, the learned centuries, Barrow and Bacon frown, he says in extenuation of his conduct that the professors take no personal interest in the students—their lectures are the drone of a bagpipe, or the monotonous note of the stormcock, and so uninteresting. 'None indeed but dryheaded, calculating, angular little gentlemen' can take delight in them.[1] FitzGerald, indeed, made an indifferent machine. He was not the sort of man to win honours at a university. He studies the classics, not because they are to advance him, but out of sheer love for them. Virgil is to him a living man; he gathers real crocuses with Sophocles at Colonus. He has no intention, like so many others, of

[1] Tennyson.

flinging his books away after taking his degree; but he will read what interests him and that only, let Henry and the centuries think what they like, and even if he should never get his degree at all.

'The Union' of FitzGerald's time met in a 'low, ill-ventilated, ill-lit, cavernous, tavernous gallery' at the back of the 'Red Lion Inn' in Petty Cury, where, 'on stated evenings, was much logic and other spiritual fencing and ingenious collision.' Several distinguished themselves, but Spedding and one Sunderland, who treated them to too much Tom Paine, were the acknowledged luminaries. Here Thackeray 'made a fool' of himself, 'sputtering on the character of Napoleon.' FitzGerald, however, was content to listen and criticise. The undergraduates gathered in one another's rooms of evenings, and smoked, chatted, and drank coffee. Allen, Spedding, and Thackeray (FitzGerald's chief friends) often came to Mrs. Perry's, and there was much wit, pointy talk, and Baconian philosophy; for Spedding, 'the pope among us young men,'[1] had already begun the censing of his idol. Sometimes the meetings were in Allen's tower, where Allen would sit, feet in fender, folio on knee, and hold forth about Milton and Boswell's *Johnson*. Although to the ordinary Cambridge studies FitzGerald applied himself only intermittently and languidly, he was framing 'many ambitious schemes,' his principal hope being to dazzle the world with his literary productions. These projects he was wont to discuss with Francis Duncan in the course of their walks in the meadows around Cambridge.

It would be unreasonable to suppose that he who lives in the future can live in the present. Consequently it is not surprising that FitzGerald did not know how many

[1] Tennyson.

holes were in his stockings, or how many buttons on his coat, or whether he was suitably provided with boots. When his mother called at Cambridge in that superb yellow coach, with four black horses, and sent a manservant to Mrs. Perry's to bid her son come to her, he was unable to comply, his only pair of boots being at the cobbler's. Some of the university experiences of Fitz-Gerald and Thackeray are recorded in *Pendennis*. For Arthur Pendennis, Thackeray drew on himself and on another, who shall presently be mentioned; whilst in Warrington there are reflections of FitzGerald. Knowing FitzGerald's fondness for music, Thackeray presented him with an idea for a new musical instrument, a sketch called 'the Hogmagundy,' which shows a number of pigs with their tails hanging through the holes in the footboard of a wooden bedstead, whilst a girl, with music-book to guide her, is playing the instrument by pulling their tails.[1] Thackeray and FitzGerald were fond of singing together the 'rather free' Cavalier song—

'Troll, troll the merry brown bowl,'

and many years after, FitzGerald adapted Thackeray's own song, 'Ho, pretty page,' to the same tune. Thanks largely to the energy of his tutor, 'one Williams,' Fitz-Gerald finally managed to obtain his degree (January 1830). If Bury had been delightful to him, very delightful too, despite, perhaps by reason of, his indolence, were his Cambridge days. He held with Roger Ascham, whose words he quotes in a notebook: 'He that is able to mayntain his lyfe in learning at Cambridge knoweth not what a felycitie he hath,' and in Ascham's words too he could say of his intimate friends there, 'I doe salute you

---

[1] See Biographical Edition of Thackeray's Works, ii. p. xxxi.

all: I name none, because I would leave out none, and because I love all.'[1]

Of the many excursions made by FitzGerald and his friends while at Cambridge, we get hints and echoes in *Euphranor*. One of them indeed is minutely described: It is a bright day in May, and the author, whilst pretending to study, is disturbed by Euphranor, who insists on a row on the river, a walk, or a game at billiards at Chesterton, a neighbouring village. The pair break in upon the studies of Lexilogus, a thin, pale, spectacled creature, who would rather have been left alone; and presently all three run down stairs, cross the Great Court, thread the Screens, and pass through Neville's Court to the open green before the Library. Taking a boat, they presently pass the 'closely packt barges at Magdalen,' and through the locks, pull a few miles down the river, and then return to the ferry, where they surrender their boat, and foot it over the fields to Chesterton, and the 'Three Tuns Inn.'[2] On the bowling-green of this hostelry they find another student, Lycion, 'rolling the bowls about lazily with his foot.' There is much academic talk, chiefly upon education and exercise, and ranging from Don Quixote to Waller, and from Aristotle to Sir Thomas Browne, and then a dinner in the little parlour 'very airy and pleasant, with its windows opening on the bowling-green, the table laid with a clean white cloth, and upon that a dish of smoking beef-steak.' They return just in time to see a boat-race. There are townsmen and gownsmen, 'with the tasselled fellow-commoner sprinkled here and there,'

17. The 'Three Tuns' at Chesterton.

---

[1] Letter from Ascham to Mr. Raven. Copied by FitzGerald into his Museum Book, 1883.

[2] The Ferry is the Horse Grind adjacent to Roebuck House; the fields are now built upon; the Three Tuns is a private residence, 'Cambridge House,' somewhat altered, but substantially the same.

CAMBRIDGE HOUSE, CHESTERTON

FORMERLY 'THE THREE TUNS' INN

GELDESTONE HALL

reading men and sporting men, masters of colleges, ladies. 'They are off—they are coming! Bravo, St. John's! Go it, Trinity!' It is all over: the ensign of Trinity drops, the eagle of St. John rises. Questions and chatter, then a walk home 'across the meadow leading to the town, whither the dusky troops of gownsmen, with their confused voices, seemed, as it were, evaporating in the twilight, while a nightingale began to be heard among the flowering chestnuts of Jesus.'[1]

Reference has several times been made to FitzGerald's brother John. Admittedly they were not twins, but Antipholus of Ephesus and Antipholus of Syracuse were not more like each other in character and disposition, whilst their resemblance in person struck even the most unobservant. The anecdotes told of John resemble very closely those told of Edward, and it may be boldly said that if Edward did anything, John would have done pretty nearly the same thing in the same circumstances. There is no need here, however, to point out the resemblances between these 'two goodly sons,'

18. The Two Antipholuses.

> 'The one so like the other
> As could not be distinguished but by names,'

for those will be made clear enough as the book proceeds. While Edward was at Cambridge, John, whose passion was the study of the Bible, of which he had a phenomenal knowledge, was preparing sedulously for the church,[2] which had always been his ambition; but an attack of brain fever, which affected his eyes, put an end to all his hopes. By and by he married, and very happily, a

---

[1] The work *Euphranor* is dealt with in Chapters vi. and ix.
[2] 'Uncle James took it into his head that one of his brother's family should be a parson.'—*Euphranor.*

Miss Augusta Jane Lisle Phillips,[1] a lady of most sweet and beautiful character, to whom Edward pays several tributes. John had already turned to authorship, but was interested less in literature than in social and religious questions, as may be seen from his tract, *Plain Advice on Drinking and Drunkenness*, 1828, the first of a long series of books and pamphlets from his pen. He did not so much read the Bible as live in it. It became part of him. His duty, he conceived, was to write and preach against what seemed to him the most lamentable vices of the day—the slave-trade, drunkenness, and everything tending to Romanism. Against these he warred all his life and with all his might.

After leaving Cambridge, FitzGerald paid a visit to his sister Eleanor (Mrs. Kerrich) at Geldestone Hall ('Gelson'), two miles north-west of Beccles, that pleasant town on the Waveney, which has absolutely no fault except its name. FitzGerald said that it always put him in mind of hooks and eyes. But he loved the quaint irregularity of its streets, its bright river, and the grand old church tower, standing a short distance from the church itself, a circumstance referred to by the Caroline poet Matthew Stevenson—

19. Mrs. Kerrich, Dr. Crowfoot, Le Bon Pasteur, Torrijos.

> 'He does himself 'twixt this and t'other tide,
> Like Beccles steeple from the church's side.'[2]

The top of the tower commands fine views of the surrounding country. To the north-west Geldestone stands out a conspicuous little white cube embosomed in ... iage; on the south-west, one can descry some of the villages of the country of *The Nine Saints*; on the east stretches the dim blue outline of Lowestoft; on the north the wooded

[1] See Chapter v.   [2] See *Gentleman's Magazine*, 1835.

country of Haddiscoe. To reach Geldestone Hall one crosses the Waveney and proceeds by a raised path, beautiful in summer-time with the rich purple of the vetch, and passes through the village of Gillingham, with its two churches, the Norman still used, the Perpendicular (and far later church) in ruins. Geldestone Hall is a substantial mansion, and its outward appearance has not altered materially since the days when FitzGerald visited it and walked backwards and forwards to Beccles. The house contained a considerable collection of curiosities, which Mr. Kerrich took great delight in showing and explaining. Of Mrs. Kerrich, his best loved sister, Fitz-Gerald has left, in an inedited manuscript,[1] the following portrait:—' Mrs. Kerrich is a clever person, fond of literary pursuits, absent, careless, fond of educating and giving advice; is a thinking, grave, and staid-minded person, very unsophisticated in the ways of the world, not easily pleased, expects much attention.' To this lovable woman and her husband FitzGerald's letters contain many references, and he was much attached to their children. At Beccles his chief friend was Dr. William Edward Crowfoot,[2] Mrs. Kerrich's medical adviser; and he was a frequent visitor both at Dr. Crowfoot's house on the Market Place and at the Misses Crowfoot's house in Blyburgate Street. Subsequently Beccles became still further interesting to FitzGerald, as the birthplace and home of Mr. W. Aldis Wright, who was one of the most intimate friends of his latter days.

In 1830 FitzGerald was staying with his Aunt Purcell in Paris. Thackeray was also in Paris, and of course they forgathered. How they spent their time may be gleaned from Thackeray's early Essays and Ballads.

[1] In the possession of the Rev. E. Kenworthy Browne.
[2] He lived till 12th May 1887.

Their mornings were passed at the Louvre, where Thackeray pleased himself with the idea that he was studying art. FitzGerald, however, was attracted less by the pictures than by the statuary. The friends liked to visit the Louvre on a Sunday after church, to watch the crowd of shopmen, soldiers, grisettes, and livery servants enjoying the pictures. They lounged on the Boulevards and in the Bois de Boulogne, and no doubt dined together at Terré's on that rich savoury stew which Thackeray has sung in 'The Ballad of Bouillabaisse.'[1] This same year, and at Paris too, Victor Hugo was writing his *Notre Dame*, Balzac his *Peau de Chagrin*; and Thackeray refers to the Parisian littérateurs blustering about 'in velvet and mustachios and gold chains.' George Sand, who had not begun to write, was just then contemplating the dismissal of her boorish husband. One fine evening FitzGerald stopped on the Boulevards by the Madeleine to listen to a street singer. Several passing 'blouses' had stopped also, not only to listen, but to join in the songs, having bought little 'libretti' of the words from the musician. FitzGerald also bought one and assisted in the song, 'which the man called out beforehand (as they do hymns in church).'[2] This song, 'Le Bon Pasteur,' FitzGerald preserved, and copied into a commonplace book which he called 'Half-Hours with the Worst Authors.'[3] It begins—

> '*Bons habitants de ce village
> Prêtez l'oreille un moment*,'

and each stanza ends—

> '*Et le bon Dieu vous bénira.*'

---

[1] Biographical Edition, xiii. p. 62.
[2] *Letters to Fanny Kemble* (Bentley), p. 31.
[3] Subsequently called 'Half-Hours with Obscure Authors.' Mr. Aldis Wright showed me this at Cambridge.

Balzac compared 'luxurious Paris' that year to a sand-pit—once in, escape was impossible. Soirees, breakfasts, theatres—a perpetual whirl. FitzGerald and Thackeray, however, managed to get away at the end of May. Fitz-Gerald, full of Utopian ideas about Society, and resolved to become 'a great bear,' crossed to Southampton, whilst Thackeray made for Germany. John Allen, who happened just then to be staying at Portsmouth, having heard that 'the most dear FitzGerald' was at Southampton, walked over with a friend to see him (10th August 1830). Arriving late, however, they found that FitzGerald had gone to bed. Says Allen of the next morning: 'Got up and went to FitzGerald's room, who jumped up and almost cried for joy to see me, dear affectionate fellow! After breakfast, though very stiff, walked with him to Netley Abbey, and tried to make him steady in his views on religion.'[1] Thackeray wrote to FitzGerald from Weimar, and sent a picture of himself in breeches and cocked hat, as he had appeared before the Grand Duke,[2] and was able to boast that he had been introduced to Goethe.

These were the days of the Torrijos fiasco. A number of needy Spanish political refugees in London, under the leadership of the courtly and accomplished General Torrijos, determined to make a descent on Spain with a view to bringing about an insurrection and the establishment of a constitutional government. FitzGerald's friend, John Kemble, had seemed inclined to enter the church, and Tennyson had addressed to him a fine sonnet, which proved, however, to be only poetry and not prophecy. Instead of becoming a 'later Luther' and a 'soldier priest,' he caught the enthusiasm of Sterling and other

---

[1] *John Allen*, by R. M. Grier (Rivingtons), p. 33.
[2] There are reminiscences of this visit in *Vanity Fair*.

hot-headed Cambridge democrats, and, embracing a quarrel not his own, followed Torrijos to Spain. These youths, however, 'helped the cause,' not by fighting, but by sight-seeing and drinking ale; and Fanny Kemble pictures her brother 'holding forth upon German metaphysics,'[1] which grow dense in proportion as the tobacco fumes grow thick and his glass grows empty. Having spent their money, they returned home, scathless, but full of fervour.[2] John Kemble, indeed, could talk of nothing but Torrijos, and he sang in FitzGerald's room in Russell Street the insurrectionary song, 'Si un Elio[3] conspiro allevo.' The end of poor Torrijos and his forty-five fighters was a melancholy and inglorious one. They were all captured near Malaga, and summarily shot.[4] Thackeray returned from Germany, and, very thick with Kemble, was now perched on a stool in a lawyer's office, from which giddy eminence he sent Fitz-Gerald a picture of himself, stool, desk, and all.

About this time FitzGerald's father purchased, subject to a life-interest in it of an aged lady, Madam Short, the old manorial house, Boulge Hall, situated about a mile from his former residence, Bredfield White House. Of Madam Short, an imperious and tetchy old lady, many odd tales are told, and one of them concerns us here. She and her husband, Colonel Short, often fell out, and at such times the Colonel would speak only to his dog, she to her cat. After a particularly bitter quarrel, Mrs. Short declared she would live with her husband no longer. She therefore built herself, near the Hall gates, a two-roomed thatched cottage, with apartments in the

---

[1] *Records of a Girlhood*, ii. p. 282.
[2] Kemble returned 21st May 1831.
[3] Elio, a Spanish general, executed in 1822.
[4] November 1831. See Carlyle's *Life of Sterling*, and Fanny Kemble's *Records of Later Life*, p. 133.

rear for servants; and the rest of her life was spent there, or at the Hall, according as she and her husband happened or happened not to be on good terms. This was the cottage which became for so many years the home of Edward FitzGerald.

CHAPTER III

NASEBY AND TENBY

NOVEMBER 1830—MAY 1834

Bibliography

1. The Meadows in Spring,	. . .	*Written*	1831
2. Will Thackeray,	. . . . .	,,	1831
3. Canst thou, my Clora?	. . . .	,,	1832
4. On Anne Allen,	. . . . .	,,	1833

IN November, FitzGerald is at Naseby ensconced in a comfortable farmhouse. He looks round the old home, 'The Woolleys'; hobanobs with Watchams, John Linnet (whose daughter Sarah is weak in the head and 'can't abear Cromwell'), the blacksmith, who is a great repertory of tradition respecting the battle, and understands it as well as if he had trailed a pike there, and the aged and venerable vicar, the Rev. John Marshall. He dines also with Ringrose the carpenter—Naseby is full of Ringroses; hears Miss Ringrose play the piano; visits the battlefield for bones, bullets, and fossils; writes to John Allen, 'I am quite the king here, I promise you'; and makes a sensation at church with a magnificent blue surtout or frock-coat (he loved splendid colours), which not only astonished Naseby but afterwards proved the theme of infinite jest among his friends. Most memorable event of all, however, he composes that pleasant poem with the Elizabethan flavour

20. At Naseby. 'The Meadows in Spring.'

NASEBY AND TENBY

entitled 'The Meadows in Spring.' The poet begins with references to the amenities of winter—

> 'When such a time cometh,
> I do retire
> Into an old room
> Beside a bright fire.'

He then goes on to tell us how he reads, smokes, and talks to a friend whilst nought passes between them 'save a brown jug'; but when the clouds part and spring comes—

> 'I jump up like mad,
> Break the old pipe in twain,
> And away to the meadows,
> The meadows again.'

These verses appeared in Hone's *Year Book*, 30th April 1831, and a variant in the *Athenæum* on July 9th had the honour of being praised by Charles Lamb, who said, ''Tis a poem I envy—that and Montgomery's "Last Man"—I envy the writers because I feel I could have done something like them.' How soon FitzGerald began to write poetry we do not know, though he may be said to have been cradled in it. A whole galaxy of poets and poetesses, most of whom were his intimate acquaintances, sang the vales, and pittering brooks, and broad estuaries, and vanished cities of his native Suffolk. Indeed the south-eastern portion of the county was a veritable Bœotia, with the Deben and the Alde for its Hippocrene and Aganippe. Of Crabbe, Barton, and Mitford we have already spoken; but there were others who, if less famous, were no less familiar to FitzGerald. There was James Bird of Yoxford (1788-1839), bookseller and giant, 'six feet his stature, as an arrow straight,' whose themes were the Vale of Slaughden[1] and Dunwich, which he credited with

[1] Published in 1819. 'There winds a vale beside the rolling sea.'

Arthurian splendour; and there was G. W. Fulcher, 'the Crabbe of Sudbury,' who in touching verse proclaimed the hardships of the deserving poor. Nor was the gentler sex mute. Mrs. Biddell, Mrs. Fulcher, and Miss Charlesworth (whose poems FitzGerald used to revise, and who addressed verse to his sister Isabella) added to the harmony. Mrs. Biddell's house at Playford was a Suffolk literary salon where all the local wits and poets met to talk about the Muses and say smart things over dinners that lasted from three in the afternoon till nine in the evening. An occasional guest at those gatherings was Robert Southey, whose poem on a 'Holly Tree'[1] at Playford is among the best of his rhythmic productions. If it be urged that Mrs. Biddell's poets are most of them forgotten, it may be claimed for most that fame was not their aspiration. Indeed they did all they could to avoid it, coyly hiding their identities behind initials, asterisks, and anons—quite content to see their effusions in print in some 'Annual' or 'Pocket Book.' Silly (that is 'guileless') Suffolk, dropping for the moment her ribboned crook, was making her valleys tuneful with the oaten flute. All the members of this coterie being FitzGerald's acquaintances, and some his intimate friends, it is not surprising that he too turned poet. But he did not adopt their literary manners, did not even try to imitate his much-admired Crabbe—harking back rather to the melodious Elizabethans and the linked sweetnesses of the Caroline

---

[1] This tree is still standing. The lower leaves, as the poem states, have prickles, the higher leaves are smooth. One passes it going from Little Bealings station to Playford by the footpath—

> 'Below, a circling fence, its leaves are seen
>   Wrinkled and keen;
> No grazing cattle through their prickly round
>   Can reach to wound;
> But as they grow where nothing is to fear,
> Smooth and unarmed the pointless leaves appear.'

lyrists. Now came more sketches from Thackeray, and among them a portrait of FitzGerald in that wonderful blue frock-coat or surtout which fluttered all hearts at Naseby. Thackeray also represented his friend in a Weimar court dress, and 'In after life.' In the latter picture E. F. G. is made to assume John Bull proportions and is surrounded by a demonstrative family.[1]

In May 1831 Thackeray suggested that he and Fitz-Gerald should go to Spain or Germany together, and sent some sketches representing the pair combating brigands. One of the sketches shows 'Captain FitzGerald' in the act of running a terrific Spaniard through the body, whilst Thackeray is slashing at two others. In October Fitz-Gerald sends his friend the spirited lines called 'Will Thackeray.'[2] They commence with the declaration, written at a moment when his heart was warm with a glass of port, that till he and Willy met, life was not life at all. The thought of Willy gives the wine new flavour, makes the fire burn clearer—

21. Lines on Will Thackeray.

'The chair that Will sat in I sit in the best,
The tobacco is sweetest which Willy hath blest.'

Though the wind blows cold, he can laugh at the storm and think of his Willy. Even old age will make no difference to their friendship—

'Let him make me grey, gouty, blind, toothless, or silly,
Still old Ned shall be Ned, and old Willy be Willy.'

But while thus exercising his poetical gifts, FitzGerald continued to delight himself also with painting and music. He makes friends with Perry Nursey of Little Bealings, who, with his son Claude Lorraine and his daughter

---

[1] See Biographical Edition of Thackeray, vol. ix., 'Christmas Books,' p. xxiii.
[2] *Ibid.* p. xx.

Marietta, lived in the house which is now (1902) the residence of Archdeacon Lawrence. Perry Nursey is remembered on three accounts—as an artist, as an accomplished violinist, and as having introduced into Suffolk that glorious tree, the black Italian poplar, or as Woodbridge folk affectionately style it, the Nursey poplar. He made for FitzGerald among other things, 'a very pretty oil sketch' of Bredfield House, and 'a small picture of a breaking wave.'[1] Another friend was Robert Newton Shawe of Kesgrave Hall, a military man, and chairman of the bench of magistrates at Woodbridge.

22. Perry Nursey and Newton Shawe.

FitzGerald's brother John, who now leaned towards Nonconformity, and occupied himself much in evangelistic work, preaching in schoolrooms and chapels, was often at Naseby—generally at Naseby Woolleys—and with him frequently was the Rev. Timothy Richard Matthews, of whom Edward speaks so much. Matthews was born at Long Sutton, Isle of Ely, in 1795, and entered at Sidney Sussex College, Cambridge, in 1815. After taking his degree he was appointed to the curacies of Colmworth and Bolnhurst, in Bedfordshire, where his earnestness as a preacher caused a furore and drew immense congregations, gathered from all the surrounding country. He was a man of splendid physique, and the possessor of a stentorian voice. In 1830 he was appointed chaplain to the House of Industry at Bedford, and here again—outsiders being permitted to attend—he attracted crowds. The chapel connected with the House of Industry was subsequently closed, but Matthews' congregation, un-

23. Matthews and his Trumpet.

---

[1] The Nurseys, and among them 'Claude Lorraine,' Perry's son, lie in Little Bealings churchyard, which is about three miles from Woodbridge. Miss Marietta Nursey died in 1891, being then in her ninety-first year.

REV. T. R. MATTHEWS OF BEDFORD
'FITZGERALD'S PREACHER' (BORN 1795. DIED 1845)

willing to lose their pastor, made strenuous exertions, and, 'sowing carnal things to reap divine,' erected for him, in less than six months, a spacious chapel in the Bromham Road, with rooms underneath for a residence, two of the round-headed windows of which can be seen in our illustration. In this underworld Matthews and his family lived, and in the chapel he henceforth officiated, using, with trifling alteration, the service of the Church of England. He was occasionally assisted by John Fitz-Gerald. In the week Matthews preached in his black gown and bands in the open places of Bedford or elsewhere, first blowing a trumpet to attract hearers. He visited at different times many towns and a vast number of villages in the Midlands. To the zealous companies he had gathered together it was his custom to write pastoral letters, which were read aloud by one of their members, and some of these letters have been preserved. In a large town he usually hired the town hall, and preached to immense congregations. Opposition he had, as do all men who are in earnest. 'The quality,' whose polite ears objected to such words as 'judgment and hell,' 'except when quoting Milton'—a society phrase snapped up by FitzGerald—would have none of him; rubicund farmers, who could see no harm in a 'merry mill'; fox-hunting clergymen, and even Charles Dickens, with his 'Sunday under Three Heads'[1] (1836), all had their hostile say, and employed against him their various arts. His manner was most impressive. To use the words of Edward FitzGerald, who became acquainted with him a little later: 'He believed in Christ, and had no misgivings whatever.' Matthews, as we have pointed out, often visited John FitzGerald at Naseby Woolleys, and,

[1] A considerable portion of this diatribe was, I believe, directed specially against Matthews.

arrayed in black gowns, both of them preached in the space between Naseby churchyard and the FitzGerald Arms. Lest in his earnestness he should forget himself and preach too long—a frequent failing—Matthews would say to Mr. FitzGerald before commencing, 'My friend, when I've preached long enough, kindly pull my gown.' These sermons, especially one about 'Three Sticks,' are still spoken of with enthusiasm by old folks in the village. After sermon the preachers would mingle with the people, and say, first to one and then to another, some word of injunction or encouragement. To John Linnet the valiant, for example, Matthews once observed, 'John, be sure you are in the first resurrection.' On cottage tables at Naseby you may still see religious books with John FitzGerald's handwriting in them—generally 'A token of Christian friendship to [So-and-so] from J. F. G.,' with the date 1832 or 1833. A little to the west of Naseby is a huge reservoir, the property of the Grand Union Canal Company, and Matthews and John FitzGerald often held baptism services there, sometimes immersing eight or nine persons in one day.

In FitzGerald's family there was little change; his father was as enthusiastic as ever in the hunting-field, and Mrs. FitzGerald still retained her passion for the theatre. We hear of her exciting both admiration and envy in London drawing-rooms with her 'green velvet gown trimmed with sables.' This was the period of the beginning of railways, and presently Edward FitzGerald had his first train ride. 'So you've seen the railway,' writes Fanny Kemble to a friend in 1831; 'I'm so glad you have seen that magnificent invention.' Edward FitzGerald spent three weeks of October and November 1831 in town with Thackeray, and later visited the west country in order to see Salisbury

24. Tenby and the Allens, 1832.

THE TRUMPET BLOWN BY THE REV. T. R. MATTHEWS
'FITZGERALD'S PREACHER'
NOW PRESERVED IN A CHAPEL AT RAVENSDEN, NEAR BEDFORD

NASEBY AND TENBY

Cathedral and Bemerton, George Herbert's village. In the spring of 1832 John Allen, who had just lost his father,[1] left Cambridge, and FitzGerald and others presented him with an armchair; and in the summer and autumn of that year we find FitzGerald visiting Tenby, where Mrs. Allen resided, and making journeys with Allen to Freestone Hall,[2] near the village of Milton. Freestone Hall was the residence of Mr. James Allen (a cousin of John Allen). This family consisted of a son, Thomas,[3] and three daughters, Fanny,[4] Anne, and Mary. The FitzGeralds and the two Allen families were most intimate, and Edward's sister Andalusia became engaged to John Allen's brother, Bird. From Tenby to Milton is about six miles, and FitzGerald afterwards remembered every inch of the road—the water-mill, the picturesque tower of Gumfreston church, Ivy Tower, the main road to Narberth, and Carew Mountain, Carew Castle,[5] and Freestone Hall at the end. He carried away mental pictures of pretty 'sweet-throated' Anne Allen, twenty-three years of age, with china rose complexion and lilac gown, who gathered flowers from the garden and made nosegays for every one, placing 'the fairest at her father's side,' and went about the house singing; as well as of Mary[6] (who became the wife of John Allen's brother

---

[1] Rev. David Bird Allen, buried at Burton in Rhos, 1831. Mrs. Allen died ten years later.

[2] One and three-quarter miles from Carew Church. A great part of Freestone Hall has since been demolished, and the remaining portion has been converted into a farmhouse by its owner—the Hon. Robert Cranmer Trollope.

[3] To Mrs. Thomas Allen, who is still living, I am indebted for most of this information.

[4] She became the wife of the Rev. William Allen, Rector of Bosheston, Pembroke.

[5] There is no village of Carew. The village is called Milton, half a mile or more to the west of Carew church. The few cottages on the north side of Carew churchyard are called Cheriton, probably a corruption of Churchtown.

[6] She lived till 1884.

Charles), poring over some wholesome book, an old turnip of a watch in front of her, in the tree-surrounded and sombre schoolroom at the west of the house. Other places that he visited were Penally, distant a mile and a half, with its watch-tower and its cave, declared to be that of Cymbeline, and the romantic cliffs and caverns of Bosheston. Allen and he often sauntered together on the sands, among the ruins of the castle, and on St. Katherine's rock. Their talk was of Shakespeare, Milton, George Herbert, the Greek poets, and religion, for Fitz-Gerald still leaned to Agnosticism, and his views disquieted Allen, who in his gentle way endeavoured to change them. FitzGerald, though unconvinced, loved him the more for his pains, and often in outbursts of affection called him 'best of friends,' 'dear fellow,' 'my Johnny,' 'dear good Allen.' To Tenby Thackeray sent more letters for his 'dear Teddekin,' 'dear old Teddibus.' In one of them he refers to a clergyman who objected to pictures in churches. 'These fellows in the shovel hats,' he says, 'are greater bigots than the Catholics. When you turn parson, dear Teddibus, you won't refuse to see merit even in a Presbyterian.'

Staying in the same boarding-house as FitzGerald was a handsome, merry-eyed, wildish lad of sixteen, William Kenworthy Browne, who is pictured with longish auburn hair, a pink complexion set off with a touch or two of white, the result of contact with the billiard-table cue, a fawn-coloured waistcoat, a bright blue tie, and a dark coat; son of Mr. Joseph Browne of Cauldwell House,[1] an alderman, and one year Mayor of Bedford. Between this youth and FitzGerald commenced a friendship which was severed only by death. The Tenby visit brightened many an after hour

25. William Kenworthy Browne.

---

[1] In Cauldwell Street, Bedford.

W. KENWORTHY BROWNE

by its delightful memory. Browne, John Allen, Anne, Mary, and Fanny—youth, beauty, and good-humour—the scent of the October leaves, and the distant sound of the band on the pleasure-vessels making for Bristol, were all recollections which abided with him.

About this time FitzGerald and Allen started a series of commonplace books, to which they gave the name of 'Paradise,' a place in which to insert choicest extracts. Nothing mean was to sully these pages. FitzGerald puts into his Carew's lines, 'Ask me no more where June bestows,' and many of Shakespeare's sonnets, 'giving each a fair white sheet' to itself. One of these 'Paradises' has been described by Miss Batch in *The Bookman*:[1] 'It is a long, thin book with a marbled cover, worn leather back, and time-stained pages.' The watermark in the paper is 1831, the last entry bears date 26th April 1840. FitzGerald evidently carried it about with him, for entries were made in different places—London, Boulge, Geldestone, and Halverstown (Ireland). It contains, among other matter, cullings from Crabbe's *Life of the Rev. George Crabbe*, Lockhart's *Scott*, Bryant's *Mythology*, and Wilkinson's *Egyptians*, character sketches of Wolsey and others, and Hayward's translation of Margaret's song in *Faust*; while there is a long catalogue of collections of poetry, showing his predilection for antique authors, with examples from *England's Helicon*, Churchyard's *Jane Shore*, which is pronounced 'very fine,' and Michael Drayton's friend William Browne. Fiction is represented by two passages only, one from *Joseph Andrews*, where Adams 'strongly asserted that there was no such thing as pleasure in the world, at which Pamela and her husband smiled on one another'; and one from

26. 'Paradise-making.'

---

[1] The book was given to Miss Batch by Mr. John Loder, bookseller, of Woodbridge.

Plumer Ward's *Tremaine* (1825). As his *Letters* and the Omar reveal, FitzGerald had a 'haunting sense of Time's continual speed, of the slipping from our grasp of day after day, of the shortness and insecurity of life'; and in the 'Paradise' there are several pages of this tincture gleaned chiefly from his favourite Owen Feltham,[1] who had the additional virtue of being a Suffolk man. Feltham's essay on Poverty is called 'very fine,' and the remark, 'He is twice an asse that is a riming one,' 'very acute.' Several passages deal with religion, and one by Rowland Hill on Prayer is held to breathe 'a spirit of sweet and childlike trust in a Heavenly Father.'

In 1831 FitzGerald visited Lowestoft — the town of herrings and saffron-buns—which, to use the words of an old chronicler, 'hangs, as it were, over the sea'—a town with which he was destined to become closely connected. Lowestoft boasts association with two other distinguished writers, the Elizabethan poet and satirist 'sweet Tom Nash' and George Borrow. Nash, who, among other things, sang the good red herring, wrote a spirited tale, *The Unfortunate Traveller*, and two breezy plays, not to mention a host of miscellaneous works. George Borrow, the third of Lowestoft's *dii majores*, did not settle in the neighbourhood until several years after FitzGerald's first visit; but he had already gone through his experiences with his Brynhildic queen, the gigantic Isopel Berners, as related in *Lavengro*, and was now a bookseller's hack in London.

27. At Lowestoft, 1831.

FitzGerald loved to stroll among the marrams or coarse sea grasses of the Denes or on the North Beach, with the red-roofed, picturesque old town, pierced with narrow 'scores' or lanes, rising high behind, and the glorious

---

[1] Author of *Resolves: Divine, Moral, and Political.* 2nd ed. 1628; 12th ed. 1709. Reprinted in 1806 by James Cumming.

NASEBY AND TENBY

sea in front. To him the sea was always glorious, whether by day, when he could watch the stately parting fishing-boats with their red or bistre sails; or by night, beautiful with the silveriness of the 'moonway'; and he liked to think of the old sea-fights, when the cannon of Opdam, De Ruyter, and York boomed in Sole Bay,[1] and Dorset wrote his dainty song, 'To all you Ladies.' He noticed that very many of the herring luggers which then lay on the beach bore testimony to the influence on the place of John Wesley, who had last visited Lowestoft in 1790—the occasion probably when Crabbe, the poet, heard him apply to himself the lines from Anacreon—

> 'Oft by the women I am told,
> Poor Anacreon, thou grow'st old.'

In 1831 Lowestoft had just begun to obtain a reputation as a seaside resort. The daffodil and the violet grew wild in the wooded pleasaunce in front of the old Suffolk Inn. There was not a single house between the bridge and Kirkley, and, to reach the latter, one had to pass over ditches from which, at low water, shrimps used to be taken. A 'Blue Coach'—for as yet there was no rail—plied between the town and London.[2]

The herrings for which the town was famous were landed on the North Beach (the harbour was not opened till about 1840); the luggers, which stood off at about a hundred yards, being relieved by boats. Mackerel was sold by auction on the spot, and the herrings[3] were carried in wagons to the fish-houses on the Waplough Road to

---

[1] 1665. Battle between Opdam and Duke of York.
1772. Battle in Sole Bay (Southwold Bay) between De Ruyter and Duke of York.

[2] I am not sure, but I think the railway to Norwich was opened about 1845, that to Woodbridge about 1865.

[3] Mackerel season began 13th May, and lasted ten weeks. The herring season occupies the months of October and November.

be cured. When the season was over the luggers were hauled on to the beach by horses, and shored up. In all the life of the beach and the fishery FitzGerald took a continual interest.

He was fond of walking to Kirkley, with its ruined church,[1] and so on by the cliff—since so ruthlessly damaged by the sea—to Pakefield. He fraternised much with the sailors, and particularly with a Pakefield man, 'Lew' Colby, and his son William, 'Dickymilk,' who was to become owner of the *Au Revoir*, called by the beachmen 'Horrywaur,' and to finish life on 'stilts.'[2] With 'Dickymilk,' whom he calls in his *Sea Words and Phrases* 'a good fellow,' FitzGerald sometimes walked on a Sunday to Pakefield church, an edifice that pleased him because of its 'delightful mouse-coloured thatch' roof. Colby would go in, and FitzGerald would remain outside in the porch—his attitude towards professed religion during almost the whole of his life. The preacher at Pakefield was the Rev. John Rumph, who, we are told, was accustomed, when the lifeboat was wanted, to close his book immediately, and go off with his flock to render help. Another of FitzGerald's beach acquaintances was one Harry Norman, 'Old Brawtoe,' who got his living and his nickname by picking up and selling odds and ends of rope. FitzGerald explored all the neighbouring villages—Hopton, with its laig or chasm in the cliff; Corton, dear to sailors homeward bound for Lowestoft; and Covehithe with 'The Blue Anchor,' known to

---

[1] Now restored.
[2] The passage in *Sea Words and Phrases* refers to events that occurred, not in 1831, but between 1831 and 1840. 'Dickymilk' was only fifteen in 1831, and did not become owner of the *Au Revoir* till about 1840. FitzGerald is only speaking approximately. When I met 'Dickymilk' in the spring and autumn of 1902 he was eighty-six years of age, lived in Surrey Street, and went about on crutches, which, Suffolk fashion, he called 'stilts.'

amphibians, no doubt after some old sign, as 'The Naked Man of Cothy.'

The year 1831 saw the country agitated over the much-debated question of Parliamentary Reform. George Crabbe, the poet—FitzGerald's 'great gun'—waiting for death, was not at all sure that the proposed change would be advantageous. He felt the degradation when he saw at Trowbridge Fair 'four hundred and eighty-five human beings' (Cuyp-like exactness in letter as well as in poem) 'with painted faces and crazy dresses and gestures, trying to engage and entice the idle spectators to enter their poor show-houses.' Crabbe died 3rd February of the next year, 1832, when FitzGerald was just twenty-three. The Reform Bill became law in the following June.

<small>28. Death of the poet Crabbe, 3rd Feb. 1832.</small>

The poem, 'To a Lady Singing,' was written, apparently, after FitzGerald's return from Tenby. One feels that Clora was Anne Allen. If so, the prophecy had the sad misfortune to be fulfilled all too speedily—too soon she followed her sweet song. The poet asks—

<small>29. Canst thou, my Clora.</small>

> 'Canst thou, my Clora, declare
> After thy sweet song dieth
> Into the wild summer air,
> Whither it falleth or flieth?'

and answers his own question—

> 'Melody, dying away
> Into the dark sky closes,
> Like the good soul from her clay,
> Like the fair odour of roses,
> Therefore thou now art behind it,
> But thou shalt follow and find it.'

Subsequently (December 1832) FitzGerald added two more stanzas which, however, are less beautiful. In this poem, like 'The Meadows in Spring,' can be discerned the influence of the old lyrists Carew and Vaughan; but not only did these poets and the earlier and equally sweet Elizabethans influence his verse, they coloured his whole existence. Indeed, Sir Henry Wotton's poem, 'The Character of a Happy Life,' which was one of FitzGerald's great favourites, reads so like FitzGerald's own life that one is tempted to assume, though there is certainly the trifling difficulty of dates, that Wotton had FitzGerald in mind—

> 'How happy is he born and taught
> That serveth not another's will;
> Whose armour is his honest thought,
> And simple truth his utmost skill.'

'It is very beautiful,' comments FitzGerald, 'and fit for a Paradise of any kind.'

While on a visit to Cambridge this year, FitzGerald met his friend J. M. Kemble, who had commenced in earnest the Anglo-Saxon studies which were to make him famous; and perpetrated 'a wretched sketch of Kemble reading something, with a glass of ale on the table.'

The year 1832 saw the publication of Tennyson's second volume of poems. Says FitzGerald of *The Lady of Shalott*:—'Well I remember this poem read to me before I knew the author at Cambridge one night in 1832 or '33, and its images passing across my mind, as across the magic mirror, while half asleep in the mail-coach to London in the creeping dawn that followed.'[1]

In November we find him in London frequenting bookshops, and buying Bacon's *Essays*, Evelyn's *Sylva*, and Browne's *Religio*. He had plenty of time at his disposal, always wrote more letters than he received, and confessed

---

[1] Quoted in the *Life of Lord Tennyson*.

to a 'very young lady-like partiality' for writing to those he loved. In the letters of this period he tells of his books and his thoughts, and returns again and again to the subject of Shakespeare's *Sonnets*. 'I had,' says he, 'but half an idea of him, demi-god as he seemed before, till I read them carefully.'[1] We gather, too, that he applied himself to Wordsworth, though without enthusiasm, but heartily admired Bacon's *Essay on Friendship*.

With his old schoolfellow, W. B. Donne, who lived at Mattishall, in Norfolk, FitzGerald often corresponded. It is 'Our Donne,' 'My Dear Donne, who shares with Spedding my oldest and deepest love.' In later years, Dr. Thompson, Master of Trinity, said of Donne: 'He is one of the finest gentlemen I know, and no ordinary scholar—remarkable also for his fidelity to his friends.' Cheerfulness and meekness were his salient characteristics, and of the former he had much need, for the world often treated him with more than customary harshness, though he never complained. 'When,' asks FitzGerald, 'does he complain?'

30. W. B. Donne. Castle Irwell.

In February 1833 FitzGerald went to stay at Castle Irwell, his father's Manchester seat—an old-fashioned, but not ancient, house, built on a natural mound of red sandstone, which crops out of the flat land of the Irwell valley, just opposite the cliff at Higher Broughton on the east side of the Irwell. The rooms were small; there was a private chapel in the house, and tradition spoke of a secret passage leading under the river to Broughton. In the meadows to the north of the house races were held, the nearest way to the course being over a private suspension-bridge of the FitzGeralds, which was open to passengers on payment of a halfpenny. Westward lay the fatal colliery ground of Pendleton. At Castle Irwell

[1] *Letters*, vol. i. p. 14 (Macmillan).

FitzGerald chiefly spent his time in a re-reading of Bacon's *Essays*.

In September he is in lodgings in London—17 Southampton Row—so as to be near the British Museum; sees Spedding, Thackeray—who used to come singing into his rooms—Pierce Morton, an Irish gentleman of estate and fortune, which, of course, went the Irish way; and Tennyson. These were 'our younger London days,' in which—long after, addressing FitzGerald—Tennyson says—

> 'You found some merit in my rhymes,
> And I more pleasure in your praise.'

The meetings of these friends—and Browne often joined them—were usually at 'The Cock' in Fleet Street, that famous hostelry whose 'plump head-waiter' has been so often talked about; but apparently nothing of the conversation has been preserved except a few feeble witticisms. A friend of FitzGerald's tells me that on one occasion upon leaving 'The Cock,' a little merry after the chop for which that house was celebrated, they all squeezed into an omnibus. Another passenger having come up, the conductor put in his head and asked, 'Are you full inside?' 'Yes,' cried Tennyson, 'the last glass did for me.' On another occasion FitzGerald referred to the fact of his sister Jane having married 'a Mr. Wilkinson, a clergyman.'[1] 'Why,' said Tennyson, 'that's verse,' and then they contended humorously for the authorship 'of the worst line in the English language.'

31. Word Portraits.

It was about this time that FitzGerald wrote a number of word pictures of his friends. In the course of my researches among the papers to which I was given access by the Rev. E. Kenworthy Browne, I had the good

[1] An elderly man. She made him 'very evangelical—and tiresome—and so they fed their flock' at Holbrook, near Ipswich.

fortune to come across a manuscript containing a number of these sketches, and I here reproduce two of the most important, namely those on Tennyson and Thackeray.

Of Thackeray FitzGerald says: 'A great deal of talent, but no perseverance or steadiness of purpose; very indifferent, almost cold in his feelings; a very despairing mind; quick in most things; impatient; exclusive in his attachments; very unaffected, and has great want of confidence in his own powers.'

Of Tennyson we get the following: 'Very well informed; just and upright; a rectifier or setter to rights of people; diligent, constant, sincere; has great discernment; industrious, decided, and possesses great strength of mind; a very valuable friend; generous, but not extravagant; punctual; cool and clear in judgment.'

It was in London that FitzGerald read that puzzling but original genius William Blake, and several of the letters contain references to him. He expresses himself gratified, too, on hearing fresh tidings of the discoveries in Anglo-Saxon MSS. at Cambridge made by Kemble, who was indeed madly devoted to 'his Mistress Learning.' 'I wish,' sighed Charles Kemble (his father), 'John had taken up something more lucrative.' His sister Fanny too was troubled. 'Poor John' indeed had a fatality for following unremunerative courses. First Torrijos, and now this Anglo-Saxon enthusiasm! Yet he was the one man in England with a head for the work, which, besides, really wanted doing.

FitzGerald now begins to interest himself in vegetarianism. He reads every available book on the subject, especially Cheyne[1] on Health and Long Life, and Cheyne's essay on Regimen, with extracts from which he crowds his notebooks and letters;

32. Vegetarianism, Oct. 1833.

[1] George Cheyne (1670-1742), *Essay on Health and Long Life*, 1724.

he inquires about 'Dr. Lambe's book,'[1] goes to hear a lecture on the subject, and can talk of nothing else. He would himself live on 'seeds, bread, milk, mealy roots and fruit,' being persuaded that such a course leads to health and longevity. He makes lists of persons who have attained to great age,—St. Jerome to 109; Simeon Stylites 109; and other Eastern Christians who are reputed to have eaten only 'twelve ounces in the twenty-four hours, with water for drink.' Then he tabulates abstemious moderns,—'One Lawrence, who lived to 140 by extreme temperance'; Thomas Jenkins to 169, and Old Parr to 152. Though Cheyne, who had been 'fat, lethargic, and listless,' restored himself to health and comfort, and reduced the diameter of his waistcoat by a vegetable diet, which he consequently recommends, he would nevertheless allow animal food to certain persons on alternate days. In short, he contradicts himself—here advocating a vegetable diet, there an animal. FitzGerald, who exposes Cheyne's inconsistencies, is resolved to give vegetarianism 'a year's trial.' How long he persevered is not stated, but for many weeks he ate meat only once at a party where he 'did not like to be singled out.' Life through, though never a strict vegetarian, his diet was mainly bread and fruit.

During 1833 he spent much time whetting his wits at the British Museum, and copying extracts that pleased him into a little manuscript book bound in maroon-coloured leather.[2] On the first page are the words 'E. FitzGerald, October 15,

33. The Museum Book, 15th Oct. 1833.

---

[1] 'The Return to Nature, or a Defence of the Vegetable Regimen' appeared in *The Pamphleteer*, No. 38. It was dedicated to Dr. W. Lambe, not written by him.

[2] This commonplace book was presented by FitzGerald to W. Kenworthy Browne, and it is now in the possession of his son, the Rev. E. Kenworthy Browne. Previous writers on FitzGerald do not appear to have been aware of its existence, and its contents are now for the first time made public. They throw most valuable light on the trend of FitzGerald's mind at this period.

NASEBY AND TENBY

1833. Museum Book, 1833,' and a pen and ink sketch of a flask, with 'SACK, 1661,' written across it, and a wine-glass with the foot left in pencil. The extracts show FitzGerald's insatiable appetite for old English writers. There are passages from Roger Ascham, Blunt Master Constable, and Sir R. Carey. Richard Corbet's 'Farewell to the Fairies' is given in full, and there is a paragraph from Ellis's account of the execution of Mary Queen of Scots, in which it is said that 'her lippes stirred up and down a quarter of an hour after her head was cut off.' Here is a quaint song, there a snatch of a ballad. One page is filled with Michael Drayton's address 'To his friend William Browne,'[1] and we may be sure that in copying it FitzGerald was thinking of his William Browne. The 'Museum Book' also contains a number of carefully executed illustrations (a few in colours) copied apparently from some old illustrated manuscript—cardinals, soldiers, ladies, and other figures in crimson and gold, blue and silver, with the laced ruffs, ornamental top boots, and purple gowns incident to the sixteenth and seventeenth centuries—all very pretty and very dainty.

In November 1830 came sad news from Freestone Hall. Anne Allen was dead. Alas, what a stroke was there! She had passed away at the early age of twenty-five. Her broken-hearted parents buried her in Carew churchyard, where may still be seen a stone to her memory with the inscription—

34. Death of Anne Allen.

ANNE ALLEN,
Daughter of James and Mary Allen.
Born January 12, 1808.
Died November 4, 1833.[2]

---

[1] Poet, 1590-1645. Wrote *Britannia's Pastorals*, *Shepherd's Pipe*, etc.
[2] Her father, who died in 1855, and her mother, who died in 1856, are buried in the same grave, and the dates of their births and deaths are inscribed on the memorial stone. The family graves are on the east side of the churchyard.

Edward FitzGerald deeply mourned her loss, and presently we find him writing that touching and lovely little poem which takes its title from her name—

> 'The wind blew keenly from the western sea
> And drove the dead leaves slanting from the tree—
>   Vanity of vanities, the Preacher saith—
> Heaping them up before her father's door,
> When I saw her whom I shall see no more—
>   We cannot bribe thee, Death.
>
> . . . . .
>
> Idly they gaze upon her empty place,
> Her kiss hath faded from her father's face:
>   She is with thee, O Death.'[1]

So touching are the lines, that one cannot help wondering whether FitzGerald ever bore towards the dead girl any more intense feeling than that of mere friendship.

On 19th November, FitzGerald refers to the marriage of his old schoolfellow Arthur Malkin (son of Dr. Malkin, Master of Bury School), 'a very clever person, and very reserved about himself—firm to his purpose, resolute, a great courtier.'[2] There is more frequenting of the British Museum, much theatre-going with Spedding, and a good deal of time is spent with Thackeray. Two mornings at the house of Thackeray's stepfather, Carmichael Smith,[3] are particularly remembered, seeing that Thackeray occupied them in enriching FitzGerald's copy of *Undine* with sixteen water-colour drawings.' Says Mrs. Ritchie: 'At a time of great trouble [the illness of Thackeray's wife], it was FitzGerald's extraordinary goodness that brought help through the saddest days of Thackeray's life. FitzGerald gave him orders for drawings which brought money into the empty purse, and "shared his troubles with a liberal heart."'[4]

---

[1] For complete poem see *Miscellanies* (Macmillan), p. 205.
[2] FitzGerald's Word Portraits, Rev. E. K. Browne's MS.
[3] Albion Street, Hyde Park.
[4] The Biographical Edition of Thackeray's Works.

CHAPTER IV

HARP AND LUTE

MAY 1834—JULY 1835

Bibliography

5. 'The Old Beau' in *The Keepsake*, ... 1834
6. 'The Merchant's Daughter,' *Ib.*, ... 1834

FITZGERALD owes his immortality in a great measure to his keen passion for retaining only the concentrated essence of things. In his writings he endeavoured always to keep before himself the example of Gray's *Elegy*. He was always saying, 'Abridge, concentrate, distil.' Scissors and paste were his harp and lute. The passion exhibits itself in everything he does. He must have a 'Paradise' into which can be admitted only the finer part of literature. He reads the *Spectator*, and would like 'to publish all the papers about Sir Roger de Coverley alone.' He has a parrot's skill in extracting kernels and scattering the shells. Favourite authors he would himself abbreviate with scissors and paste. By and by we shall find him so employed with Richardson's *Clarissa*, Crabbe's *Tales of the Hall*, and a host of inferior books. Wesley's *Journal*, always a favourite with him, required, he thought, the same treatment; and as late as 1877 he was suggesting to Fanny Kemble that she should condense her 'Gossip,' which had appeared in the *Atlantic*

35. Genius for concentrating.

Magazine. This feature in his character was of paramount service to him when, in middle life, he approached Omar Khayyam. Much as he admired Omar—who for brevity was an absolute Gray among Persian poets, most of whom wrote tens of thousands of lines—his perfect taste suggested that the essence would be far more delectable then the whole. Hence that poem of only a hundred and one quatrains. To this habit of fastidious selection and pitiless condensation, and to his custom of tearing out of books leaves which he considered valueless, and welding a dozen thus attenuated volumes into one, we shall have again to refer.

In the summer of 1834 FitzGerald paid a visit to the home of W. Kenworthy Browne at Bedford, and he visited Bedford nearly every summer up to the time of Browne's death. The Brownes, as we have said, resided at Cauldwell House in Cauldwell Street, on the left as you proceed from St. Mary's Street, and just opposite the residence of Mr. Browne's friend, the late nonagenarian, Mr. George Hurst. A narrow channel called, after King Offa, the King's Brook, which takes its course from the Ouse, and borders what was formerly Mr. Hurst's garden, crosses under the road, runs down the east side of the garden of Cauldwell House, and joins the Ouse again at a spot called Duck Mill. The house has been altered since Browne's time, but recently, when I visited it, the room on the left of the entrance-hall had seen little change; and the walls were coloured, not inappropriately, a rich brown, ornamented with gilding. Here the friends spent many a happy hour together talking, reading, and smoking, while Browne's top boots, polished like a mirror, stood on a chair, with his scarlet coat hung over the back —all ready against the hunting-season. Browne's smart,

36. Cauldwell House, Bedford. Frank Edgeworth.

CAULDWELL HOUSE, CAULDWELL STREET, BEDFORD
RESIDENCE OF THE BROWNES

handsome, dapper little figure made a striking contrast to the larger, shambling, carelessly dressed form of Fitz-Gerald. A large room in the rear opened into a conservatory, which again led into a garden adjoined by a close which then extended to Pilcroft Street. 'This house,' says FitzGerald, 'is just on the edge of the town: a garden on one side skirted by the public road, which again is skirted by a row of such poplars as only Ouse knows how to rear—and pleasantly they rustle now—and the room in which I write is quite cool and opens into a greenhouse which opens into said garden: and it's all deuced pleasant.'[1] Browne was then eighteen years of age, 'full of confidence, generosity, and the glorious spirit of youth.' The friends spent much of their time riding and fishing, and FitzGerald found himself very 'much in love with Bedfordshire.'

Now and again he heard from Allen, who was married and settled in London, and in one of his replies he tells how very welcome these letters were, and adds, 'I am an idle fellow, of a very lady-like turn of sentiment, and my friendships are more like loves, I think.'[2] He is often at his mother's (he never calls it his father's), 17 Gloucester Street, Queen Square; he smokes a pipe with Frederick Tennyson and the impecunious Morton in Mornington Crescent; and meets at the British Museum his old Cambridge friend Frank B. Edgeworth, youngest son of Richard Lovell Edgeworth. The genealogical table of the Edgeworths is as puzzling as that of the man we have all met 'going to St. Ives.' Richard L. Edgeworth, it is true, had only four wives, but these four had among them, at what was apparently the last time of counting, twenty-two children.[3] His first wife

---

[1] *Letters* (Macmillan), vol. i. p. 61.   [2] *Ibid*. (Macmillan) vol. i. p. 30.
[3] For list, see *Life and Letters of Maria Edgeworth*, vol. i. p. 243.

was the mother of 'the great Maria,' his fourth the mother of Frank.¹ The sister and brother (who looked like grandmother and grandson) were at this time aged respectively sixty-seven and twenty-five. Frank Edgeworth, who married a Spanish lady, Rosa Florentina Eroles, is pictured by FitzGerald as 'a very intelligent and agreeable person; very generous; . . . gets through a great deal of business with ease, and is quiet in manner, but very cheerful spirits; warm-hearted and affectionate.'² Carlyle describes Edgeworth—'Poor little Frank'—as 'a short, neat man: of sleek, square, colourless face, with small blue eyes, in which twinkled curiously a joyless smile.' He had a croaky, shrill voice, was deeply read in Plato, Kant, and other philosophers, and looked coldly on all creeds. Edgeworth's philosophy paired well with Kemble's combined philosophy and Anglo-Saxonism. It was as much as their pockets could do to bear the strain.

To *The Keepsake*, an annual edited by Frederic Mansel Reynolds, FitzGerald, in 1834, contributed two poems which do not appear in any collection of FitzGerald's works. One, 'The Old Beau,' has vigour and humour; but the other, 'The Merchant and his Daughter,' has neither; and both, wonderful for him, are signed with his name in full. The first commences—

37. 'The Old Beau,' 1834.

> 'The days we used to laugh, Tom,
>   At tales of love and tears of passion;
> The bowls we used to quaff, Tom,
>   In toasting all the toasts in fashion;
> The heaths and hills we ranged, Tom,
>   When limb ne'er fail'd, when step ne'er faltered;
> Alas! how things are changed, Tom,
>   How we—and all the world—are altered!'

---

¹ Born 1809; married 19th December 1831; died 1846.
² The unpublished manuscript in possession of the Rev. E. Kenworthy Browne.

His college days are recalled, and his college friends—

> 'And some their race have run, Tom,
> And some are ruin'd—some are risen,
> And some have had their fun, Tom,
> In parliament and some—in prison.'

He then goes on to lament the degeneracy of the present times compared with the past. Tradesfolk give trouble now if you delay them a year or two; at any ball you may notice 'the falling off in face and figure.' Gazing on the young ladies of to-day, we are obliged to say with a sigh, 'You're nothing to your mothers!' He looks forward, however, to a little pleasure from two visits from a couple of ancient relics—'Jekyll' and 'Lady Aldboro'.'

> 'Out on the greybeard Time, Tom,
> He makes the best turned leg grow thinner;
> He spares not sex nor clime, Tom,
> Nor *us*—the old relentless sinner!
> But come down and be gay, Tom,
> At the old Hall, and banish sorrow;
> For Jekyll comes to-day, Tom,
> And Lady Aldboro' to-morrow.'

'The Merchant and his Daughter' is altogether inferior. An old Jew, surrounded by his deeds and money-bags, has a presentiment of ill. He expresses his detestation of the Christians, and goes out to work them 'spite,' whereupon his daughter announces that she herself has become a Christian. She rejoices in Jesus, who

> 'Makes light the wearied sinner's yoke
> And comforteth the weak.'

She looks forward to the time when the stain that has defiled God's chosen people shall be cleansed, and when

> 'The harp of Judah's tribe again
> Shall welcome Judah's child.'

The verses were written to an accompanying plate,[1] which represents Shylock handing Jessica the keys, whilst Launcelot stands in the background; and a number of Shakespeare's expressions—'wry-necked fife,' 'fast bind, fast find,' 'by Jacob's staff'—are worked in. Despite its poverty, however, 'The Merchant and his Daughter' is no worse than the other 'sweet' things 'in the *Keepsake*, by Lord Diddle'[2] and his fellow-contributors with imposing titles and feeble intellects.

38. In the Lake Country.

In April 1835 FitzGerald is visiting Spedding—'that mad wag,' 'old Jem Spedding the Wise,' 'my sheet anchor,' Thackeray's 'Jeames Spending'— at Mirehouse by Bassenthwaite lake, just under the 'double-fronted head of Skiddaw'—a region of fells, cascades, white cottages nestling under crags, and 'streams more sweet than Castaly.'[3] Bassenthwaite lake and Derwentwater lie like two pears, the taper end of each pointing to the other, and the Derwent river joining them. The vicinage is all classic ground. At Keswick, on the Greta, just before it enters Derwentwater, stood the cottage in which Coleridge resided from 1800 to 1804, and here he was visited by Lamb and Southey. To the south-east, and in Westmorland, are two other smaller pear-shaped lakes, also lying stalk to stalk—Grasmere and Rydal Water—sacred to Wordsworth and De Quincey.

It was the time of daffodils, which yellowed the field in front of the house. Spedding's father was at his farm most of the day, and in the evening settled to a

---

[1] A common custom in the 'Annuals' period. In the same volume, for example, Mrs. Shelley writes a tale, 'The Mortal Immortal,' to go with Briggs's well-known picture of 'Juliet and the Nurse,' who become 'Bertha' and a 'high-born hag.'

[2] Biographical Edition of Thackeray, xiii. p. 601.

[3] Wordsworth.

book, saying little—a practical man, who liked neither poets nor their vagaries—and therefore not too pleased that his son found no better company than 'The Cock' coterie. The old man suffered in company with Charles Kemble and the relatives of Frank Edgeworth. 'Jem' Spedding was one more sheep (one more of FitzGerald's friends) gone astray into the wilderness of unremunerative literature. But Spedding had a mastery of himself that would have extorted praise from an Epictetus. Stoicism and a quiet melancholy were his chief characteristics. He could not quite drive out the sadness brought about by the loss of friends—and death had already removed friends from him—but that verse of Horace's, so ably translated by Dryden, always lined his melancholy with gold—

> 'Happy the man, and happy he alone,
> He who can call to-day his own';

and especially the concluding lines—

> 'Not Heaven itself upon the past has power,
> And what has been, has been, and I have had my hour.'

Later he could write, 'The past is sacred and sanctified, nothing can happen hereafter to alter or disturb or obliterate it. . . . To me there are no companions more welcome, cordial, consolatory, or cheerful than my dead friends.'[1]

Subsequently there joined the party Alfred Tennyson, 'Hercules as well as Apollo,'[2] 'a sort of Hyperion,' powerful, serene, with a great shock of dusty dark hair, bright, laughing, hazel eyes, massive aquiline face, and sallow brown complexion.[3] The poet found little favour with the elder Spedding, who cared nothing for Lords

---
[1] *Autobiography of [Sir] Henry Taylor.*
[2] Brookfield.　　　　　　　　　　　[3] Carlyle.

of Burleigh; preferred a sheep's fleece to the hair of a mermaid; and did not even want to know 'where Claribel low lieth.' 'Well, Mr. FitzGerald,' Mr. Spedding would say, 'and what is it? Mr. Tennyson reads, and Jem criticises, is that it?' Tennyson read aloud a great deal of Wordsworth (he particularly admired 'Michael'), Keats, and Milton; and Spedding not only read aloud too 'as if bees were about his mouth,' but drew a picture of Tennyson in an armchair. With Mrs. Spedding —a motherly body—FitzGerald used to play chess; and there was also present a Mrs. Bristowe, who would have them call the place Mērehouse. The three friends ascended the 'mountain called Dod,' rambled over Grisedale Pike, and at the end of May went to lodge for a week at Ambleside, within a mile of Wordsworth, who then resided at Rydal Mount. But neither FitzGerald nor Tennyson, much as they admired 'the Daddy,' as they called him, would pay the veteran poet a visit. Says Spedding: 'I could not get Alfred to Rydal Mount. He would and would not (sulky one), although Wordsworth was hospitably inclined towards him.' Tennyson's 'little humours and grumpinesses' provoked frequent laughter, especially from FitzGerald, who, as Spedding said, 'loved to see a man in his weaknesses,'[1] and FitzGerald amused himself with his pencil, producing, among other sketches, a chalk drawing of a back view of Tennyson's head and shoulders.[2] He writes to Thackeray, who is in Paris, to say how happy he is; and Thackeray in a reply proposed that they should take a château in Normandy and be nothing to the world for a year—accompanying the text (as was his wont) with an illustration of the imagined

---

[1] Unpublished letter of Spedding's.
[2] There is an engraving from it in the *Life of Lord Tennyson*.

château. 'We would fit it up in the old style, and live in it after the manner of Orestes and Pylades.'[1]

After leaving Ambleside, FitzGerald stayed again at Castle Irwell, and later, for a month, at Warwick—drawn thither by Sir Walter Scott's story. He sketches, reads Dante, and poetizes. Hearing that Tennyson, whose income was small, needed a certain sum by a particular date, he wrote and offered, in a delicate manner, to send it. In one of his references to Tennyson, FitzGerald, revealing an extraordinary weakness, observes: 'I felt what Charles Lamb describes, a sense of depression at times from the overshadowing of a so much more lofty intellect than my own.' Yet FitzGerald, take you his gifts as poet, letter-writer, and critic, stands at least Tennyson's equal; just as Lamb does not occupy a plane inferior to that of Coleridge and the other bright particular spirits by whom he was surrounded, and of whom he occasionally stood in awe.

As we noticed, FitzGerald's father had, some years previous, purchased Boulge Hall, subject to the life-interest in it of Mrs. Short. That acrimonious old lady being now dead, he decided to make it his home. FitzGerald gets up early one July morning, slips on an ancient red dressing-gown, goes to his battered rosewood desk, and writes a letter to Thackeray telling the news. The whole family, he says, is collected there—all his brothers and sisters, with their wives, husbands, and children, including his brother John's wife Augusta, the idol of her husband, sweet, cheerful, and Christianly as ever, who, though only twenty-four, is marked for death. There is then nothing but packing up sofas and pictures; and all left very regretfully—after a connection of ten years—a beautiful home, in which they had experienced much happiness.

39. Farewell to Wherstead.

[1] Biographical Edition of Thackeray, vol. ix. p. 41.

BOOK III

BOULGE
EIGHTEEN YEARS (JULY 1835-1853)

CHAPTER V

BOULGE HALL

JULY 1835—AUGUST 1838

FITZGERALD describes Boulge, with its pollards and regular hedges, as one of the ugliest and dullest places in England; but matters have since improved. Thus the local mania for felling trees has spent itself, and in spring and summer, whatever it may be in winter, the country round has many a quiet charm. As regards company, if there is not the roar of Cheapside, there is the song of the thrush; and I saw at Boulge in an hour more cowslips than I had before seen in all my life. It is truly a land of cowslips. Boulge Park was yellow with them, stretching away like a sea as far as the eye could reach, and loading the air with their refreshing perfume. And the cowslip reminds of FitzGerald's great love for our English wildflowers—'for all deare Nature's children sweete.'[1] He took the trouble to underline in his copy of Ainsworth's *Anglo-Saxon Dictionary*[2] the name of every wildflower mentioned. He loved the heavenly blue rosettes of the succory which star the road between Boulge and Woodbridge, and especially loved the violet, 'fearing to be looked upon,' which he made the subject of a short poem.[3]

40. Boulge Hall.

On the way from Woodbridge to Boulge you pass 'The

---
[1] Lines from an old poet, copied by FitzGerald into his 'Museum Book.'
[2] Now in possession of Mr. Vincent Redstone of Woodbridge.
[3] *Miscellanies*, p. 207.

White House,' FitzGerald's birthplace, on your left, and Bredfield village and church on your right. At the gate of Boulge Park is Mrs. Short's thatched cottage, and following the drive one reaches the Hall, a handsome building of Queen Anne date, with a spacious porch, standing on a balustraded terrace, and picturesquely surrounded with flower gardens and ornamental trees. Climbing plants cover the walls—one a cascade of delicate blue, and so lovely that the gardener, when passing it, religiously doffs his hat; whilst there are ample kitchen gardens and modern greenhouses in the rear. The house was scarcely a convenient one in the FitzGeralds' time, though some of the rooms were of noble proportions. In the library were glass cases with relics from Naseby, and at the head of the stairs were two large oil paintings, one representing Edward FitzGerald and his brothers John and Peter as boys,[1] and another (which is still in the house) a view of Naseby Woolleys. The stables and the room adjoining—'the chapel,' where John FitzGerald held his evangelistic services, and Edward sometimes taught the village children—are little altered, whilst 'Old Nelly,' the clock referred to by Edward in his letters, still keeps very good time—'ten of the clock, by the chime now sounding from the stables.'[2] The filmy forms of Colonel and Mrs. Short, who lived and died so miserably, are said to haunt the park, but in the spirit they are as disobliging to visitors as they were in the flesh to each other, for though we have been there at dusk, and have even looked out of a window at Boulge Hall near midnight, they never once vouchsafed us a sight of their persons. The church, approached from the Hall by an avenue of beeches, is of

[1] It was at Boulge Hall in 1851.
[2] To F. Tennyson, 10th December 1843.

BOULGE HALL

BOULGE CHURCH

BOULGE HALL

flint, with an ivy-covered brick tower, near which are the mausoleum of the FitzGeralds, and the tomb, of which we shall have occasion to speak particularly in the last chapter of this work.

If FitzGerald did not eulogise his own corner of Suffolk, he at any rate preferred Boulge to his town lodgings; and handsome Mr. Osborn Shribb Reynolds, the venerable white-headed rector, to old Lady Morgan, who in her powders and paint then dominated literary London. Boulge was at least clean (how often in later years he urged Carlyle to leave his filthy London), and it was pleasant too to sit 'on the banks of the dear old Deben,' distant only a mile or two, 'and watch the collier sloop going forth into the wide world as the sun sinks.' While, indeed, FitzGerald, whether in earnest or not, deprecates very frequently Boulge and Woodbridge, he can never speak glowingly enough of the Deben, which inspired at least three of his friends—Mitford, Barton, and John Hindes Groome. Mitford, then editor of the *Gentleman's Magazine*, wrote 'The Walk' on the banks of the Deben, and 'The Farmer's Daughter,'[1] about a pleasant young lady who on a Sunday gives to all a modest greeting, 'except' (deliciously) 'the folks who came from meeting'; Barton sang 'No stately villas';[2] Groome 'Deben! no cloud-capped mountains,'[3] confining his attention to the river before it broadens out into its wide estuary. FitzGerald, however, instead of sitting at home and writing about the Deben, went out in boat or yacht and enjoyed it.

About the time the FitzGeralds removed to Boulge, the Rev. George Crabbe, son of the poet, was appointed to

---

[1] 'On Deben's banks our little farm.' *Gentleman's Magazine*, November 1835, December 1836.
[2] *Household Verses*, p. 234.   [3] *Gentleman's Magazine*, September 1839.

the vicarage of the adjoining parish of Bredfield. As we shall have occasion to speak of three Crabbes, all clergymen, and all named George, a word or two may be required to prevent confusion. The first George Crabbe was the poet, and very much FitzGerald's idol, who, as we saw, died at Trowbridge in 1832. George Crabbe the second, son of the poet, was vicar of Bredfield. George Crabbe the third was son of George Crabbe the second, and rector of Merton, in Norfolk. George Crabbe the second, 'The Radiator,' as FitzGerald dubbed him, from the gleams of wisdom and mirth he emitted, was at this time about fifty, or almost double the age of FitzGerald, who had just passed twenty-six. He was a strong, muscular man of the Parson Adams type, with a prominent Wellington nose. Like FitzGerald, he was careless of personal appearance, his clothes did not fit, his hat was never in the right place. As he could not be trusted with money (for when out he invariably gave away all he had to the needy or the plausible), his daughters used to take the precaution of emptying his pockets before he quitted the house. He was loved by all in the parish, and he loved all and prayed for all, 'including Mary Ann Cuthbert,' the only black sheep in his flock. FitzGerald calls him heroic,[1] noble-minded, rash in judgment and act, liable 'to sudden and violent emotions, and morbidly self-distrustful, though over-confident in the success of causes near his heart; with simple habits' and a Cervantic humour. He had a passion for botany and fine trees, and once pleased FitzGerald hugely by saying of a landowner who had felled some oaks that he had 'scandalously misused the globe.'

His *Life* of his father, written in 1835 is, of course, a

[1] *Gentleman's Magazine*, November 1857.

classic, and FitzGerald considered it 'one of the most delightful memoirs in the language.' Yet for the muse George Crabbe the second cared so little that he did not even take the trouble to read his father's poems till late in life. One of his first actions on settling at Bredfield was to erect a new vicarage at a cost of £1400. He loved to sit and meditate in a dismal little study, reeking with tobacco smoke, and smelling like an inn-parlour, which he called 'The Cobblery.' Here he prepared his sermons and entertained his friends, smoking unintermittently and increasing in happiness as their forms became more indistinct. Such was the man who for twenty-two years was to be FitzGerald's neighbour and intimate friend. Crabbe, whose wife was dead, had a large family, including three daughters, and with the eldest, Caroline Matilda—a tall, fair girl with two large curls, one on each side her face—FitzGerald presently fell deeply in love, a fact that has never before been recorded. She was pious and amiable, and, like FitzGerald, musical. By Crabbe's wish FitzGerald went in and out of Bredfield vicarage as if it was his own house. The younger children were fond of him and proud to go into the garden, where he used to sit and write, and call him to lunch, 'but he was sure not to come if called, though he would come if not called'; and he made them happy by praising their gardens because they were overrun with nasturtiums, his favourite flower.

Among the books dear to FitzGerald was the Rev. John Newton's *Letters to a Wife*, his unstinted praise of which has had the effect of reattracting attention to a delightful and once popular work. People are rather apt to regard Newton as a kind of satellite of Cowper, whereas he had a notable and distinct individuality, and, leaving out of consideration his prose

42. **Newton and Cowper.**

masterpiece, ranks as a hymnist with the very greatest; for if his worst hymns, like the worst of **Wesley**, **Watts**, and **Cowper**, are feeble and unpoetical, his best—for example, 'How sweet the name of Jesus sounds,' and 'Begone, Unbelief'—are second to none in the language. Another error that many, and FitzGerald among them, have fallen into is that of regarding Newton's influence over Cowper as deleterious—the bright, witty, almost jovial Newton, that delightful fountain of sound divinity and unconsidered *bons mots*, that ecclesiastical Charles Lamb, who spent all his life, as his letters to Symonds and others show, in trying to cheer up souls less buoyant than his own! Southey blackened Newton to posterity, and hundreds since, without taking the trouble to investigate for themselves, have echoed his words. FitzGerald himself, whilst expressing admiration for Newton, was carried away by Southey's diatribe. Writing on 31st October 1835, he says: 'I have just read Southey's *Life of Cowper*—that is to say, the first volume. . . . It is a fearful book. Have you read it? Southey hits hard at Newton in the dark; which will give offence to many people; but I perfectly agree with him. At the same time, I think that Newton was a man of great power. Did you ever read his life by himself?[1] Pray do, if you have not. His journal to his wife,[2] written at sea, contains some of the most beautiful things I ever read: fine "feeling" in "very fine" English.'[3] FitzGerald found the second volume of Southey dull, seeing that 'one is naturally impatient of all matter that does not

---

[1] The *Authentic Narrative*, etc., August 1764.
[2] *Letters to a Wife.* 2 vols. April 1793. Vol. i. written during three voyages to Africa (from 1750 to 1754); vol. ii. written in England (from 1755 to 1785).
[3] *Letters of Edward FitzGerald*, vol. i. p. 41. Quoted by permission of Messrs. Macmillan.

BOULGE HALL

absolutely touch Cowper'—a reference to Southey's wearisome and interminable digression on the history of poetry; but observes that he is glad W. B. Donne had read the work with satisfaction. In March (1836) Donne was exhibiting interest in the reputed common ancestor of himself and Cowper, namely the Rev. Dr. Donne, the distinguished Dean of St. Paul's, and FitzGerald urged him to secure a copy of his 'ancestor's sermons.'

Spedding had just furnished chambers in Lincoln's Inn Fields, and FitzGerald in company with him one day paid a visit to their common friend R. J. Tennant at Blackheath, where they met Frank Edgeworth, who had taken a large house at Eltham, near King John's Palace, and was advertising for pupils to prepare for the University. 'Poor Edgeworth,' writes Carlyle, who about this time[1] paid a visit to Eltham, 'tried this business for a while, but found no success at all. . . . I very well recollect the big Edgeworth house at Eltham; the big old palace now a barn.' A few years later Frank returned to his native Edgeworthstown and took charge of the estates of his famous half-sister.

In January 1837 FitzGerald is at Geldestone Hall again, taking Christopher Wordsworth's advice and surrendering himself to Aristophanes, who makes him laugh heartily. Wherever FitzGerald goes he finds—and for such research he had a perfect genius—some dear old lady who delights him by her conversation and agreeable manner, and who, on her side, is charmed with his good nature and chivalry. Thus at Gillingham, near Geldestone, he makes friends with a Mrs. Schutz, who imparts to him 'the names of the stars and other chaste information'; and to his conversations with her may be traced

---

[1] Spring 1836. FitzGerald was at Blackheath, middle of March 1836. Carlyle's *Life of Sterling*, chap. iv.

his reference to the 'zodiacal constellations which Aries leads over the field of Heaven,'[1] and some other effective allusions in his works. He gets for her, and at her request promptly, for she did not expect to live through the year, a copy of Taylor's *Holy Living and Holy Dying*, but as a matter of fact she lived another ten years, and imparted additional astronomical information. FitzGerald's pleasure in the society of cheery and cultured old ladies continued right on until he became an old lady himself—until he was numbered (his own expression) among the 'dowagers' of Woodbridge.

To the thatched cottage erected by Mrs. Short close to the gates of Boulge Park we have several times alluded. FitzGerald, who had spent the last seven years of his life rambling about the country with friends or staying with relatives, now felt a desire for a home or den of his very own, and made up his mind to take up his abode there.

43. The Cottage at Boulge, April 1837.

It was, and is, a single storied tenement of two apartments separated by a passage. He made the room on the right of the entrance his study, that on the left his bedroom. He complained that the walls, which are of lath and plaster, were as 'thin as a sixpence,' and damp. In the rear were trees, including a walnut—the last a doubtful advantage, owing to boys not being unknown in those parts. The tenement at the back of this cottage, and adjoining it, was occupied by a Waterloo man named John Faire,[2] who worked for FitzGerald's father; whilst Mrs. Faire, a snuffy but vain old woman, with very red arms, who wore, besides other vanities, an enormous

---

[1] *Euphranor.*

[2] The name is thus spelt on his tombstone in Boulge churchyard, but I have also seen it spelt 'Faiers.' He died in 1860, aged seventy-seven.

BOULGE COTTAGE (SIXTEEN YEARS THE RESIDENCE OF FITZGERALD)

bonnet full of flowers, looked after 'Mr. Edward.' Fitz-Gerald had in his heart a soft corner for all Waterloo men, and he esteemed John particularly because he had not only fought in the battle but had also guarded Napoleon at St. Helena. Save for the loss of a thumb, the good man was none the worse for his military experiences; moreover, as another man in the parish had three thumbs, matters, as John remarked, could not possibly have been more nicely adjusted. By April FitzGerald had got the garden in order, put his books on the shelves (as you passed along the drive you could see them through the window), set Stothard's *Canterbury Pilgrims* over the fireplace, Shakespeare's bust in a recess, and begun with a cat, a dog, and a parrot called 'Beauty Bob' a very pleasant Robinson Crusoe sort of life. His wants were few. He had books and pictures, a barrel of beer, and his snuffy, red-armed, finely-bedizened old woman; and he wanted nothing more. His bedroom was furnished as simply as the prophet's chamber at Shunem. Wardrobe he had none—for he could always hang the few clothes he possessed on his own person, and badly hung they were. The study, on the other hand, was crowded. Order not being one of his weaknesses, the books that would not go on his shelves were heaped on the floor. Here were portraits on wall or easel, there large pictures, boots, music, tobacco pipes, walking-sticks, mingled in pleasing confusion on table, chair, and piano (for the new Robinson Crusoe had a piano, and played excellently). With his window open to let in the odour of the cowslips or the garden flowers, FitzGerald sat in dressing-gown and slippers, pipe in mouth, and let time slide—troubling about, and being troubled by, nobody, except the Woodbridge man who brought him his letters and thrice a week shaved him, and the matchman, with his bundles of great sulphur-tipped matches, whom 'you could smell a mile off.'

On Sundays he occasionally attended church with the other members of the family, but, for the reason that it was damp and given over to toadstools and mice, which ate the pew curtains, he more frequently took a walk, preferring to study Nature, if at all, out of doors, or settled himself in his cottage to literature whilst the sounds of the distant Grundisburgh bells floated musically in at the window.

Of a week evening he would, often as not, light a lantern, and cross the fields to spend an hour or two with Crabbe in the 'Cobblery,' the chief joys there being, of course, pipes, at which old Shribb Reynolds, the Boulge rector, in his spectacles with circular eyepieces, sometimes assisted. When they joined the ladies (FitzGerald liked to sit next to Caroline), pleasant talk and music occupied most of the time, though—the vicar's family included—they had not a voice among them. At home he read the fine sacred poems of Henry Vaughan, in a collection of the Rev. John Mitford's, Plutarch's *Lives*, in which he revelled, and Theocritus.

That there was a strain of indolence in FitzGerald (as in the other members of the family) is clear enough; but he was also, as we have before intimated, a man of ambition—he had an intense desire to excel in composition, both prose and poetry; and, to bring about this, took infinite pains. Few men read more voraciously, and everything that was excellent in what he read he copied out or made note of. He was as ambitious in his way as Spedding, Carlyle, or Tennyson, and he succeeded. His writings, whether in prose or poetry, have taken their place in the first rank. His fine letters, the *Euphranor*, the *Salaman*, and the *Omar*, are the result of assiduous study. Men do not write classic English by accident; and FitzGerald was no exception. Whatever he did he subjected to continual polish—even his earliest poems betray this—and, like all really great souls, he was never satisfied with himself.

In the August of this year (1837) died the sweet and lovable Augusta, wife of his brother John, who never really recovered from the blow. She was only twenty-six, and left three children, Olivia, who died the following year, Gerald, and Maurice.[1] John FitzGerald possessed a large painting of his wife which he greatly prized, and every night he had it taken from its place on the wall and put at the foot of his bed, so that he could see it first thing in the morning. Some of her clothes, too, he would always have near him. Indeed all his life he mourned his loss; and this distressing event, acting on a nervous nature, was probably responsible for the eccentric conduct that marked his subsequent years.

By 1838 FitzGerald and Bernard Barton[2] had become bosom friends, and not only met but often wrote to each other, chiefly on literary matters. Barton was at this time fifty-four, his daughter thirty-one, and FitzGerald twenty-nine. In 1824 the Quaker fraternity had presented Barton with £1200, so with his income at the bank he was now in comfortable circumstances. His poems were known in every Suffolk homestead, and good little maidens by the Deben liked to see a copy lying in their chair beside their prayer-book before going to sleep. Charles Lamb praised the verses to the Memory of Bloomfield; Fitz-

44. Bernard Barton and his daughter Lucy.

---

[1] John married a second wife, Hester, daughter of Mr. William Haddon, who outlived him, dying in 1888. 'I should never have married again,' he used to say, 'but to give my children a mother.'

[2] Barton lived first in Cumberland Street, afterwards at the back of Messrs. Alexander's bank, and lastly near the Quakers' Meeting.

Gerald those to Joanna, and 'some on the decline of life and the religious consolations attending it.' Barton was very regular in his habits, and might be seen every day at precisely the same moment, in his broad-brim, spectacles, gaiters, white stockings, and low shoes, journeying in the direction of, or returning from, the bank. He sometimes made excursions on the Deben with FitzGerald, but got most happiness at his own cosy fireside. There, a glass of wine, and the 'working box and table companion' of the poet Crabbe at his elbow, snuff-box in hand, and Cowper's poems or one of Scott's novels on knee, he purred like the sleek, scrupulously clean, self-satisfied kitten which he precisely was. Year after year he inclined more to his books and pictures, and less to heath, cornfield, and river, and at last went but rarely from home except to his bank and the meeting-house. Let him be summed up in FitzGerald's words: 'A very strange character; a good-hearted and benevolent person, with a good deal of pride and caution, with a pretence at humility; perverse, formal, strict, plain, and unpresuming in his dress—a great many contradictions of character.'[1]

Lucy Barton, afterwards FitzGerald's wife, tall, angular, and pleasant (though plain), was her father's right-hand, managing his house and interesting herself in his literary work. She is the busy bee, 'the gentle stream-let, the flower making fragrant the meadow,' of his poems. These, says he, 'are types of thee and of the active worth thy modest merit hides.' The partiality of the father did not notice that she was a rather peremptory busy bee, and his verses clothe her with a personal beauty which in the eyes of others she did not possess. She wrote verses herself, some of which appeared in Fulcher's *Sudbury Pocket-Book* and other volumes, but in after years

[1] Browne MSS. Word Pictures.

repudiated, and justly, the insinuation that they were poetry. Early in the twenties she had accompanied her father on a visit to Charles Lamb, then domiciled at Colebrook Cottage, Islington, and Lamb furnished for her album the lines beginning—

> 'Little Book surnamed of white,'

and ending—

> 'Whitest thoughts in whitest dress,
> Candid meanings, best express
> Mind of quiet Quakeress.'

To Lamb's beautiful essay, 'A Quaker's Meeting,' also inspired by his friendship for Bernard and Lucy Barton, one need do no more than refer. Barton was more than once advised to leave Quakerism and join the Church of England. Writing on 1st September 1837, he says: 'I am now almost the sole representative of my father's house, . . . left as an adherent to the creed he adopted from a conscientious conviction of truth. . . . Lucy tells me I must turn too. . . . I love them not a whit less for abandoning it, . . . still I must e'en be a Quaker still. My Lucy was, comparatively, a chit when she apostatised'; and later, 'the longer I live, the more I prize Quaker principles.' After Lamb's death, which took place on 24th December 1834, Lucy Barton in an un-Quakerly dress of blue muslin, called on Mary Lamb, who took her hand, stroked down her skirts once or twice, and said, with a look of surprise and perhaps of slight reproach, 'Bernard Barton's daughter!'[1]

A model housekeeper, and an excellent conversationalist, prim, exact, and masterful, Lucy Barton went through life authoritatively. Every one liked her—even her Sunday-school scholars, though in the street they called after her, at a safe distance, 'Step-a-yard,' in allusion to the long

[1] Article by E. V. L. in *The Academy*, 3rd December 1898.

strides she used to take. Primarily for her Sunday-school scholars she wrote, and in 1831 published, a book entitled *Bible Letters for Children*, with introductory verses by her father: an 'unpretending little volume,' submitted to the public 'with the distrust natural to a first attempt in so important a field of labour.' The letters are addressed to 'My dear children.' 'I have thought,' says the writer, 'that if you had a few letters written by one who loves you very dearly, that ... you would take them up and read them, and might chance to find therein ... something that would lead you early to think upon that great and good Being who made you and me, and all this beautiful earth, and not these things only, but also a glorious and happy heaven, where such of you as love to obey Him will live in His presence for ever.' The introductory lines by Bernard Barton end with a striking verse. After giving an epitome of Old Testament history, he comes to Jesus Christ, the Resurrection, and the Gift of the Comforter; and concludes happily—

> 'While such stupendous themes remain
> For wonder, love, and praise,
> Who shall ungratefully maintain
> These are *not* Bible days?'

The letters, twenty-nine in number, cover Bible history from Genesis to the Captivity. In the closing address the writer asks the children if they wish to have for their friend the Almighty Being whose goodness and mercy are so conspicuously evident in these narratives. 'I hear you all say Yes; for what would become of us if He were against us? Oh, then, pray to the Saviour, that He may fill your hearts with His Holy Spirit, which will lead you to God.' The *Bible Letters* give us a good idea of one of the sides of the character of her who was to become FitzGerald's wife. At the time of their publication, however, though he was intimate with Lucy Barton, FitzGerald's heart was with Caroline Crabbe.

In 1837 appeared Carlyle's *French Revolution*, of which FitzGerald, who did not like it on account of its absence of repose and equable movement, says: 'I don't know a book more certain to evaporate away from posterity than that, except it be supported by his other works.' The only pity is that Carlyle did not treat Cromwell and Frederick in the same way as the *Revolution*, and give compact and perfect works of art with a beginning, a middle, and an end, instead of huge, shapeless, sprawling masses, terrifying to all save the most venturesome and intrepid. FitzGerald, however, when these came to be written, liked them no better than the *Revolution*. Later, Alfred Tennyson, 'very droll and wayward,' visited Fitz-Gerald in his Boulge den, and sat and smoked late with him; and in May of the next year (1838) FitzGerald was in London, where he heard Carlyle lecture on Hero-Worship. He spent the 28th of June (Queen Victoria's Coronation Day) at Kitlands, near Leith Hill, having been, with Spedding and W. F. Pollock, invited there by Douglas Heath, a Trinity tutor, and son of its owner. In the grounds was a long open bath, secluded by trees, and at the sound of the distant cannon announcing that the coronation ceremony had been performed, the four took headers into the water, and swam about, singing 'God save the Queen.' FitzGerald's friend, Fanny Kemble, who had married and settled in America, was now back in London again, just in time to see her father leave the stage and close his professional career. Anglo-Saxon Kemble continued to get fame enough for two men, but not half enough money for one; Dickens had just published *Pickwick*; and Sydney Smith was delighting the drawing-rooms of London with his humorous sallies.

CHAPTER VI

CHIEFLY BEDFORD

AUGUST 1838—JUNE 1841

Bibliography

7. 'Bredfield Hall,'. . . . . . *Written* 1839
8. 'Chronomoros' in Fulcher's *Poetical Miscellany*, ... *Signed Anon.* 1841

As we said, FitzGerald seems to have spent part of the summer of every year at Bedford. Browne, the Ouse and its poplars were never long out of his mind. He interested himself in the literary associations of the town and vicinity, and particularly in Bunyan, whose native village, Elstow, is distant barely a mile. The *Pilgrim's Progress* was one of his favourite books. 'Next to the Bible parables,' says he, 'I believe John Bunyan remains the most effective preacher among the poor to this day.'[1] Bedford was then not half its present size. Browne's house, now some distance from the fields, was on the edge of the town. A large portion of the east side of the High Street formed the boundary of a spacious garden, and sombre trees cast their shadows on the pavement. The Grove and Grove Place were, in nature as well as name, sylvan ways—of which now remain here a few yews and there a chestnut. The old Grammar School,

45. 'Flowing Rivers full of Fishes.' 'The Falcon' at Bletsoe, August 1838.

[1] Preface to *Polonius*.

though converted to other uses, still stands. It is an unpretentious building, with a dismal figure of Sir William Harpur, roll in hand, in a niche, on its front. A row of shops screened St. Paul's Church from the High Street, and the picturesque front of the Pre-Reformation old George Inn was not the only ancient house in that thoroughfare. The four ancient churches of the town present much the same appearance now as then. The liliputian St. Cuthbert's Church had not yet given place to the present edifice; Trinity Church was building; Bunyan Meeting was a quaint structure, with three gables in a row.

'Fitz,' writes Spedding, 'is on his way to Bedford, in a state of disgraceful indifference to everything except grass and fresh air. What will become of him (in this world)?' A favourite haunt of Browne and FitzGerald was 'The Falcon' at Bletsoe, a village eight miles north of the town, to which they generally drove in a morning with their fishing-rods. FitzGerald, however, who never went without his colour-box, painted more pictures than he caught fish; and wished nothing better than to lie at his ease under some gnarled willow among the rich red spires of loosestrife, and within view of the gently rocking water-lilies. Usually they fished for perch and pike. When they went after the bream, they had to be at Bletsoe while the dew was still heavy on the grass, and get their fishing over, or the better part of it, by breakfast-time. Bletsoe boasts a picturesque church and a ruined castle, but it was the river rather than the antiquities that attracted FitzGerald. 'The inn,' says he, 'is the cleanest, the sweetest, the civillest, the quietest, the loveliest, and the cheapest that ever was built or conducted. On one side it has a garden, then the meadows through which winds the Ouse: on the other, the public road, with its coaches hurrying on to London; its market people halting to drink, its farmers, horsemen, and foot travellers. So, as one's humour is, one can have whichever phase of life one pleases: quietude or bustle, solitude or the busy hum of men. One can sit in the principal room with a tankard and a pipe, and see both these phases at once through the windows that open upon either.'[1] Browne's fondness for rod, scarlet coat, and buckskins led FitzGerald to write—

> 'Heaven would answer all your wishes,
> Were it much as earth is here;
> Flowing rivers full of fishes,
> And good hunting half the year.'

After tea at the Falcon and a song—frequently 'Bobby Shafto's gone to Sea'—they would walk leisurely home through Milton Ernest, by the massive church tower of Clapham, past 'The Angler's Rest' (less easy to get by), and so, whistling towards Bedford, down the same hill that R. L. Stevenson's St. Ives and Dudgeon danced so merrily; whilst the cry of the corncrake in the meadow mingled with the peevish call of the plover circling over the cornfield, and the westering sun in a sea of violet, grey, and silver made spindle-legged silhouettes of them on road and bank. 'Those Bedfordshire villages!' They were FitzGerald's dear delight. Bletsoe, Sharnbrook, Keysoe, Turvey, Goldington—the very thought of them sent the blood singing through his veins.

During this visit to Bedford, FitzGerald presented to Browne a copy of a work with whose contents he had been exceedingly struck, and which he had pondered deeply, namely *Godefridus* — the first part of Kenelm Henry Digby's[2] book *The Broad Stone of Honour*—his reason for making the

46. 'Godefridus' and Keysoe.

---

[1] *Letters*, vol. i. p. 74. Quoted by permission of Messrs. Macmillan.
[2] Kenelm Henry Digby, born 1800, died 22nd March 1880.

'THE FALCON,' BLETSOE, NEAR BEDFORD

gift being, as he afterwards said, because page 89 and the following pages seemed to delineate the character of Browne.[1] On the fly-leaf he wrote, ' W. Browne from E. F. G., "sed tu noli deficere: quod ille quaerit, tu esto"—St. August.' Digby's book (the copy given to Browne is in grey-coloured boards) is a 'philosophic history of chivalry'—' a history of heroic times, arranged chiefly with a view to convey lessons of surviving and perpetual interest to the generous part of mankind.' Its style probably influenced FitzGerald's prose more than that of any other work. For example, the first section of *Godefridus* and the last few paragraphs of *Euphranor* might have been written by the same man; and practically *Euphranor* is a blend of the substance of this book and the personal traits of W. Kenworthy Browne. The passages which in FitzGerald's opinion were applicable to Browne are the following: ' Chivalry is only a name for that general spirit or state of mind which disposes men to heroic and generous actions, and keeps them conversant with all that is beautiful and sublime in the intellectual world. . . . Every boy and youth [and FitzGerald maintained that Browne was always young] is, in his mind and sentiments, a knight, and essentially a son of chivalry. Nature is fine in him.' ' There is no difference,' says the philosopher, ' between youthful age and youthful character; and what this is, cannot be better evinced than in the very words of Aristotle: " The young are ardent in desire, and what they do is from affection; they are tractable and delicate; they earnestly desire and are quickly appeased; their wishes are intense, without

[1] It is curious to note that this copy of *Godefridus* contains besides a small allegorical vignette on the title-page only one illustration—namely a picture of two naked horsemen (Greek evidently), the front one of whom is turning round and flourishing a whip. It was a similar action on the part of one of Browne's friends that led to Browne's premature death. See chapter xiii.

comprehending much ; ... they are passionate and hasty, and liable to be surprised by anger ; for, being ambitious of honour, they cannot endure to be despised ; ... they love honour, but still more victory ; ... they are sanguine in hope, for, like persons who are drunk with wine, they are inflamed by nature ; ... they live by hope, for hope is of the future, but memory of the past, and to youth the future is everything, the past but little ; they hope all things and remember nothing ; ... they have lofty souls ; ... they live by affection rather than by reason ; ... they are warm friends and hearty companions ; ... they chiefly err in doing all things overmuch, for they keep no medium ; ... they are full of mercy, because they regard all men as good, and more virtuous than they are, for they measure others by their own innocence."' Indeed, the moral of the book is 'keep young.' The whole of this passage of Aristotle, as quoted in Digby's *Godefridus*, is given in *Euphranor*, which is simply and solely a glorification of W. K. Browne, and a pressing home to the youth of England of the lessons to be learned from his breezy and strenuous life. FitzGerald's intense admiration for Browne would be incredible to any one who was not minutely acquainted with the facts. To him Browne was at once Jonathan, Gamaliel, Apollo—the friend, the master, the god—there was scarcely a limit to his devotion and admiration ; and literary history offers no parallel to the conjuncture.

And how did Browne, 'Phidippus'[1] (for Phidippus is Browne), 'my Master,' receive all this incense? Just as one might expect that an honest, warm-hearted, practical and sensible man would. He devotedly loved his friend, and gave him such welcomes at Bedford as satisfied even Edward FitzGerald ; attributed all the virtues that he was

[1] In *Euphranor*.

accredited with to a friend's partiality, and quietly assumed that in every matter FitzGerald was a more competent authority than himself. More than all, he received without retort the unkind and acrimonious sayings which FitzGerald sometimes inflicted upon him. No other man would have uttered them with impunity. Of these displays of pique, peevishness, and temper FitzGerald never failed to repent speedily, and with moist eyes. 'I hate myself for them,' he would say.

Sometimes the excursions of FitzGerald and Browne extended to the 'uncouthly named town of Biggleswade,'[1] and to Keysoe, of which village FitzGerald's Bury and Cambridge friend, the Rev. William Airy, brother of the Astronomer-Royal, was vicar;[2] and occasionally they indulged in pistol practice, FitzGerald using oak-trees as targets, and generally missing at ten yards. At Keysoe he used to sing remarkable and old-fashioned songs—picked up in the British Museum and elsewhere—accompanying himself on the piano. One began—

'Like Macedon's madman my cup I'll enjoy';

and another—

'The stwuns, the stwuns,'

though what stones they were my informant, the Rev. Basil Airy,[3] son of FitzGerald's friend, cannot recollect. 'I remember,' continues Mr. Airy, 'his being at Keysoe when there was a general Fast Day, and my childish surprise at seeing him go off for a walk with a pipe in his mouth while we were all starting for church.' On the west front of Keysoe church is a very odd inscrip-

---

[1] FitzGerald.
[2] Presented in 1836. He was also Rector of Swynshed, four miles from Keysoe, Rural Dean and Domestic Chaplain to the Duke of Manchester.
[3] Vicar of St. John's, Torquay.

tion which FitzGerald often used to quote with unction. It commemorates the preservation of the life of William Dickens, who, on 17th April 1718, 'when he was pointing the steepol,' fell 'from the rige of the middle window in the spiar over the south-west pinackel,' and when he was falling called out to his brother, 'Lord, Daniel, wot's the matter!'[1] The good man lived over forty years after this accident.

Another of FitzGerald's haunts was Sharnbrook, one of the visits to which is described so pleasantly in the preface to *Polonius*. 'I had started,' says he, 'one fine October morning on a ramble through the villages that lie beside the Ouse. In high health and cloudless spirits, one regret perhaps hanging upon the horizon of the heart, I walked through Sharnbrook up the hill, and paused by the church on the summit to look about me. The sun shone, the clouds flew, the yellow trees shook in the wind, the river rippled in breadths of light and dark; rooks and daws wheeled and cawed aloft in the changing spaces of blue above the spire; the churchyard all still in the sunshine below.'

Woburn Abbey—the Duke of Bedford's place—FitzGerald found little to his taste. He appreciated the pictures, especially the Canalettos, but preferred an old squire's gabled house as much more English and aristocratic than the Duke's establishment. Luton Hoo, Lord Bute's mansion, with its splendid library, grand hall supported by Ionic columns, and chapel with Gothic wainscotting and carved ceiling, pleased him better,[2] and he afterwards dreamt of the fine pictures there. Indeed, he and Browne went picture-hunting in all direc-

---

[1] See Appendix.
[2] Three years later, November 1843, Luton Hoo was destroyed by fire. The chapel was utterly ruined, but the pictures and other valuables were saved.

CHIEFLY BEDFORD

tions, and if one made a present to the other it was almost sure to be an oil painting. Much, however, as he enjoyed these excursions in the sleepy villages by the Ouse, FitzGerald 'began to have dreadful suspicions' that this fruitless way of life was 'not looked upon with satisfaction by open eyes above,' though Keats's words might then have given him some comfort—

> 'He who saddens
> At thought of idleness cannot be idle.'

Still it was evident that life ought not to be all leather breeches and fishing-rod.

The happier he was at Bedford with Browne the more unpleasant he found the parting, and perhaps he was thinking of this when he copied into his Museum Book, 'So good disport you have made me, against my wille I take my leve.' *47. At Lowestoft with Browne.* At any rate, on this occasion he put off the evil day as long as possible by taking his friend away with him to Lowestoft. They amused themselves with boating, going about with 'Dickymilk' and FitzGerald's other sailor friends, teaching 'Bletsoe'[1] to fetch and carry, and shooting gulls. If they did little good, at any rate they did no harm, and when their consciences pricked them they found what comfort they could in Browne's dictum that it is better to repent of what is undone than what is done. FitzGerald's comment was: 'All this must have an end; and as is usual, my pleasure in his [Browne's] stay is proportionately darkened by the anticipation of his going. . . . Well, Carlyle told us that we are not to expect to be happy.' After Bedford, Woodbridge, where there 'was no river Ouse and no jolly boy to

---

[1] This dog, a big black retriever, was a present from Browne to FitzGerald. FitzGerald named it after the Bedfordshire village of Bletsoe.

whistle the time away with,' seemed painfully dull. In writing to Pollock of the little disasters and miseries under which he laboured in Suffolk, he says, 'This all comes of having no occupation or sticking-point.' But life through he bemoaned his lack of enforced occupation, and repeatedly declared that no one who is not employed can be really happy.

About this time FitzGerald met Frederick Denison Maurice, whom he heard preach. 'Maurice,' observes FitzGerald to Allen, 'seems to say in his demeanour, "You may trample on my body, I lay it on the road for you to walk over."'

The agent of the Boulge Hall estate and principal tenant was Mr. Job Smith of 'Hall Farm,' on whom FitzGerald used often to call, while the farmer's little son Alfred would waddle up and play with 'Bletsoe.' FitzGerald took to the boy as he grew older and was very kind to him, often making him presents—sometimes, however, creating embarrassment as well as gratitude, as, for example, when he once gave him half a crown to buy so cheap a toy as a ball.

In the autumn of 1838 or earlier FitzGerald made the acquaintance of Samuel Lawrence the portrait-painter, who was subsequently indebted to him for several commissions, one of the first being a portrait of Browne. He talks to Lawrence about going to Italy, but the proposed visit never came off, for in his heart of hearts he infinitely preferred Suffolk turnips to Campania lemons, and Naseby to Naples. He still applied himself to drawing and painting, and got many hints on collecting, and some on technique from his new friend, whom he describes as 'a dear little fellow—a gentleman—made of nature's very finest clay—the most obstinate little man—incorrigible, who wearies out those

48. Samuel Lawrence and Geldestone.

who wish most to serve and employ him, and so spoils his own fortune.' Spedding spoke of Lawrence as a portrait-painter of real genius and worthy of all men's love. 'His advantages of education were such as it pleased God (who was never particular about giving His favourite children a good education) to send him.'

In April 1839 FitzGerald is again at Geldestone, and he writes to tell John Allen, who is living in London (Coram Street), how he had spent one very happy day. All the morning he had been lying full length on a garden bench in the sun reading about Nero, in Tacitus. 'A funny mixture all this: Nero, and the delicacy of Spring: all very human, however. Then at half-past one lunch on Cambridge cream cheese; then a ride over hill and dale; then spudding up some weeds from the grass; and then coming in, I sit down to write to you, my sister winding red worsted from the back of a chair, and the most delightful little girl in the world chattering incessantly. So runs the world away. You think I live in Epicurean ease; but this happens to be a jolly day: one isn't always well or tolerably good, the weather is not always clear, nor nightingales singing, nor Tacitus full of pleasant atrocity.'[1] 'Give my love to Thackeray,' he goes on, 'from your upper window across the street.'

As we have seen, FitzGerald had for some time been in love with Miss Caroline Crabbe,[2] eldest daughter of his friend, and they were very often in each other's company. The lady, however, after a time came to the conclusion that marriage with FitzGerald would not be prudent. What her actual reason was we do not know. A profoundly pious girl, it is possible that FitzGerald's

<small>49. In Love with Miss Caroline Crabbe. 'Bredfield Hall,' 1839.</small>

[1] *Letters*, vol. i. p. 60. Quoted by permission of Messrs. Macmillan.
[2] These statements, which are all new, are founded on most trustworthy authority.

agnosticism may have troubled her; but the reason given, I am told, was that as she was the eldest of a large family, it would not be right for her to leave home. FitzGerald felt the refusal very keenly, though doubtless it was worded in the kindest possible way, and it was whilst suffering under this blow that he wrote those charming and realistic though mournful lines entitled 'Bredfield Hall.'

He refers to the well-timbered lawn and gardens, the distant sea and the solemn surrounding woods, and recalls the bygone owners and guests—the knight in ruff and doublet, and the cavalier—

> 'Languid beauties limn'd by Lely,
>   Full-wigg'd Justice of Queen Anne,
> Tory squires that tippled freely,
>   And the modern gentleman.'

Here they gathered round its hospitable fires—

> 'Till the bell that not in vain
>   Had summoned them to weekly prayer,
> Called them one by one again
>   To the church and left them there.'

Almost every stanza contains beauties and felicities of expression. The 'gilded vanes still veering,' the crocus breaking the mould, and the coat of paint and plaster hiding the wrinkles of decay, give us almost as vivid a picture of the old mansion and its surroundings as was possessed by the writer, whose youth was 'buried there' —a reference to his disappointment in love. Although Miss Crabbe could not marry FitzGerald, she continued to be his friend, and, as will be seen, was at her brother's house when FitzGerald died there.

John Allen was this year made Inspector of Schools, the commission being a roving one for the whole of England and Wales.

CHIEFLY BEDFORD

In October 1839 FitzGerald and Browne took a trip to Ireland, and visited Dublin. Dublin was attractive enough even in those days, with its quayed river, its parks, its circular road, and memories of Goldsmith, Swift, and Stella.[1] The friends made their stay at the Imperial Hotel, and often recalled the hours spent together there. From Dublin they go by coach and jaunting-car to Halverstown, Kilcullen, 'a little town that tumbles down a hill and struggles up another,' in Kildare. There they are the guests of Mr. Peter Purcell, FitzGerald's uncle, subsequently beloved of Thackeray, who said of the Purcell family, 'Such people are not to be met with more than a few times in a man's life—nothing but laughter and sunshine from morning till night.'[2] While they are amusing themselves among the round towers, ancient crosses, the 'clane-skinned girls' and 'dacent boys' of Mr. Purcell's farm (he employed 110 persons), Browne is suddenly summoned back to Bedford, but FitzGerald continues his stay, spending his time reading Homer's *Iliad* and De Quincey's paper on Southey and others in *Tait's Magazine*. He hears of the publication of Carlyle's *Essays*,[3] and he hopes, after returning to England, to read them. He dearly loved Ireland, with its suggestion of Spain, and declared prettily that the airs of Moore's Irish Ballads are the spirits of its beautiful women made into music.

After observing that when at Geldestone he lived quietly, FitzGerald says: 'People affect to talk of this life as very beautiful and philosophical, but I don't:

50. In Ireland with W. K. Browne, October 1839.

---

[1] There is a monument to Swift and Stella in St. Patrick's Cathedral.
[2] *Irish Sketch-Book*, chap. ii. (Biog. Ed., vol. v. p. 292), where there is an amusing description of Mr. Purcell's home and family.
[3] *Critical and Miscellaneous Essays*, collected and republished (4 vols.) 1839.

men ought to have an ambition to stir and travel.'[1] Elsewhere he calls his besetting indolence the salient feature about him, and confesses that he himself and nobody else is blamable for his inaction and its evil consequences. 'But I have made my bed and must lie on it, and die on it.'[2] He does not excuse himself even on the ground that indolence is the family complaint; and he speaks of his sister Andalusia's desire to exert herself as 'the highest wish a FitzGerald can form.' However, he finds comfort in Herodotus—tremendously interesting if 'slippery and mendacious,' and Newman's *Sermons*; and it is with a passage from Newman that he closes one of his commonplace books: 'One secret act of self-denial, one sacrifice of inclination to duty, is worth all the mere good thoughts, warm feelings, passionate prayers in which idle people indulge themselves'—a passage which, from the fact that the place and the exact time of entering it (Geldestone, April 26, 1840; Sunday evening, half-past nine o'clock) are recorded, evidently entered deeply into FitzGerald's soul. This passage is also quoted in *Polonius*.

[51. At Geldestone. J. H. Newman, April 1840.]

At the beginning of June, FitzGerald is at Leamington, where he chances on Alfred Tennyson. They go excursions together, visiting Kenilworth Castle (Sir Walter Scott was a never-failing loadstone) and Stratford-on-Avon, where FitzGerald is more moved by the old footpath leading to Shottery—so often trodden by Shakespeare—than by the house, or even Shakespeare's tomb.

The earlier portion of the nineteenth century was the golden age of 'Annuals,' which were generally collections of verse by a number of hands, and were issued both by London and country booksellers. Thus we

---

[1] *Letters* (Macmillan).   [2] Unpublished letter.

hear of the *Literary Souvenir*, edited by Alaric A. Watts; *Raw's Pocket-Book*, and many others. A publication of this order was the *Sudbury Pocket-Book*, first issued by George W. Fulcher[1] in 1825, Fulcher himself, Bernard Barton, and other Suffolk men contributing. A selection from these Pocket-Books was published in 1841 under the name of *Fulcher's Ladies' Memorandum - Book and Poetical Miscellany*. The contributions included an unsigned poem called 'Chronomoros,' by FitzGerald, but in which number of the Pocket-Book it appeared we have not been able to discover. Its subject, the evanescence of human life, was one that constantly haunted FitzGerald's mind, and had the effect not of stimulating him to greater activity, but of benumbing him and making him ask himself whether there was really any use in doing anything. His life is a succession of sighs, each stifled ere half-uttered; for the uselessness even of sighing is as evident to him as the reason for it. He was more apt to cry *Eheu fugaces* than *Carpe diem*. The poem is prefaced by a passage from his favourite Owen Feltham: 'In all the actions that a man performs, some part of his life passeth. . . . Nay, though we do nothing, Time keeps his constant pace—whether we play or labour, or sleep or dance, or study, the sun posteth, and the sand runnes.'

52. 'Chronomoros.'

The writer is represented as making various attempts to prevent Time from flying, and at last smashes his hour-glass, breaks his watch, and hides his sundial under a cloak—

> '"Now," I shouted aloud, "Time is done,"
> When suddenly down went the sun;
> And I found to my cost and my pain,
> I might buy a new hour-glass again!'

---

[1] George W. Fulcher (1795-1855). He wrote some touching lines entitled 'The Dying Child,' 'The Village Paupers,' and commenced a *Life of Gainsborough* which was completed by his son E. S. Fulcher.

Nay, whatever we do, time will go on, and all are treated alike—

> 'The king in a carriage may ride,
> And the beggar may crawl at his side;
> But, in the general race,
> They are travelling all the same pace.'

Among the contributors to this volume besides FitzGerald were Mrs. Fulcher, whose poems Mrs. Edward FitzGerald used to speak of as 'very beautiful,' Bernard Barton and Miss Elizabeth Charlesworth (subsequently Mrs. Edward Cowell, FitzGerald's correspondent and friend), who signs herself author of *Historical Reveries*.

CHAPTER VII

NASEBY EXCAVATIONS

JULY 1841—JULY 1844

FITZGERALD now purchases more pictures and concocts tar-water—to be tried first on the vain and ruddy Mrs. Faire. He writes to his old Cambridge acquaintance W. H. Thompson (subsequently Master of Trinity), sending remembrances to Blakesley, Douglas Heath, and such other potentates whom he knew before they 'assumed the purple'—a phrase stamped on his mind by his recent study of Gibbon. June saw him in Ireland again, staying first with his uncle, Mr. Peter Purcell of Halverstown, Kilcullen—riding in stage-coach and jaunting-car; and afterwards at Edgeworthstown, where he is the guest of the 'great Maria,' who lives in a country mansion approached by an avenue of venerable trees. Other members of the household are her half-brother Lovell and Mrs. Edgeworth, her father's widow, mother of Fitz-Gerald's friend Frank. Maria is seventy-two, the widow seventy-four. The chief room is the library, with its oblong table at one particular corner of which the aged authoress sits and writes undisturbed by the conversation, in which, looking up, she now and again joins. Jars of Nankin china and 'shells from ocean knows where are on the mantelpiece.' She is a lively and dapper little

53. In Ireland again, July 1841. The Edgeworths.

body, with thin, pale, and irregular features, and 'grey hair which shows, through her cap behind, but a dark frisette'—a sort of 'whippity stourie' or fairy, 'who comes flying through the window to work marvels'[1]—delighting to talk about Sir Walter Scott, whom she adores, and whose pen lies always before her. She is now owner of Edgeworthstown, bought (with a fortune won by literature) of Lovell, who, however, still remains the apparent owner, just as Mrs. Edgeworth is still nominal mistress of the house. She gives FitzGerald—'and all her thoughts were intent upon making her friends happy'—a copy of her 'Frank'[2] in German and English. Though the Lady Bountiful of the neighbourhood, she meets with little sympathy from priest or peasant—'no bows, no touching of hats, no pleasant looks.' She sells a legacy of diamonds to build a market-house in the village, but she might have kept her diamonds for all the thanks she got. The people had no love for Protestant landholders.

In September (1841) FitzGerald is at Naseby again, and, writing to F. Tennyson in Italy, facetiously addresses his letter from 'No. 0 Strada del Obelisco,' in allusion to the situation of the house of Mr. Watchams (formerly his mother's coachman) where he was lodging. Here he reads Congreve, Vanbrugh, and Farquhar, flying when tired to an old tub of a piano, the blacksmith's forge, or to tobacco at the FitzGerald Arms, or with a tenant of his father's named Love. Later he is in London, where he meets Allen, Thackeray, Spedding, and Tennyson. Of Tennyson, who is 'finer in appearance than ever,' Mrs. Carlyle leaves us a vivid picture at this time. 'A tall

54. Strada del Obelisco. A Drive with Dickens.

---

[1] Sir Walter Scott.
[2] He many years after presented it to Mr. Frederick Spalding.

NASEBY EXCAVATIONS

man leaning to a wall, with his head touching the ceiling like a caryatid.' 'You ought to be a dragoon,' cries FitzGerald to him, 'or in some active employment that would keep your soul stirring instead of revolving in its own idleness and tobacco smoke.'[1] The chief meeting-place of this junto was now Spedding's room in Lincoln's Inn Fields, where they would sit up till midnight smoking, discussing Lord Bacon with Spedding, or listening to Tennyson's poems read from a foolscap folio parchment-bound book. As the poems were written towards one side of the paper, they used the unoccupied edges as pipelights; and a few of these leaves when they returned with the proofs from the printers were taken possession of by FitzGerald, who afterwards presented them to the Library of Trinity College, Cambridge. In October (1841) John Allen lost his brother Bird, commander of H.M.S. *Soudan*, in the poetical and heroic Niger expedition. For several years Bird had been engaged to FitzGerald's sister Andalusia.[2] About this time W. Kenworthy Browne fell in love with Miss Elizabeth Elliott, the beautiful sixteen year old daughter of Mr. Robert Elliott of Goldington Hall, near Bedford. Browne's acquaintance with her was probably made through her brother Robert, a comrade of his in the hunting-field; by and and by they became engaged.

To this date I assign a very interesting unpublished letter of FitzGerald's, which refers to a drive with Dickens —the only occasion, apparently, on which FitzGerald and Dickens ever met. It is written to Browne, and commences, 'Dear Stubby.' After remarks that need not be quoted, it proceeds: 'Alfred [Tennyson] is just left us in a cab: he, like me, has had and has yet the damned influenza. To-night I go with my mamma to the Opera.

[1] *Life of Lord Tennyson.*   [2] Afterwards Mrs. De Soyres.

We get on very well together, by help of meeting very little. Lusia had her eyelid cut by Guthrie. As to your picture, I will not send it till Lawrence has seen if something cannot be done to it. As I have such abundance of pictures I shall not be solicitous to keep it for myself, much as I like it, that is, I will leave it quite to your papa's will without saying a word. I have lately had a very charming head by Reynolds sent up from the country. You would like it much. Give me some account of the house you spoke of at Bedford.' (FitzGerald contemplated settling at Bedford.) 'Is there any sitting-room looking out to the back? I went on Thursday with Alfred and Thackeray to drive with Boz. He is like Elliott,[1] only rather on a smaller scale—unaffected and hospitable. You never would remark him for appearance. A certain acute cut of the upper eyelid is all I can find to denote his powers, but you would doubtless see much more than I do.'

It was this year (1841) that FitzGerald's friend Major Moor published his curious work *An Account of the Mysterious Ringing of Bells at Great Bealings, Suffolk, in* 1834. As there are persons still living who know more about the occurrence than they care to tell, we need not inquire whether it was due to the agency of spirits. Though neighbours smiled at what they regarded as one of his many crotchets, the Major, to his dying day, maintained that his 'bells were rung by no human hand.'

Some of FitzGerald's best letters are written to Frederick Tennyson (eldest brother of Alfred), 'a noble man in all respects,' though haughty and passionate, who now lived in Italy, wrote monotonous poetry, chiefly sonnets, dwelt in a world of spirits—Swedenborg's world—and

[1] Robert Elliott, brother of the young lady who became Browne's wife.

turned earth into heaven by sitting in his spacious hall in the midst of forty fiddlers. Another correspondent was Pierce Morton—scholar, artist, journalist, etc.—'that mad man of genius Morton'—who was chronically in need of ten pounds—and travelled much, but delighted chiefly in Rome, in the soil of which he found something glutinous. FitzGerald, who liked to hear about foreign places, declared that he would himself travel if he had the eyes of Frederick and Morton. 'The eye,' he says, quoting Goethe, 'can but see what it brings with it the power of seeing.' So he sat at home under the cinereous skies of Suffolk, dreaming about the blue of Tuscany. Of Morton's letters he was a particular admirer, and copied a number of extracts from them into a commonplace book. In return he had nothing new to tell his distant friends except that Carlyle had published 'a raving book about heroes.' But despite his condemnation of Carlyle's book at the first reading, its influence on him was extraordinary. Naturally a hero-worshipper, he puts his friends—and especially W. K. Browne—on higher pedestals than ever; and this book was certainly in a considerable degree responsible for the apotheosis of 'Posh,' with which we shall deal in subsequent chapters. He quotes Carlyle in condonation of Posh's faults.[1] He calls Boulge 'Malebolge,' after the 'Malebolge Pool,' with its gloomy circles that Carlyle, handling Dante, talks so much about. Passage after passage appeals to him; especially the declaration that 'The poet who could merely sit on a chair and compose stanzas, would never make a stanza worth much,' and the reference to the

55. Frederick Tennyson; Pierce Morton; and Carlyle's 'Hero-Worship.'

---

[1] 'David, the Hebrew king, had fallen into sins enough. . . . Is this your man according to God's heart?'—*Hero-Worship*, Lecture II.

dawning on Dante that he would some day die,[1] which is echoed in the preface to *Polonius*. In the body of *Polonius* he quotes in full the fine passage in Lecture II. answering the question, 'What is a man's religion?' together with several other passages. Thus FitzGerald was evidently a very great admirer of a work which he is usually credited with having regarded slightingly. Let us note, however, that he quotes with approval in this same *Polonius* Carlyle's saying: 'The commonest quality in a true work of art, if its excellence have any depth and compass, is that at first sight it occasions a certain disappointment.'

In December 1841 FitzGerald is at Brighton, and in January at Geldestone again, where he gets an invitation to lecture at the Ipswich Mechanics' Institution, on 'any subject except controversial divinity and party politics'—a phrase which for days he rolled round his tongue. He pretended that Donne, who had not been asked, was mad with envy; and though he hoped to see Barton in February, he adds, 'You need not, however, expect that I can return to such familiar intercourse as once (in former days) passed between us. New honours in society have devolved upon me the necessity of a more dignified deportment.'[2] From January to April 1842 he was in London, visiting theatres and picture-dealers' shops, but feeling all the time that his life was unsatisfactory. He describes himself as living 'in a very seedy way, reading occasionally in books which every one else has gone through at school,' reading, moreover, 'just in the same way as ladies work: to pass the time away.' He often sees Thackeray, who has just finished his *Irish Sketch-Book*, and is trying to get appointed editor of

56. In London, Spring 1842.

[1] *Hero-Worship*, Lecture III. [2] *Letters*.

'a new foreign review' projected by Chapman and Hall. Thackeray thinks he could suit them, unless they want 'a great man like Mr. Carlyle.' At any rate, he knows two languages, and is not given to 'deep philosophising' —that unfortunate faculty which ruined the journalistic career of J. M. Kemble.[1] Thackeray, for his part, delighted to be with FitzGerald, but observed, 'I am afraid his society makes me idle; we sit and talk too much about books and pictures, and smoke too many cigars.'

Later, FitzGerald ruralises first at Geldestone, where he gets up at five in the morning to read Ecclesiasticus, and afterwards at Bedford, where he names Browne's pictures, writing down 'awful calumnies about Cuyp and others.' Moreover, they named the subjects rashly as well as the artists—calling one 'General Wolfe' for no reason except that he wore a scarlet coat and looked brave. Then there was 'a little Crome cottage' bought by FitzGerald at Norwich, and a hawking picture, the finest FitzGerald ever got, both apparently presents to Browne.[2]

57. At Bedford, Yardley Hastings, and Castle Ashby, August 1842.

From Bedford he makes trips with Browne and others to Keysoe, their favourite Bletsoe, and through Turvey and Lavendon to Yardley Hastings, in order to see the Marquis of Northampton's seat,[3] with its Inigo Jones architecture, Italian vistas, and associations with Samuel Johnson, who at Easton Maudit, close by, visited his friend Dr. Percy. FitzGerald found fault with the pictures, and took no note of the quaint and wonderful Dutch tapestry, but admired the fabric of the house, with the parapet balustrade round the roof carved into the letters 'NISI DOMINUS CUSTODIAT DOMUM, FRUSTRA

---

[1] Letter of Thackeray, 10th March 1842.
[2] From an unpublished letter (undated).   [3] Castle Ashby.

VIGILAT QUI CUSTODIT EAM.' 'This,' he observes, 'is not amiss to decipher as you come up the long avenue some summer or autumn day, and to moralise upon afterwards at the little "Rose and Crown" at Yardley, if such good home-brewed be there as used to be before I knew I was to die.'[1] Naturally he did not leave Yardley without visiting the famous Yardley Chase; and in his commonplace book, 'Half-Hours with the Worst Authors,'[2] he devotes a large space to an abridgment from Grantley Berkeley, entitled 'The View Hulloa of Yardley Chase,' an anecdote of deception practised on the writer by 'a fine young farmer.' Back again in Bedford, more journeys were made to the Bletsoe 'Falcon,' this time in company with Herr Teufelsdröckh —for there is always a copy of *Sartor Resartus* sticking out of FitzGerald's pocket.

The study of *Sartor Resartus* not unnaturally led to a desire to meet the author—a desire that was realised on

<small>58. Carlyle in a 'Branglemess.' Naseby Excavations.</small> the 15th of September 1842, when FitzGerald called upon Carlyle—'Gurlyle,' according to Thackeray—with Lawrence the artist. Carlyle, who was engaged upon his *Letters of Cromwell*, had a little before, in company with Dr. Arnold, made a journey to Naseby with a view to going over the battlefield. Knowing the place well, as was natural, seeing that most of it belonged to his father, FitzGerald discovered that, misled by Naseby's lying bully, the obelisk, Carlyle and Dr. Arnold had seen nothing, having walked over what was not the field of battle at all—that, in short, to use an expression common enough at Naseby, Carlyle was in a 'branglemess.'

<small>[1] *Euphranor.* *Cf.* Carlyle's *Hero-Worship*, Lecture III., which FitzGerald had just been reading. 'One day, it had risen sternly benign on the scathed heart of Dante, that he . . . would full surely die,' etc.
[2] Afterwards altered to 'Half-Hours with Obscure Authors.'</small>

'THE ROSE AND CROWN,' YARDLEY HASTINGS (NORTHAMPTONSHIRE)

NASEBY EXCAVATIONS

Though very reluctant to admit that they had been deceived, Carlyle had no objection to further evidence; consequently FitzGerald, who was just then going to Naseby, resolved to settle the matter once and for all. Before he could start, however, there came a letter from Carlyle asking a number of questions, and concluding with: 'On the whole, my dear sir, here seems to be work enough for you! But, after all, is it not worth your while on other accounts? Were it not a most legitimate task for the proprietor of Naseby, a man of scholarship, intelligence, and leisure, to make himself completely acquainted with the true state of all details connected with Naseby battle and its localities? Few spots of ground in all the world are memorabler to an Englishman. We could still very well stand a *good* little book on Naseby! *Verbum sapienti!*'

Before going further, it will be necessary, if we are to understand the communications between Carlyle and FitzGerald, to give a very brief account of what really happened on that famous 14th of June 1645. Fairfax, who had marched out of Buckinghamshire, was joined at Flore, in Northamptonshire, by Cromwell, who had come from the eastern counties on 12th June; and on the 13th they reached Naseby and took possession of Mill Hill, half a mile north of Naseby. The king's army was on Dust Hill, a rising parallel to Mill Hill, about a mile further north, and divided from it by a plain—Broad Moor. The battle began at ten on the morning of the 14th. Prince Rupert, who led the right wing of the king's army, charged across Broad Moor and up Rutput and Fenny Hills, fired upon, as he passed, by Colonel Okey and his dragoons hidden in Lantford Hedges, a thicket which ran northward at right angles to these hills. He reached the Parliament's left wing under Ireton and Skippon, and put them to flight. Ireton, whose horse was shot under him, and who was wounded in the thigh and in the face, was taken prisoner, and the Cavaliers then made for the Parliament's baggage, which was under the protection of firelocks close to the village. In the meantime the Parliament's right wing under Cromwell had charged down Mill Hill on to the king's left under Sir Marmaduke Langdale, who fled through the furze in the direction of Dust Hill and Longhold Spinnies. The Parliament's centre, under Fairfax, which was opposed by the king in person, now wavered and 'mostly all fled.' The officers, however, snatched the colours and fell into the reserves with them. The reserves rushed on, and others, encouraged by Cromwell's success on the right, rallying to them, they attacked the Cavaliers vigorously, and drove them pell-mell down the hill. At Dust Hill the king made a final attempt to rally his flying forces, but in vain, and they fled in panic towards Harborough. Not until he had reached the baggage did Rupert discover that the rest of the king's army was being repulsed. He then hastened to render help, but too late. The battle was irretrievably lost. The number of slain is unknown, but five thousand were taken prisoners. When the battle was found to be going against the king, Ireton offered his keeper pardon in return for freedom, and so got released.

On arriving at Naseby, FitzGerald had spade and mattock taken to a spot some considerable distance from the 'Blockhead Obelisk,' a spot on a hill 'pitted with hollows and overgrown with rank vegetation,' where, according to the blacksmith, the principal local authority, many of the slain lay. On opening one of the hollows this declaration was proved true, for there lay the remains of skeletons packed closely together. Carlyle now plies FitzGerald with questions. He wants to know whether there was a windmill at Naseby (yes, on Mill Hill). Are there any traces of such names as these: Lantford Hedges, where Okey's dragoons hid; Rutput Hill, Lean Leaf Hill? What steeples, etc., can be descried from Mill Hill? and so on—just the questions to be asked by a man desirous of writing a vivid account of the event. Replies to the best of his ability being sent by FitzGerald, Carlyle again writes urging a continuance of the investigations, and observing, 'It is long since I read a letter so interesting as yours of yesterday. Clearly enough you are upon the very battleground; and I, it is also clear, have only looked up towards it from the slope of Mill Hill.' In the intervals of excavating, FitzGerald read Virgil's *Georgics*, and felt that they attuned perfectly with his bucolic surroundings. He sits at breakfast at Mr. Watchams', and looking out of window sees the old stump of a cross grown round with long grass, great high hedges ramped over by clematis and briony, and labourers taking their horses to plough—up the long road that leads past the obelisk; then turning to his book he reads the passage in which the swains are bidden to work their steers and sow barley in the fields, '*Libra die somnique*,'[1] etc. Next day he goes out with two farmers and the venerable vicar, the Rev. William Marshall, who was old enough to have spoken to the sons of the men who took part in the fight. A great trench was dug, with the result of more skeletons—most of them naturally incomplete—and a large number of sound teeth, a few of which were afterwards sent to Carlyle. FitzGerald's idea of opening another grave was apparently not put into execution. He quite satisfied Carlyle, however, but con-

[1] *Georg.* i. 208-211.

fessed that all this digging up of dead Cavaliers and Roundheads was little to his taste; although it certainly gave him satisfaction to feel that he had been able to discover where the thickest of the fight had taken place. Unfortunately the *Cromwell* was not being constructed in the same way as the *French Revolution*; and Carlyle, instead of giving a vivid description of the battle, for which he had all the materials, contented himself with a short *pasticcio* of it, which he put, not in the body of the book, but in the appendix of the third volume.[1]

Carlyle wished to erect over the principal grave a block of Portland stone, and suggested for inscription: 'Here, as proved by strict and not too impious examination, lie the slain of the Battle of Naseby'—a project that was talked about for thirty years, but owing to various difficulties never put into execution. FitzGerald often calls at 24 Cheyne Row to see Carlyle about this Naseby affair, or about nothing in particular, and he and Carlyle, in dressing-gown and straw hat, each with half a yard of pipe, stroll by the hour up and down the flagged court and 'poor sooty patch of garden,' and under the 'old scrag of a cherry-tree.'

In July 1843 FitzGerald paid a third visit to Ireland, reaching Dublin on July 11th, to find the people going about in their cars or standing idle just as ever. At his hotel occurred an odd and inconvenient incident. It was a hot day, and he ordered a tepid bath. By and by he went to the bathroom, where the attendant, instead of leaving him to lock the door inside, by mistake locked him in; and, to crown the trouble, the water was scalding hot. How long FitzGerald was left in this predicament history does not record, but it is relieving to read of his setting out next day for his Uncle

59. In Ireland again.

---

[1] *Oliver Cromwell's Letters and Speeches*, vol. iii. p. 344. Ashburton Edition.

Peter's at Halverstown, Kilcullen. For his cousins Margaret, Honoria, and Mary Frances, who were amusing themselves with private theatricals, he wrote a prologue to one of Calderon's plays. He passed most of his time, however, at Ballysax, close to the Curragh Camp, and Kildare, 'one of the wretchedest wild villages' that Carlyle, who visited it a little later, 'ever saw, full of ragged beggars, and altogether like a village in Dahomey.' We may judge that FitzGerald visited the cathedral, and the ruins of Grey Abbey, the burial-place of the ancient FitzGeralds, and was shown the site of the nunnery of St. Bridget, famous for its inextinguishable fire. Then followed another visit to Edgeworthstown. Frank Edgeworth, having given up his unprofitable school, if indeed he ever had any pupils, at Eltham, had come back to Ireland to take charge of his sister's estate, and 'be a good country gentleman'—'to Mrs. Edgeworth's and all our inexpressible comfort and support,' adds 'the great Maria,' 'also for the good of the country as a resident landlord and magistrate *much* needed.' So Frank at last found his niche in the world and could, when not sitting on the bench, receiving rents, or going into accounts, bury himself in Kant, Spinoza, and 'deep philosophising' in general. FitzGerald thinks Miss Edgeworth is wearing away; still she has six more years to live. He sets sail from Dublin on September 1st, bearing with him 'the heartfelt regrets of all the people of Ireland.'

Back again in Boulge he walks out with 'Bletsoe'; visits Crabbe; takes tea with Barton; strolls over to Hasketon to taste some of Squire Jenny's fresh air; goes on Sunday to church, where the parson and the clerk—among the fungi and the mouse-bitten curtains—get 'through the service sea-saw, like two men in a saw-pit'; papers his rooms a 'still green,' so as to agree with his 'Venetian pictures'; places his chair against the window, hangs his legs out over the window-ledge, reads Seneca, and feels happy. This method of disposing of his legs used to be taken advantage of by two naughty village boys, who would watch until they saw him comfortably settled, and then steal round to the back and climb his walnut-tree. On one occasion, when they were helping themselves, they saw, on looking down, FitzGerald walking backwards and forwards in his loose blue coat, book in hand, under the tree, but never raising his eyes. He kept them there the better part of an afternoon. In March he hears of the death of his old friend and pensioner Mrs. Chaplin of Wherstead, and looks out another old lady to supply her place. In April he writes to Mrs. Charlesworth of Bramford,[1] chiefly with a view to helping Carlyle on the subject of Cromwell's Lincolnshire campaign; and late in the year he hears of the presentation of John Allen to the living of Prees, in North Shropshire.[2]

[1] Near Ipswich.
[2] In October 1847 Allen was appointed Archdeacon of Salop.

JOHN ALLEN, 1844

CHAPTER VIII

REV. T. R. MATTHEWS

APRIL 1844—SEPTEMBER 1845

In the meantime, the Rev. T. R. Matthews had been continuing with more energy and fervour than ever his evangelistic work, wearing himself out with preaching, six sermons a week being no uncommon occurrence. One particular service, at which FitzGerald was present, excites our interest above others. It was on the night of Good Friday (April 1844). The worshippers had gathered early in front of the Bromham Road Chapel. The traffic was impeded, vehicles having a difficulty to get past. As soon as the doors were opened the crowd (FitzGerald among them), or as many as the building would hold, poured in, while the rest stood with heads craned in at the door, or went away disappointed. In the middle of the far end of the chapel was a panelled pulpit with red cushion and tassels, and 'S' shaped gas bracket and globe. Close to this sat FitzGerald. Matthews, a Saul of a man, with prominent eyebrows, aquiline, high-bridged nose, and hair curling up at the neck, in black Genevan gown with white bands, ascended the pulpit steps, a wooden cross in his hands. The subject of the sermon was the Crucifixion. Raising the cross, and fixing his eyes on it, Matthews commenced with a calm and minute description of the tremendous event, describing the approach to

60. The Bromham Road Chapel.

Golgotha, the driving of the nail into one hand, into the other, through both feet, the raising of the cross, God in man's image distended, the tears of the women, the terror of the disciples, the sneers of the priests. 'He saved others, Himself He cannot save.' No fine words, no affectation, but the preacher's earnestness was terrible. A grand sermon with a flavour of the old monkish days, though even Peter the Hermit, with all his eloquence and with *his* wooden cross, was less powerful to move the masses. At the end ensued a few moments of profound silence. Then Matthews earnestly begged that some of his hearers would express their belief that Christ had died for them. One after another, with tear-stained face and with sobs, rose up and declared their faith in the Redeemer. 'I was quite overset,' observes FitzGerald, 'all poor people: how much richer than all who fill the London churches. Theirs is the Kingdom of Heaven!' FitzGerald was greatly impressed, too, by Matthews' enthusiasm and intense feeling. He preached with all his soul and with all his might, and he quitted the pulpit 'as wet as if he had been in a tub.' In fact, he was slowly killing himself.

In May 1844 Browne and 'Monsieur Jem' (that is Spedding) were at Boulge visiting FitzGerald, who calls them good representatives—Browne of the Vita Attiva, Spedding of the Vita Contemplativa: the former one of the busiest men in Bedford, 'farmer, magistrate, militia officer—of more use,' says FitzGerald, 'in a week than I in my life long'—being all for action; the latter all for persistent and unwearied study. Browne, however, could spare odd half-hours for contemplation; and Spedding, 'that literary sportsman,' was, as his letters show, fully appreciative of the pleasures of country life. In one of his letters,

<small>61. Browne's Marriage, 30th July 1844.</small>

written just before a visit to Browne, he says: 'I hope that before the partridges or hares are all shot we may make it suit each other to have a pop at them together. We never quite settled the question which of us could miss a hare cleanest.'[1] This, however, was pleasantry, each being a first-rate shot. Spedding clearly came into the world for only two purposes: to edit Bacon and to shoot grouse and snipe—grouse in his plantations at Corrybrough, and snipe among the reeds of the Ouse.

Browne, as we have seen, had become engaged to Miss Elizabeth Elliott. The death of her father took place on 21st February 1844, and by and by the date of the wedding of Browne and Miss Elliott was fixed. FitzGerald wished his friend every happiness, using the words of Michael Drayton to *his* William Browne: 'So mayst thou thrive as thou, young shepherd, art beloved by me'; but his heart was sore all the same. No more Bedford, he thought, and no more poplars, or Clapham Tower, or 'Falcon' at Bletsoe, or pottering alongside the Ouse with book and colour-box. Ten years had elapsed since his first visit, and this of 1844 was surely to be the last! He need not have troubled himself with apprehensions, for Bedfordshire was to be his yet another fifteen years. 'When I heard,' says he, 'that they could not have less than five hundred a year, I gave up all further interest in the matter. I could not wish a reasonable couple more. W. B. may be spoilt if he grows rich: that is the only thing could spoil him.' The wedding, at which FitzGerald was present, took place at Goldington, all the village being in gala, on 30th July 1844. Browne, who was twenty-six (his wife was nineteen), is described at this time as having a very clear, pink, and white complexion, a full, large, blue-grey eye, and a square

---

[1] Unpublished letter of Spedding's.

and rather massive forehead. Then he was shaven; subsequently he wore full moustache and whiskers. Four portraits of him are in existence: (1) A water-colour—head and shoulders—a very young man in fawn waistcoat, darkish coat, light overcoat, light blue tie, longish hair, shaven chin and lip. (2) Sketch by Thackeray—three-quarters, cutaway coat, cane in left hand, stock and big coat collar; Swiss church in background. (3) An unfinished oil painting by Lawrence — side face, auburn hair, slight side whiskers. (4) A photograph of him outside his hut at Aldershot. All are given in this book. FitzGerald portrays his friend thus: 'Has very good abilities; a smooth-mannered person; more surface than depth; quite a man of the world; fond of argument, but not ill-tempered; careful, thoughtful for others, and a good contriver; gentlemanly; would not do a mean thing.'[1] 'He had rare intuition,' says FitzGerald in a letter of 7th February 1883, 'into men, matters, and even into matters of art; though Thackeray would call him "Little Browne," which I told him he was not justified in doing.' The epithet 'Little' seems, however, to have been suggested rather by Browne's stature, for he was only five feet seven, whilst Thackeray himself was big and burly. Moreover, FitzGerald in his playful moods did not spare his friend either, often calling him 'Dear Stubby.' Even six months later (December 1844) FitzGerald was lamenting his supposed loss. 'Browne,' says he, 'is married, and I shall see but little of him for the future. I have laid by my rod and line by the willows of the Ouse for ever. "He is married and cannot come." This change is the meaning of those verses—

> "Friend after friend departs;
> Who has not lost a friend?"'

---

[1] Unpublished manuscript in the possession of the Rev. Kenworthy Browne.

TURNPIKE COTTAGE, GOLDINGTON

GOLDINGTON HALL (BEDFORD), FROM GOLDINGTON GREEN

But in the summer of 1845 FitzGerald is again off to 'dear old Bedfordshire,' the marriage having made no difference whatever; and presently we hear of Mr. and Mrs. W. Kenworthy Browne taking up their residence at Goldington Hall.

The village of Goldington is situated about two miles north-east of Bedford, which in that direction, as in others, is rapidly extending. On the left, one passes the 'Fox and Hounds' inn and spacious nursery gardens, and on the right the road leading to the ruins of Newnham Priory, with the site of Turnpike Cottage,[1] the picturesque residence of the common friend of the Brownes and FitzGerald, Captain Addington. Addington was a retired naval captain—a little, pursy, bald-headed, kindly, catty old gentleman in brown coat and brass buttons, much given to blazing fires, a luxurious arm-chair, and other 'seductive comforts' or discomforts. He divided his time between Turnpike Cottage and his London club, the United Service. His cats, which he treated like human beings, and taught numerous accomplishments, were the talk of the neighbourhood, and FitzGerald extended their fame to Woodbridge. Goldington is built round a green or goose-common. On the west is the vicarage (a modern erection occupying the site of its low and picturesque predecessor), on the north Goldington Hall, on the east Goldington Bury, and on the south are the majority of the cottages, with several inns. The church, St. Mary's, is a little to the north-east of the Hall, and beyond, near the Ouse, is a conical mound—the remains of Risinghoe Castle. The Hall, dating from 1650, is a spacious house, embosomed in shrubs and lofty trees, but its chimneys and upper windows appear conspicu-

62. Goldington Hall. The Bloody Warrior.

[1] Pulled down in December 1902, just after our photograph of it was taken.

ously and picturesquely above the foliage as one approaches it from the green. The south or principal front, like the rest of the house, is of old red brick, but on the right of the entrance-porch is a patch of stone, evidently the remains of an earlier house. Noticeable, too, are the two curious round-headed recesses in the wall to the left of the porch. There are fine old yews, chestnuts, hawthorns, walnuts, and firs. An old-fashioned garden, with mounds of topiary work, and gay with flowers, extends northward, and is succeeded by a pretty pightle or paddock of classic fame, from which is obtained a view of the gables of the house. There have been considerable alterations and improvements at the Hall of recent years, but all in keeping with the Cromwellian building. The staircase and the decorations of the hall are modern, but the massive carved oak doors are of Browne's time ; whilst on the first floor is a room with the original oak wainscotting, and untouched, except that the ceiling has been raised. The furniture is modern. In FitzGerald's day one of the charms of the place was the fact of its being filled with furniture from Mrs. Piozzi's house at Streatham, which Mrs. Browne's father had bought as early as 1810. Dr. Johnson's own bed was included, and in the room in which, during his visits here, FitzGerald slept, stood the Great Cham's 'own bookcase and secretaire ; with looking-glass in the panels which often reflected his uncouth shape.'

FitzGerald was never happier than when at Goldington sauntering in its elmy fields and dreaming in the pightle;[1] and in his letters, both published and unpublished, he speaks with feeling and affection of the village and the friends he there made. If inclined for sport, and it was

---

[1] See chapter xii. of this work, 'When in Bedfordshire I put away almost all books except Omar,' etc.

GOLDINGTON VICARAGE

(THE FIGURE IS THE REV. WILLIAM MONKHOUSE)

to fishing that he was always most addicted, he could generally — if Browne was busy with his tenants, at a true-blue dinner, or at his hundred and one other occupations — fall back on Harry Boulton,[1] the gentleman farmer of Puttenhoe, married to Browne's sister Anne; or Robert Elliott of Goldington Bury, Mrs. Browne's brother. If studiously inclined he could, as he so often did, look in at the vicarage, and talk philology with the Rev. William Monkhouse.[2] To Mr. Monkhouse, a tall, handsome, nimble man with an aquiline nose, who had been a great athlete, and who at fifty had never seen a gate he could not jump, the vicarage was a sort of Little Ease. He could not stand upright in any of the rooms without brushing the ceilings with his hair or bumping his forehead against the beams. Being more solicitous, however, for the spiritual and educational advancement of the village than for the preservation of the charms of his person, the situation gave him small concern. He was an enthusiastic antiquary, his speciality being Druidic Remains, which he held to be entirely unconnected with Druidism, and he was the author of a scholarly work on the etymologies of Bedfordshire, which appeared in 1857. Very sensibly, he did not keep his learning to himself, but, by way of lecture and conversation, imparted it to his thick-soled, but not unintelligent, parishioners, who thus became not only good Christians but respectable antiquaries. The Rev. William Airy, FitzGerald's Keysoe friend, and Monkhouse were kindred spirits and boon companions. Airy compiled a *Digest* of the Domesday Book as it concerned Bedfordshire. If FitzGerald did not interest

---

[1] Henry Dyott Boulton.
[2] Born 1805; curate of Goldington and Willington 1831, rector of Goldington 1835.

himself much in their archæology, he was ever ready to discuss with both questions relating to philology. Old Captain Addington of Turnpike Cottage cared nothing for philology, but FitzGerald found him also excellent company, and he would often visit the little thatched homestead, which must have reminded him of his cottage at Boulge, which, however, was less ornate, and in which one could walk without treading on cats. Captain Addington's family had owned Goldington Bury, indeed most of the village; but the estate had become encumbered, and when it was sold—Mr. Robert Elliott, Mrs. Browne's father, being the purchaser—the captain had seven-and-sixpence to take. With his seven-and-sixpence, his Government pension, his servants, 'Big Isaac' and 'Little Isaac' (father and son named Joyce), his dog Badger, his tortoise-shell cat Tom, and his other but less illustrious cats, the choleric little captain then retired to Turnpike Cottage. His delight was to drive about in a gig, dressed in a blue coat and white waistcoat, with 'Little Isaac,' and to terrify children, 'often threatening to ride over them.' This, however, was only his fun, for 'he was a very tender man for a captain.'

A favourite excursion with FitzGerald at this time was to Turvey, four miles out, where lived Mr. George Boulton, Harry Boulton's brother. Here FitzGerald made a number of sketches, which for years were among his most cherished treasures. The guests at Goldington included Thackeray; and he, FitzGerald, and Browne, by their different heights, formed three steps as they walked down Bedford High Street. Thackeray made a good many sketches with Bedford scenes for background; moreover, presently, when engaged on *Pendennis*, he drew largely on Browne, and in a minor degree, as we

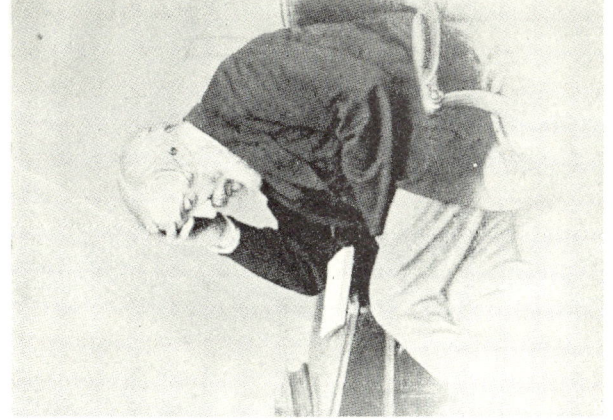

REV. W. AIRY

REV. W. MONKHOUSE

have already observed, on FitzGerald. Bedford does not altogether correspond with Chatteris, which is apparently a mixture of Bedford and some sleepy cathedral town; but Arthur Pendennis is clearly enough Browne's double. 'Arthur's hair was of a healthy brown colour which looks like gold in the sunshine; his face was round, rosy, freckled, and good-humoured; . . . in fact, without being a beauty, he had such a frank, good-natured, kind face, and laughed so merrily at you out of his honest blue eyes, that no wonder Mrs. Pendennis thought him the pride of the whole county.' Then again, Pendennis was only five feet eight—a mere dwarf in the eyes of the gigantic Thackeray. He rode a very good mare with uncommon pluck and grace, and took fences with great coolness, had an 'honest taste for port wine,' was an enthusiastic fox-hunter and angler, loved art and literature, and had political ambitions. Such also was Browne, and one could easily point to plenty of other parallels. As Mrs. Anne Thackeray Ritchie observes, 'There was a little likeness in Warrington to Edward FitzGerald.'

That Browne was a man of culture is evident from his commonplace books. One of them, a 'Book of Extracts made in 1833,' contains among other entries 'A Paper on Diet,' 'Virgil's Tomb,' 'Remarks on Hogarth by Horace Walpole,' and extracts from the poets, principally Scott. Being now ambitious to distinguish himself in politics, he often spoke at the meetings of the Bedford Conservative Society, and nursed the hope of getting into St. Stephen's. Fitz-Gerald's ideal man in *Euphranor*, it will be remembered, 'is qualified not only to shoot the pheasant and hunt the fox, but even to sit on the Bench of Magistrates—

or even in Parliament—not unprovided with a quotation or two from Horace or Virgil.'

On August 20th FitzGerald is in London with Thackeray, who is busy on *Barry Lyndon*,[1] and they dine with Quin at a party where 'FitzGerald is in wonderful cue.' Later FitzGerald is at Geldestone again, visiting Mrs. Schutz, and making for a niece 'a Nelly-ad,' or abstract of Nell's wanderings from the *Old Curiosity Shop*. In September he is at Leamington to see his sister Andalusia married to the Rev. Francis de Soyres, and gives a day to looking over the field of Edgehill. 'If war breaks out in France,' says he, 'I will take up arms as a volunteer under Major Pytches.[2] Pytches and Westminster Abbey!' Back at Boulge, he wishes F. Tennyson were with him to quarrel—that is 'in the sense of a good strenuous difference of opinion, supported on either side by occasional outbursts of spleen'; and in November he declares, 'I certainly love winter better than summer. Could one but know, as one sits within the tropic latitude of one's fireside, that there was not increased want, cold, and misery beyond it.' So he cuddles round the fire in his solitary Boulge Cottage, his cat and the dog 'Bletsoe' on the rug, and his old woman, with her beautiful red arms, in the kitchen, just as if it were an Apuleius's or Gil Blas's robbers' cave, save that the prison is his by choice, not necessity. 'We are never very much displeased,' he cries, echoing La Rochefoucauld, 'with our neighbours' misfortunes'[3]—but that is a libel on himself, for he can scarcely enjoy his fire for thinking of the sufferings of the poor in the biting cold

63. Andalusia's marriage.

---

[1] Appeared in *Fraser's Magazine*, January to December 1844.
[2] His friend at Melton Grange.
[3] Unpublished letter.

W. KENWORTHY BROWNE

weather, though he thinks they are much to blame too —'they will have such enormous families.'

In May 1845 Bernard Barton, after a silence of nine years, published his eighth volume of poetry, *Household Verses*, which is interesting to us on account of its frontispiece, 'Gainsborough's Lane,' and vignetted title-page, 'Scene on the Deben,' both from paintings by FitzGerald's friend Thomas Churchyard; also for the verses to Lucy Barton and the stanzas[1] suggested by a gift which Barton received from FitzGerald's mother.[2] Thomas Churchyard —'my little friend Churchyard,' 'le petit Churchyard'— was a solicitor and amateur artist of Woodbridge, who did not, FitzGerald used wickedly to say, paint in 'body' colour. Churchyard, 'our great judge on art,' had a poetical mind—once pleased FitzGerald, for instance, by calling the pretty yellow aconites in front of Boulge Cottage 'New Year's Gifts'—and was an authority on Gainsborough, Constable, Crome, and other East Anglian artists. In his own profession Churchyard, despite, or perhaps owing to, his gifts made little headway. Had he loved parchment more and canvas less, he would have had a plumper purse, though not necessarily a more joyous existence. In short, his was the poetic and artistic, not the business temperament. He embroidered even the law; his nervous eloquence, to use the words of his friend John Loder, 'often lending a positive grace to the dry details of many an uninteresting case.' His devotion to the fine and impoverishing arts was, indeed, to him the very 'breath of life.'

Matthews the preacher had persevered in his work with an earnestness which even his herculean frame could not stand. In three years, says John FitzGerald, he preached

64. Bernard Barton's eighth volume. 'Le petit Churchyard.'

[1] *Household Verses*, p. 86. [2] *Ibid.* p. 83.

over a thousand sermons—an average near upon of one a day, but the preaching was but a part of his self-imposed labour.[1] Take a glimpse at him at half-past five in the morning on Easter Sunday, 1842. He is in a meadow by the river Ouse, for seven persons are to be baptized. There are one hundred and fifty present. 'A little while,' he says, 'before I baptized, the sun had risen with peculiar splendour, his bright rays threw a lustre over the solemn scene and met the faces of our baptized brethren and sisters as they came out of the water, making their faces sparkle again, as the dewdrops in the morning sun; it was a glorious time, the sun shining, the children of God rising out of the water, the animating voices of friends by the river-side singing "glory, honour, praise, and power," made the whole scene truly solemn.' The sick he anointed with oil, *Omne oleo tranquillari*—'Everything can be calmed with oil,' he used to say with Pliny. And he prayed over people afflicted with deafness and other complaints, though not always with success. 'One for deafness of seventeen years standing, and on Sabbath could hear better than for a long time,' but on another occasion, though he prayed for two hours and a half over a poor deaf woman, whose friends were anxious 'that she should have the use of her hearing,' his efforts availed nothing, for 'there was a lack of faith.' A Mrs. Symes of Ravensden, among others, is said to have been the subject of a miraculous healing. 'She was so weak that she had to be carried to the river, but on emerging from the water was able to walk home without assistance.' Fired with gratitude to God, she built at Ravensden the

65. Death of Matthews, 4th Sept. 1845.

---

[1] Mr. John FitzGerald tells us that in 1841 Matthews preached 328 times; in 1842, 320 times; in 1843, 360 times; in 1844, 280 times; and in the eight months of 1845 (the year he died), 158 times.

THOMAS CHURCHYARD
'LE PETIT CHURCHYARD'

chapel which still stands. Bedford became the English Lourdes. Matthews advocated the frequent reiteration aloud of the more precious verses of Scripture. Thus he would say, '"The blood of Jesus Christ, His Son, cleanseth us from all sin" should be frequently repeated by our *lips*. . . . I have found faith greatly increased by taking the word into my mouth.'

On the 22nd August 1845 he was at Walham Green, London. The chapel was crammed, the doorway filled up, the crowd extended so far across the road that the omnibuses had difficulty in passing, and he got home at ten, wearied out. On the Monday and Tuesday he exerted himself even more, and his appetite failed. On the Wednesday he went to dine with a gentleman, but could eat nothing; nevertheless he preached as usual in the evening to a huge congregation. The exertion, the heat, the closeness of the atmosphere, the exposure to the cold air afterwards, quickened his complaint, and when they brought him home to Bedford it was found that typhus fever had set in. FitzGerald, who was then paying his usual visit to the Brownes, deeply sympathised with his 'noble preacher,' but feared for the worst. Conformably to a plan made some time previous, he took a three days' trip to Naseby. On his return on Friday, September 5th, passing through Bedford at dusk, he saw a coffin carrying down the street. It was for Matthews, who had died the previous day in one of the apartments of his toad paradise under the chapel in the Bromham Road. Says Fitz- Gerald, writing on the following Sunday : ' I knew whose it must be. I would have given a great deal to save his life, which might certainly have been saved with common precaution. He died in perfect peace, approving all the principles of his life to be genuine.'

Matthews was buried on Monday, September 8th, in

the graveyard at the back of Bromham Road Chapel, both Edward and his brother John being among the mourners. His trumpet was placed before the pulpit in the chapel built by his arch-disciple Mrs. Symes at Ravensden, where it still hangs. Subsequently his remains were removed to Colmworth, where his followers raised a tomb to his memory.[1] Silhouettes of Matthews preaching in his pulpit were eagerly sought after, but they are now scarce. Indeed I have never seen but one, which is here reproduced.

On the Sunday after Matthews' death, John FitzGerald 'improved' the death of his friend in an address delivered in the Bromham Road Chapel. This was subsequently printed,[2] and for a time John FitzGerald continued Matthews' work at Bedford, preaching regularly in the chapel. Though sealed of the tribe of Matthews, and sincere and staunch as to his principles, 'a sinner called to be the Lord's delight,' John FitzGerald lacked the evangelist's energy. Edward said wittily, that when his brother wrote 'D.V.' (his constant habit) he was taking the Lord's name in vain, the 'D.V.' merely meaning, 'If *I* happen to be in the humour.' John FitzGerald was nevertheless a very earnest man, and whenever he preached commanded a large auditory. Yet he had an impediment in his speech, which gave his voice a hissing

---

[1] See Appendix ix. He was at Colmworth twelve years, at Bedford fifteen.

[2] There is a copy in the British Museum :—

'The Apostolic Minister's Preparation for Departure; a Funeral Address on the Death of the Rev. T. R. Matthews, by John FitzGerald, M.A.' In slate-coloured paper covers. Price 4 shillings. 140 pp.

Contents—
Funeral Address, pp. 1 to 49.
Appendix 1: On the Authority of the Canons, and how far they bind the Clergy, pp. 51 to 81.
Appendix 2: On the Presumption of Attempting to Condense the Whole Scheme of Divine Revelation in a Smaller Globe than itself, pp. 82 and 83.
Appendix 3: On Dissent, pp. 84 to 140.

'MATTHEWS' CHAPEL,' BROMHAM ROAD, BEDFORD

or whistling sound, and his sermons were of inordinate and wearisome length. A man well read in the scriptures, 'his chief aim,' says a hearer, 'was not to display his abilities, but to lead his hearers to the fountain of life and blessing in Jesus Christ.' In Bedford, owing to his preaching, he was long a well-known figure. His eccentricities, both in and out of the pulpit, were many. 'I sat with him once,' observes an informant, 'in a pew at Bunyan Meeting. To my surprise, when the preacher (it was the Rev. John Jukes[1]) entered the pulpit, Mr. FitzGerald began to undress. He did nothing worse, however, than remove his boots and stockings and a few other minor articles of attire, and empty the contents of his pockets on to the cushions of the seat; after which he seemed comfortable and thoroughly to enjoy the service, though he, unwittingly, whistled now and again, but not more, it seems, than usual.' John FitzGerald was never happy unless preaching, listening to sermons, or arguing about and criticising them. 'I wish,' said Edward plaintively, one day, after patiently listening to one of John's tremendous harangues, 'I wish my brother wouldn't always be talking about religion.'

[1] Minister at Bunyan Meeting, 1840-1866.

CHAPTER IX

E. B. COWELL

OCTOBER 1845-1853

Bibliography

9. Notes to the *Table-Talk of John Selden*, 1847.
10. The 'Bernard Barton' contributions to the *Ipswich Journal*, 1849. February 24—Death of Bernard Barton; March 3—Funeral of Bernard Barton.
11. 'Memoir of Bernard Barton,' prefixed to *Selections from the Poems and Letters of Bernard Barton*, 1849.
12. *Euphranor*, 1st edition, 1851.
13. *Polonius*, 1852.
14. Six Dramas from Calderon, 1853.

THE farm, 'Hall Farm,' at which Mr. Job Smith lived, situated a little to the north of Boulge Hall, was a frequent resort of FitzGerald's. It was an old-fashioned, low thatched building, 'provided with all the things in Bloomfield's poems.' The good folks made their own candles (though they didn't tell it at 'The Bull'[1]), and Alfred, Mr. Smith's son, used to go down to the brook to fetch the rushes. The chimney-corner was the snuggest nook in the parish, and the most corpulent of pots hung from the hake. One table served for the family and the labourers, who sat together at the end, and the place reminded FitzGerald of Mr. Tovill's farmstead in the *Life of George Crabbe*. Of a winter's evening a noise would be

66. A Peep at the Hall Farm, 1846.

---
[1] At Woodbridge.

heard at the door as of some one stamping the snow off his feet. 'There's the parson,' Mrs. Smith would say, and in walks, as white as a miller, old Mr. Shribb Reynolds—'handsome Mr. Reynolds'—with a basket of pears. Presently, perhaps, 'Mr. Edward'[1] joins the comfortable circle and smokes a long clay with the rest, whilst Alfred's brother reads aloud from the newspaper, with the Government red stamp at the corner, a speech by Sir Robert Peel on the corn laws. When the rushlight has burnt low and the log on the hearth has become mostly white ash, Mrs. Smith begins to fidget, and the evening is understood to have gone. At Hall Farm you might burn as many candles as you liked in the morning, which began with sulphur matches and tinder-box at five, but there was a limit at night. Mr. Reynolds is first to go. 'I'll send the basket up,' Mrs. Smith invariably said, and the old rector always gave the reply, 'I brought it down full, surely I can carry it back empty.' Then he would make for his house at Debach, and FitzGerald would seek his Gil Blas's den at the park gates, Colonel and Mrs. Short or no Colonel and Mrs. Short.

FitzGerald was very fond of inviting Churchyard, Bernard Barton, and the Rev. George Crabbe to his cottage, and he dubbed them and himself 'The Wits of Woodbridge.' The time passed pleasantly enough, for with each of these guests FitzGerald could always be expansive and effusive, though at the supper-table there was more hospitality than comfort. However, FitzGerald 'in his morning-coat of blue serge, cut short,' and made like the rest of his clothes—'very baggy,' and in boots 'not suitable for skates,' did the honours, and the fame of their con-

67. The Wits of Woodbridge.

---

[1] FitzGerald was always called 'Mr. Edward' at the farm.

versations reached as far as Woodbridge. Occasionally there joined this circle Captain Capper Brooke of Ufford, 'Le Grand Capitaine Brohoke,' and the Rev. Robert Groome, the very civilised, well-lettered, and agreeable rector of Monk Soham.[1] Brooke, who rode a huge chestnut charger with a long tail, was a good-looking, dapper, well-dressed, and scrupulously neat man, with very black whiskers, which were never allowed to go grey. He was the pride of his valet and his tailor, and the very antithesis in appearance of FitzGerald. This care for the person made him look much younger than his years. FitzGerald once said to him, 'You are a deceiver, mon capitaine; you falsify your years, you have no right to look so young.' Captain Brooke could talk of rare and sumptuous books, for he had a fine library, collected at enormous expense and trouble. He made no account of going even so far as Italy to secure anything he had set his heart upon, but he was more of a collector than a reader. FitzGerald sometimes visited Ufford. Once he and Groome called together. The drawing-room there had been newly refurnished, and FitzGerald sat himself down on an amber satin couch. Presently there was seen trickling over it a black stream, which came from a penny bottle of ink which FitzGerald had bought in Woodbridge and put into a tail-pocket.[2]

Groome, whose forte was folklore, wrote subsequently under the name of John Dutfen, and in the Suffolk dialect, *The only Darter*,[3] a storyette styled by FitzGerald, who reprinted it at his own expense, 'a beautiful Suffolk idyll.' Another visitor at Boulge Cottage was the Rev. H. S. Drew, Crabbe's curate. Crabbe and Drew might have

[1] Rector of Monk Soham from 1845; archdeacon of Suffolk from 1869 to 1887. He died 19th March 1889.
[2] *Two Suffolk Friends.*
[3] See *Two Suffolk Friends*, pp. 52 to 57.

been taken bodily out of *Tristram Shandy*. To hear them was, to FitzGerald, better than a play. They differed on various religious points, but particularly on infant baptism—adult baptism being in Mr. Crabbe's opinion preferable, while Drew was a pædo-baptist. They took long walks together, and most of the way argued loudly and with heat on this subject, whilst Crabbe's hat, never in its right place, would work round his head like satellite round a planet. Thus almost every field thereabouts was a battlefield, and might have been marked on the map with tiny crossed swords. FitzGerald —a capital mimic—delighted to take off these antagonists. 'Drew and Crabbe,' he would begin, 'have been taking a walk and arguing as usual upon that accursed infant baptism. Of course neither could convince the other,' and then, to the infinite amusement of all present, he would imitate their speech, gait, and gestures. Indeed when in these merry moods he never spared his closest friends, and Garrick himself was not more deliciously funny. Now and again FitzGerald used to visit his old friend Major Moor at Great Bealings, and he liked to sit in the Major's snug parlour and talk, over a glass of Shiraz wine, about India and the Hindu gods.

In 1845 Carlyle's *Cromwell* was at last published, but FitzGerald, though he read it attentively, proved unimpressible. He admired certain descriptive passages in the work—that, for example, about the battle of Dunbar, but to Cromwell himself was not drawn.

About 1846 FitzGerald became acquainted with E. B. Cowell, then a young man of twenty, and subsequently professor of Sanskrit at Cambridge. Cowell it was who unlocked for FitzGerald the treasure-house of Persian literature and showed him the way to immortality.

68. E. B. Cowell.

Born at Ipswich in 1826, Edward Byles Cowell, eldest son of Mr. Charles Cowell, corn-merchant, was brought up to his father's business.[1] Having, however, a turn for books, he had borrowed from the Ipswich Literary Institute the *Memoirs of the Life, Writings, and Correspondence of Sir William Jones*, by Lord Teignmouth,[2] a work of thirteen volumes, which he studied with assiduity, and which when the library was given up he purchased. In October 1841 his father gave him a copy of the number of the *Edinburgh Review* containing Macaulay's article on Warren Hastings, but the boy was most attracted by the list of new works advertised at the end, which included *An Introduction to the Grammar of the Sanskrit Language, for the use of early students*,[3] by H. H. Wilson, M.A. 'I saved up my pocket-money,' said Professor Cowell to me,[4] 'and I bought the book at Christmas and kept it by me as a future hope.' Every Monday he went up to Mark Lane, but his thoughts were more on Virgil than on corn, and he had always a Latin book in his pocket. His great hope was to get money in business, and then devote his life to books and reading. All his plans, however, were changed upon his acquaintance with Miss Elizabeth Charlesworth—'the elect lady' of Fitz-Gerald's letters—to whom he presently became engaged. Cowell was absolutely without ambition, and never dreamt of striving after honour; but Miss Charlesworth had ambition enough for both. Cowell must go to Oxford and make his way. So, 'a man of wit and sense,' as Kirke White would have called him, he forsook Mark Lane for

---

[1] These facts and others in this work about Cowell have not before been made public. Some were told me by the late professor, during our interview in 1901. Others are taken from his letters to me.

[2] Published 1807.

[3] London, 1841.

[4] At our meeting in November 1901.

the Aonian Maids. Together (and never was study pursued more delightfully) he and Miss Charlesworth learnt the Persian characters and then the grammar. This was in 1845. Next year they went through Johnson's *Mahâbhârata*, and Cowell made some translations from the Persian poet Hafiz,[1] which he sent to FitzGerald, who warmly praised them and expressed the hope that the labours in this orey mine would be continued. Henceforth Cowell—'a judge of everything while pretending to nothing'; a man modest—nay shy; with 'great hidden humour'; with a 'head for anything'—was 'my dear Pundit,' 'that sheikh of mine.'

The acquaintance formed with Cowell was, as we said, an event of the first importance to FitzGerald. But for Cowell there would have been no learning of Persian, let alone the writing of Omar Khayyam. Then again, as a devout student of the Bible and an optimist profoundly endued with the belief that our lives are guided by an Almighty hand, Cowell exercised over FitzGerald just the influence then needed. It was the alliance of the doubter with the man absolutely without doubt. Cowell's favourite text is alone sufficient to reveal him to us: 'This God is our refuge for ever. He will be our Guide even unto death.'

In April 1846 Carlyle was again writing about that constantly discussed, but never erected, stone for Naseby; and in October, FitzGerald, who was meditating *Euphranor*, visited his old rooms in King's Parade, Cambridge, to find the same prints hanging on the walls, and his old hostess, Mrs. Perry, unaltered. On his way back he calls at Bury St. Edmunds to see Donne, hard-working

69. Death of Edgeworth, 12th October 1846.

---

[1] Incorporated by Cowell in an article on Hafiz published (anonymously) in *Fraser's Magazine* for September 1854.

and uncomplaining as ever, who had just settled there, and to have a look at the old school in Northgate Street; and then comes news of the death of Frank Edgeworth, which occurred 12th October 1846. 'We learned next that he was dead,' comments Carlyle, 'that we should see him no more. The good little Frank.' 'I do not yet feel half so sorry as I shall feel,' writes FitzGerald. 'I shall constantly miss him.' Edgeworth's half-sister, 'the great Maria,' had about three more years to live.[1]

In January 1847 Carlyle had received a communication from a William Squire, then of Yarmouth, who professed to have in his possession a number of letters written by Cromwell. As FitzGerald, fond of the company of sailors, was often in the neighbourhood of Yarmouth, Carlyle asked him to try to see the letters; so in June FitzGerald called on Squire, whom he found 'a wholesome, well-grown, florid, clear-eyed, open-browed man' of about thirty-eight,—a choleric, ingenuous fellow, a little mad. According to Squire, an ancestor of his, who served under the Parliament, left a journal—between two and three hundred folio pages of manuscript—including thirty-seven letters by Cromwell. Squire, fearful— so he said—lest the knowledge of the fact that his family had received letters from Cromwell should get abroad and be detrimental to their interests, first copied out the letters, and then put the manuscript into the fire—a cock-and-bull story which FitzGerald, after sherry and biscuits (which it certainly wanted), came away believing. An article on these letters, from the pen of Carlyle, appeared in *Fraser's Magazine* for December 1847, the name of their possessor being withheld. The critics, however, who had the letters without the sherry and biscuits,

70. The 'Squire' Papers. Kemble at Cassiobury.

[1] She died 22nd May 1849.

showed themselves sceptical, and many pronounced them forgeries. Even Carlyle admitted that the business had an amazing look, but declared that personal knowledge of Squire, who had called twice at Cheyne Row, forced him to believe in the 'fundamental authenticity' of the man. Poor FitzGerald made no complaint about all this, so far as we know; but it must have seemed to him on the whole less agreeable even than bone-digging at Naseby. The curious will find these letters at the end of volume ii. of *Cromwell's Letters and Speeches*.[1] Another of Fitz-Gerald's occupations this year was to furnish notes for an edition of the *Table-Talk of John Selden*, edited by S. W. Singer. Of Selden, FitzGerald says in *Polonius*, 'Here we find wit, humour, fancy, and good sense alternating, something as one has heard in some scholarly English gentleman's after-dinner talk—the best English commonsense in the best common English.' There is little that is original in the notes, though here and there FitzGerald is clearly seen, as, for example, in a reference to one of his favourite books, Swift's *Tale of a Tub*, of which, he suggests, Selden's passage, 'Every man has a doublet,' etc., may be the seed. Selden is quoted eight times in *Polonius*.

Now and then FitzGerald still met 'Anglo-Saxon' Kemble, who, living, or rather languishing, 'in a poor small cottage on a wild corner of common near Cassiobury,'[2] was trying to earn bread by making a *History of the Saxons*.[3] To the smart man of business he must look a Simple Simon Kemble as well as an Anglo-Saxon Kemble, but the lover of learning will grieve that to such a man, engaged upon so important a work, England could offer no adequate reward. There were many dunces

---

[1] Ashburton Edition.   [2] Near Watford, Herts.
[3] *Records of a Later Life*, by Fanny Kemble, vol. iii. p. 151.

receiving high salaries for doing nothing, while J. M. Kemble toiled hard for a pittance in that 'poor small cottage' at Cassiobury.

In August 1847 FitzGerald visited first his sister Andalusia (Mrs. De Soyres), and afterwards his old college chum, the Rev. Francis Duncan, rector of West Chelborough, in Dorset, a quiet, saturnine man, with five children to flurry and a pipe to soothe him—the Francis Duncan with whom in the undergraduate days he had discussed his ambitions. In October, E. B. Cowell was married to Miss Charlesworth, their honeymoon at Dover being spent characteristically in reading Persian, and particularly the *Mahâbhârata*. FitzGerald opened the new year (1848) by reading Thucydides, delighting especially in the Fourth Book. 'It came upon me,' says he, '*come stella in ciel*, when in the account of the taking of Amphipolis Thucydides comes with seven ships to the rescue. . . . This was the way to write well, and this was the way to make literature respectable'—that is for the historian himself to be one of the leading figures in the story.

71. Cowell's marriage.

FitzGerald took great interest in the village children, and helped both in the school at Debach and that at Bredfield. At Debach he taught the elder children and the youths their notes from the blackboard by a simple method of his own invention, and books used in these classes may still be seen in the neighbourhood. The natives took to crotchets and semibreves as ducks to water; but when they were asked to pronounce differently the names of their vilages they became embarrassed. 'You should pronounce Debach,' FitzGerald used to say, 'as it is spelt, with the accent on the second syllable, not Debbidge, which is not at all pretty—sounds, in fact, too much like

72. FitzGerald as a Teacher of the Bible.

cabbage. Then Boulge—why don't you call it Boulge, with a long "o" and a silent "u"? Bow-widge, another sort of cabbage, is horrible!' To please him they all tried —screwing their mouths and making painful contortions with their bodies, but, despite their good-will, nothing but Debbidge and Bow-widge would come out.

The school at Bredfield was taught by a Mrs. Jasper, and FitzGerald and Miss Caroline Crabbe went at stated times to assist. FitzGerald gave lessons from the Bible, and read twice a week from the *Pilgrim's Progress*; and Miss Crabbe used to write letters to the elder children and deliver them herself, with the request that the receivers would reply in writing. One of these letters, written to Emma Cole, lies before me. 'I think,' says Miss Crabbe, 'writing letters is a very good thing for all of you that can do it, for very often, if a person can spell words perfectly and knows what she wants to say, she cannot put it upon paper.' With Mrs. Jasper to superintend, FitzGerald to teach scripture, and Miss Crabbe to encourage English composition, Bredfield school was privileged. On the other hand, when FitzGerald's back was turned Mrs. Jasper wasted a good deal of time gossiping with FitzGerald's old woman, the redoubtable Mrs. Faire, who loved to go over to the school, in her huge bonnet crowded with roses, and pass the time of day. When FitzGerald was seen coming along the road she would promptly slip away, leaving behind her a powerful odour of snuff. Miss Lucy Barton used to worship at Bredfield, and after the evening service taught the Sunday-school, which was held in the church. How soon FitzGerald became engaged to her, or whether there was a formal engagement, or merely an understanding, is not known. Apparently FitzGerald did not consider himself engaged.

On 26th February 1848 FitzGerald lost his old friend Major Moor, who died at Bealings House. They carried him down that winding drive, past the ugly pyramidal sarcophagus full of gods, to the church to which he and the *Royal George* walking-stick and little FitzGerald had so often gone together. A scholar without the gift of expressing himself acceptably, Moor is remembered rather as a good man than as a man of letters. To know him was to love him.

73. Death of Major Moor and Bernard Barton.

The remainder of the year was spent by FitzGerald in his usual way, either at Boulge or the homes of his friends. In December (1848) his mother was at Brighton, and Thackeray, who was visiting Brighton too, wrote in high spirits to FitzGerald as follows (19th December 1848): 'My dear old Cupid,—I did not come to see thee, for I was working day and night to finish that Xmas affair, and the few spare hours I had went—R! never mind where—as soon as the book and *Punch* and the plan for *Pendennis* were done. But the very day when somebody left town I came down to this Mireau Eboad. And am directly very much better. I slept well. I have laughed already twice this morning. I have begun *Pendennis iii.*, and have leisure to think of my friend and wish he was here. Come, Eros! come, boy-god of the twanging bow! Is not Venus thy mother here? Thou shalt ride in her chariot, and by thy side shall be, if not Mars, at least Titmars. How these men of letters dash off these things! *c'est étonnant, ma parole d'honneur, c'est étonnant.*' [1]

Carlyle, who had been writing on the Irish in *The Examiner*,[2] mentions in a letter to FitzGerald that

[1] Unpublished letter in possession of Rev. E. Kenworthy Browne.
[2] 13th May 1848.

Thackeray, owing to *Vanity Fair*, had become 'a great lion,' but presently FitzGerald receives a letter from Thackeray beginning 'My dear old Yedward,' and declaring that 'all about being a lion is nonsense.' Two or three prominent people ask him to their houses —nothing more.[1]

The health of Bernard Barton, which had for years been failing, now declined rapidly. He had never cared much for exercise—indeed he took 'almost as little as a milestone,' but now he rarely went beyond the town. He still, however, fulfilled his daily task at the Bank, still enjoyed reading *Rob Roy* or *The Antiquary* with FitzGerald, especially on a Saturday night. He felt no acute pain, and having 'a skeely doctor,' a good nurse, and kind friends, he declined to fret. Following the advice of Lamb and Byron he had clung to his Bank, resolved, as he said, to keep on making figures till Death made him a cipher. On the 19th of February, unable to get to the Bank, he spent most of the day on his sofa, but chatted with callers and wrote several letters. In the evening, after conversing cheerfully with a friend, he rose, went to his bedroom, and suddenly rang the bell. When his daughter obeyed the summons she found him dying. In a few minutes more that beneficent and affectionate heart was still for ever — so suddenly did Death knock at the door of Bernard Barton. His poems are now forgotten, but Fame robbed him with one hand only to reward him with the other, for the fact of his intimate friendship with Lamb and FitzGerald has given him immortality. Attended by a long train of members of the Society of Friends and others, Barton's body was borne up the street to the graveyard of the Friends' Meeting-house, and there

[1] Biographical Edition of Thackeray, vol. i. p. 35.

lowered into its final resting-place, a service being afterwards held in the chapel, 'when three or four very dull but good people spoke in a way that would have been ludicrous but that one saw they were in earnest.'[1] He lies in a spot which is now marked by a small lichen-stained stone with the simple inscription—

BERNARD BARTON

DIED

19 OF 2 MO. 1849

AGED 65

His wife Lucy, who had died forty-two years previous, lies unmemorialed a few feet to the right. The Friends' Meeting-house is still standing. Oblong in plan, it is of red brick coloured white, except in the front, which is cemented, and has a tiled roof. The interior is divided into three parts: the chapel proper, a vestry, and a schoolroom above the vestry. The chapel has two galleries, one on the right hand and one on the left as you enter, and both, as well as the benches and the other fittings, are painted white. Standing in the schoolroom we read the motto printed in bold letters, 'It is as much a Christian duty to avoid *taking* offence as to avoid *giving* offence,' and it was as if the Quaker poet had spoken to us. The portion of the graveyard that is not given over to the dead grows cabbages, and all is very quaint, and very quiet, and old world-like, and Bernard Barton like. To the *Ipswich Journal* of 24th February FitzGerald furnished an account of the last days and death of his amiable friend, and in the same paper of 3rd March a paragraph respecting the funeral, followed

[1] FitzGerald.

BERNARD BARTON

by some lines of particularly feeble verse. Barton having left his daughter almost unprovided for, FitzGerald, who deeply sympathised with her position, took upon himself to edit and publish, by subscription, for her benefit a selection from her father's poems and letters.[1] The work is dedicated to Mr. and Mrs. Newton Shawe of Kesgrave Hall, who are described as friends of Bernard Barton; and the memoir, although FitzGerald speaks of it disparagingly, is a masterpiece of its sort. The subscription-list is almost as interesting as the memoir, and shows how diligently FitzGerald strove to make the book a pecuniary success. He and other members of the FitzGerald family took altogether some fifty copies, and the names of his friends appear. Thus we notice Rev. W. Airy, Archdeacon Allen, Arthur Biddell, Major F. C. Brooke, Mrs. W. K. Browne (Goldington Hall, Bedford), Edward Cowell (Bramford), Miss Crabbe, Dr. Crowfoot, Rev. Thomas Maude (Hasketon). Spedding took ten copies, and the receipt of the parcel is thus acknowledged in an unpublished letter[2] in my possession: 'A large packet arrived ... looking from its shape like a mighty box of real Havannahs, and directed to J. Spedding, Esq., Mirehouse, Whitehaven. Being handled, however, it no longer seemed to be the baccy that I hoped, but books. What books should they be? Nobody had ordered a work of that size, and if any had been ordered they could have come from Carlisle, not from Whitehaven. These considerations passed through my mind while I was untying the knot of a parcel, and it is a weakness with me never to use a knife till I am beaten, which was no sooner accomplished than I saw how it was. The entire ten volumes of B. B.'

---

[1] *Selections from the Poems and Letters of Bernard Barton*, edited by his daughter, 1849.   [2] To FitzGerald.

Soon after the death of her father, Lucy Barton became companion to two of the grand-nieces of Mr. Hudson Gurney of Keswick Hall, Norwich, where she stayed several years. The facts that led to the marriage between her and FitzGerald are rather befogged; still we can get some idea of what really took place. The prim and busy helpmeet of her father, the enthusiastic young Sunday-school teacher, had become stereotyped as the equally prim and busy woman with a gift for tract-distributing and district visiting. A submissive man, with evangelical leanings, would have found her a model wife, but she was one of the last women FitzGerald should have thought of. They were much together prior to Barton's death, and FitzGerald certainly made to Barton some kind of promise respecting her, which Barton and she understood to mean marriage, but which FitzGerald seems to have regarded only as a promise to see that she was never in want. However, seven years were to elapse before their marriage.

In May (1849) came the news of the death of Miss Edgeworth (she died on the 22nd). Among the last words that left her pen were some lines expressing the warmth of her affection for Ireland, and the remark, 'Our pleasures in literature do not decline with age; last 1st of January was my eighty-second birthday, and I think that I had as much enjoyment from books as I ever had.'

In June, FitzGerald is reading and eulogising Keats's letters and poems, and in October he is visiting his still superb and still magnificently dressed mother at Ham, near Richmond, a spot haunted 'by the memory of princes, wits, and beauties.' Writing to F. Tennyson, he says he wishes he were at that poet's elbow so as to advise what verses should or should not be printed. FitzGerald

<small>74. The Cottage at Bramford. Spedding's Forehead (1850).</small>

THE COTTAGE AT BRAMFORD

laid claim to great taste, and in *Polonius* observes, 'Taste is the feminine of genius.' The name of philosopher he repudiates, as one undeserved by a man who resents the toothache. This same year, 1849 (June 30th to August 6th), Carlyle is in Ireland and stays for some time at Halverstown, Kilcullen, with Mrs. Purcell, widow of FitzGerald's uncle Peter.

After his marriage, Mr. E. B. Cowell went to reside in a little house, or rather cottage—for there were only two fair-sized rooms up and two down—at Bramford, near Ipswich, a modest brick building washed with stone-colour; flower garden in front, fruit garden behind. The windows had quaint-looking red Venetian shutters, and before the door stood a little monkey-tree—now a very large monkey-tree, as tall almost as the house itself. Over the front clambered a japonica (thickly studded, when I was there one May, with red blossoms); and old-fashioned flowers such as gillivers, London pride, and butter-of-witches, the last in great yellow patches, brightened the box-edged beds. The surrounding scenery is level and placid, but scarcely picturesque save in the neighbourhood of the river—the Gipping, or, as FitzGerald preferred to call it, as more poetical, the Orwell, a name which the children of men bestow on it only after it reaches Ipswich. Here Cowell and his wife—for Mrs. Cowell was equally enthusiastic as a student—studied the Greek classics, Spanish and Persian. FitzGerald often joined them, and presently he too began to 'nibble' at these languages. His first-love was Spanish, at which, helped by Cowell, he was working sedulously in 1850. Years later, in unhappy hours, when thinking of these idyllic scenes, his two beloved friends, the cottage with the monkey-tree, the pellucid river, the old mill, the footpath leading to Ipswich, Elmsett village, where they read the *Magico* together, he often repeated with a sigh Moore's lines, beginning—

> 'The days are gone when Beauty bright.'

Cowell delights in botany, and yearns after

> 'Simples with preposterous claims,
> And with yard-long Latin names,'

and is happy all day, as is FitzGerald too, out of sympathy, when he finds some new plant. Cowell had a hawk's eye for singling out resemblances in literature. He made Job with his mallows by the bushes (chapter xxx.) illustrate *Don Quixote*, and facetiously compared Hatifi's *Haft Paikar*, a poem on the seven castles of Bahram Gur, with Corporal Trim's unfinished tale of 'The Seven Castles of the King of Bohemia.' Everything in that smiling cottage was riveted on FitzGerald's memory—the green ribbon in Mrs. Cowell's hair, the slippers (Cowell's) he used to wear, even 'Keziah's cakes.' To all three—Mr. and Mrs. Cowell and Fitz-Gerald—everything at Bramford was iridescent, romantic, delightful. Mrs. Cowell wrote poems—pretty but diffuse; FitzGerald revised them. Cowell and FitzGerald sat with their heads together over some entrancing Spanish or Persian poem, and to FitzGerald (looking back in after years) it was a Salaman and Absal existence; and the little garden in the rear grew apples as rosy as those that Absal's taper fingers had gathered. How often he thought of that room in which they used to sit and study! To other eyes its furniture might seem plain, but to him, 'Oh the ebony! oh the gold!' It might have been an apartment in a palace of the Cæsars, instead of a poor little room in a poor little house with a poor little newly planted monkey-tree in front. It was well that FitzGerald enjoyed Bramford, with all its colour, sunshine, warmth, phantasm, and glamour, for a sable enough time was in store for him —sunless gloom, aching heart, hideous days, sleepless nights. It was to be a drop from mountain heights to profoundest abysses. During one of FitzGerald's visits to Bramford (in 1850), Spedding, 'that aged and most subtle serpent,' leaving his hole in Lincoln's Inn Fields and bringing with him evidence of both his pursuits (Bacon in brain, and a charge of shot in one leg), came down to join them. As usual he was witty and illuminating; indeed, wherever he went he left his aura and a sort of Platonic perfume. A willow near the old mill at Bramford, under which he explained the laws of reflection and refraction in water, was thenceforward called 'Spedding's Willow,' and FitzGerald could never see it without recalling him. The mill itself brought to FitzGerald's mind Tennyson's poem, 'The Miller's Daughter,' and often after in imagination he would lie

> ' Beside the mill-wheel in the stream,
> While *Spedding's Willow* whispers by.'

He also amused himself with the idea that Spedding in face resembled Shakespeare, declaring that he ought to have edited Shakespeare, in which case one frontispiece would have served for author and editor. The resemblance, however, was chiefly in the high forehead and the bald crown, both of which were a constant provocative of fun with FitzGerald and his friends. Fanny Kemble speaks of 'the white, round object which is the head of him,' and Thackeray, who pretended that he could find it somehow or other in all things, drew it rising 'with a sober light over Mont Blanc, and reflected in the lake of Geneva.' Instead of Spedding, it was the forehead; Spedding was swallowed up in the forehead. FitzGerald begged Frederick Tennyson to hasten back to London, that they might sit together 'under the calm shadow of Spedding's forehead.' When in 1842 Spedding accompanied Lord Ashburnham to America as private secretary, FitzGerald burst out with, 'Of course you have read the account of Spedding's forehead landing in America. English sailors hail it in the Channel, mistaking it for Beachy Head.' Later, FitzGerald felt sure Spedding was safe, believing that to scalp such a forehead was beyond any Indian's power. On his return from America, Spedding had thrown himself heart and soul into the labour of his life, the editing of Bacon; a task to which he was so devoted that in 1847 he refused an under-secretaryship and £2000 a year in order to be able to give the whole of his time to the work.

FitzGerald had not seen Donne, who still lived at Bury, for nearly a year, but letters passed, and he read of one event there with extreme interest, the celebration, on the 2nd of August 1850, of the three hundredth anniversary of his old school. The sermon was preached by Dr. Blomfield, Bishop of London, a former scholar, and 'our Donne' presided at the banquet afterwards in the Assembly Rooms.

In the letter of 31st December 1850 to F. Tennyson, FitzGerald says: 'The delightful lady' (Mrs. Cowell) 'is going to leave this neighbourhood and carry her young husband to Oxford, there to get him some Oriental professorship.' This removal took place a few days later, in January 1851. When Cowell was gone FitzGerald grew doleful. His heart sickened when he thought of Bramford all desolate.

75. Cowell goes to Oxford.

Said he, 'I shall now almost turn my head away as any road, or railway, brings me within sight of the little spire.'[1]

In 1851 FitzGerald published *Euphranor*.[2] Like Plato and Digby—and his indebtedness to both has already been pointed out—he 'took the great passport of poetry in order to enter into the gates of popular judgment.' The companionship of William Kenworthy Browne—that modern Bayard, *chevalier sans peur et sans reproche*—a man who, as we have seen, combined useful study with vigorous exercise, had forced upon FitzGerald the belief that the ordinary student pored over his books far too much. In the small seminaries, at the great public schools, and even at Cambridge and Oxford, athletics were in those days practically unknown. A student at Cambridge could take a walk into the country or indulge in a little boating, and that was all. Cricket, football, and other sports, which to-day are probably overdone, had then comparatively few votaries. University men were of two kinds: the close-working, pale, dwindled student, and the idler. What is wanted, asseverated FitzGerald, is for men to combine study and exercise judiciously—to be, in short, fine, healthy, educated Englishmen, not peaky, etiolated, angular, lank-haired little beings 'fit only to have their necks wrung.' FitzGerald would not keep a child indoors just because the ground is a little damp or the sky lowering—far better to rough it somewhat; and he thought a sounding slap and 'Don't do so any more' far better than shutting up all

76. 'Euphranor.'

---

[1] *Letters* (Macmillan).
[2] None of the facts which relate to the origin of *Euphranor* have before been published. They were discovered by me when I went through the Browne manuscripts and books.

day in a bedroom. How he pitied the wretched child committed to the tender mercies of the Educational Skythrops, who gave his pupils ten hours a day of grammar, etc., and by way of recreation two hours' daily walk and conversation with himself and his sallow and consumptive-looking pupils! Then he would improve Eton with 'good military drill, with march and counter-march,' and encampment by Father Thames, and by giving the boys, in addition to the playground, 'a piece of arable to work in,' instancing the fact that Hugh Latimer wrought with his father's hinds in Leicestershire. All young men, he held, should be taught not only to ride 'Dobbin,' but to saddle him, get a collar over his head, the crupper over his tail—and without awkwardness; in short, to arm themselves against contingencies, and especially against those minor trials of life which are so hard to encounter because of their frequency. The atmosphere about a man would then be a far more invigorating one than could be created by closet-loads of poetry, metaphysics, and divinity. More of the animal, less of the rational! His ideal poets are Chaucer, 'who could ride fair,' having already 'borne him well in chevachie' and done business as an ambassador; and Burns, who not only sang but ploughed; his ideal historians, Gibbon, who captained a body of Hampshire militia, and Thucydides, who commanded ships at Thasos.[1] He liked the studious man to be, not sickly, irritable, inactive, and solitary, but sound in wind and limb, mind and body—such a one, for example, as Phidippus (W. Kenworthy Browne), who now comes riding in on his glorious mare of illustrious pedigree, Miss Middleton. When questioned concerning

[1] *Cf.* Carlyle's remark in *Hero-Worship*: 'The poet who does nothing but sit on a stool and write poetry will never write a poem worth reading.'

some of those equestrian difficulties which had been the subject of dispute, Phidippus treats all as banter, and pretends he is no judge—I must ask older hands, and so forth. After giving his mare in charge to the hostler, with due directions as to her toilet and table, he took off the saddle and bridle himself and adjusted the head-stall, and on the way out asked, 'Was she not a beauty?' for he persisted in the delusion that his companion knew more of the matter than he chose to admit.

Two other features of Browne's character also come out in this dissertation: first his lack of taste for sporting ladies, and secondly his enthusiasm for bowls. After the game at the 'Three Tuns,' Browne, who ranks himself among 'the best of us,' instructs Lexilogus 'in the mystery of bias.'[1] The identity of Lycion is unrevealed, and Lexilogus, though a Cowperian, was, we are told by FitzGerald himself, not Donne. Later, in answer to some questions of W. F. Pollock's relative to *Euphranor* and the Calderon translations of 1853, FitzGerald observes, 'Wishing to do something as far as I could against a training system of which I had seen many bad effects, I published the little dialogue.' Three of his friends—Spedding, Cowell, and Donne—endeavoured, each in his own way, to bring the merits of the work before the public; but no great success rewarded their efforts. Even FitzGerald himself speaks of it disparagingly, calling it 'a pretty specimen of chiselled cherry-stone.' But at the time he wrote it he was thoroughly in earnest, and many years after, reflecting on the story of Carlyle's youth and early manhood, he says, 'Ah! it is from such training that strength comes, not from luxurious fare, easy-chairs, cigars, Pall

[1] Bowls was a favourite game at Goldington, Mrs. Browne's father having been one of the best players in England.

Mall Clubs, etc. It has all made me think of a very little dialogue I once wrote on the matter.' Of the copy of *Euphranor* which FitzGerald presented to Browne, and which supplied me with the key to that production, I shall have occasion to speak later. While FitzGerald was publishing *Euphranor*, Carlyle was finishing his delicate and delightful *Life of Sterling*, and pondering the advisability of undertaking the *Life of Frederick the Great*. Years later (23rd October 1870), FitzGerald spoke thus pleasantly of four of Carlyle's works: '*Hero-Worship*—I seemed to hear you talking to me . . . in that lecture-room.[1] *Sterling's Life* talks to me also; and so does *Cromwell*, and the old monk of St. Edmunds [*Past and Present*]—they all do; but these perhaps most agreeably to me.'

FitzGerald, who had used his eyes injudiciously, sitting up till midnight reading by a paraffin lamp, now found that they were giving him trouble; so in order to save them, he hit on the expedient of having a boy reader. His choice (not a difficult choice, since there was no one else available) fell on Mr. Job Smith's son Alfred, from that snug Hall Farm. Alfred, now grown a big lad, did not much care about the occupation (found it slow, indeed, compared with bird's-nesting and tearing his knicker-bockers), but FitzGerald liked him, and, as the lad loved FitzGerald, everything went pleasantly. Alfred also took to FitzGerald's Skye terrier 'Ginger,' 'whose eyes you couldn't see owing to his long hair'—the successor of 'Bletsoe'; and he honoured old John Faire as the man who had fought against, and afterwards kept an eye on, Napoleon. Mrs. Faire (notwithstanding her gay bonnet) was his abhorrence. He 'never could enjoy his tea

77. Alfred Smith, Boulge Reader.

[1] Edward Street, Portman Square; May 1838.

there, she took snuff so.' Sometimes FitzGerald carried his young friend up to London to see the sights and to eat suppers at Evans's,[1] treating him 'more like a nephew than an acquaintance'; for, lonely man, 'he was full of love, and yearned for some one on whom to bestow it.' FitzGerald's object in having Alfred Smith at Boulge Cottage was perhaps as much to do the boy good and help him with his education as anything else—at least, so Alfred himself believed. The talk was chiefly about the books they read.[2] FitzGerald was much interested in cremation, of which he was one of the earliest thoroughgoing advocates in England; and he frequently inveighed against the follies of vaults, brick graves, and lead coffins, and insisted that no method of disposal of the bodies of the dead could compare with that of burning. He advocated it for two reasons: first from a sanitary point of view; and secondly, because it would do away with the horror of being buried alive, of which he himself was always in dread. 'Better far,' he said, 'be reduced in a few moments to ashes than run such a terrible risk.' On this subject he would dilate all through life, and most of his friends have heard him express himself forcibly on it.

Meanwhile things were fast going wrong at the Manchester colliery. The elder FitzGerald had hazarded his all, and Squire Jenny had put into the concern something like £50,000. For years those engines, forcing-pumps, ventilating shafts, chimneys, blind pits, cages, and what not, had been to those two unfortunate and unhappy men an incubus and a horrible nightmare,—still success had for

78. Bankruptcy of FitzGerald's father.

---

[1] Concert and dining-rooms, Covent Garden. See Cassell's *Old and New London*, vol. iii. p. 252.
[2] The information on this subject was furnished me by Mr. Alfred Smith, with whom I spent several days at Lowestoft in October 1902.

some time seemed possible. But matters went from bad to worse,—what the particulars were, or what was the immediate cause of the collapse, does not concern this history. It is enough for us to know that the crash came, and to imagine the effect of it not only on the 'blundering Irishman' who brought it about, but also on his family, the wretched Squire Jenny and his poor parsimonious sister Anne (now with much need of her parsimony), who fared worst of all. A chariot 'with daffodil wheels' (window open for fresh air) drove one morning wildly into Playford and stopped at the door of Mr. Arthur Biddell. It was Squire Jenny's. The old gentleman rushed into the house crying, 'Biddell, I want your advice. I'm in a devil of a mess! I'm ruined!' And he said but the truth. Everything was swallowed up in that relentless vortex. FitzGerald's father was terribly troubled; he felt for himself, and he felt for the poor friend whom he had dragged down with him. It was the death of both. A few months more and each was in his grave. Mrs. FitzGerald's property was safe, but everything else had to come to the hammer. The sale at the Hall lasted six days. Of this period of stress and strain Edward says little, but he felt deeply. Perhaps he grieved most for Squire Jenny. Owing to the serious reduction in his income (his allowance from his father having, of course, suddenly ceased), he now called on Miss Barton in order to discuss their future. After weighing a good deal of conflicting evidence, I have come to the conclusion that what took place was this: FitzGerald said to Miss Barton, 'I have promised to see that you shall never want, and I hope, in spite of our misfortune, to keep that promise.' Miss Barton pointed out that she had taken it for granted that there was an engagement between them. 'You misunderstood me,' said FitzGerald, 'and I am glad now I never intended an engagement, for my present poverty would make it imperative that I should give you permission to release yourself.' 'I have no wish to be released,' replied Miss Barton, 'the change in your circumstances makes no difference to me.'[1]

Misfortunes never come singly, and during the sale, Hall Farm (Mr. Job Smith's house) caught fire and was burned to the ground. The Hall being empty, Mr. Smith and his family (including Alfred, the reader) came to reside there, and stayed about two years. Among their visitors was Miss Anna Biddell (daughter of Mr. Arthur Biddell of Playford and that Mrs. Biddell who wrote verses and entertained the wits and poets of Suffolk). FitzGerald used to say that he had three Annies: 'the tall Annie,' Miss Anna Biddell; 'the other tip-top Annie,' Annie Thackeray, now Mrs. Ritchie; and 'the short Annie,' Miss Annie Kerrich. Anna Biddell and her brother Herman presently became FitzGerald's intimate friends. So Hall Farm and its thatch, and that cosy chimney-nook where Sir Robert Peel's speeches had been read, all going up in flame and smoke was not entirely a misfortune.

Squire Jenny, whose health had been shattered by the Pendleton colliery failure, was now nearing his end, and FitzGerald, who was at this time much from home, wrote frequently to inquire after him. When Mrs. Maude of Hasketon[2] asked the Squire whether he was going to 'the Great Exhibition,'

79. Death of Squire Jenny, 1851.

---

[1] Said Mr. Herman Biddell to me: 'They were engaged in Barton's lifetime, and when FitzGerald's father became bankrupt, FitzGerald, who for a time was in poverty, asked Miss Barton to release him, but she refused. On the other hand, there is evidence to show that FitzGerald did not consider himself engaged to Miss Barton at this time.'

[2] Wife of the Rev. Thomas Maude.

he said 'No. The *Illustrated London News* will tell me all I want to know.' Contrary to advice, however, and exhibiting his natural bias to the end, he attended the Newmarket Meeting in the first week in July, and there caught a chill. On his return, passing through a hayfield at Hasketon, he said, 'I shall never see the hay put in cocks again,' and a few days later he was dead. The gospel of the open window did not, however, with his departure, cease to be preached in Suffolk; his disciple (in that respect) Edward FitzGerald continued the propaganda both by practice and precept. As every one had expected, Squire Jenny's estate was found to be hopelessly involved, and in order to pay expenses the magnificent woods that had been FitzGerald's terror as a child and his delight as a man, were cut down—a loss always deplored. The famous hampers in the attic were opened, and there sure enough was the antique china, and in abundance, but all broken to fragments. And so ends the melancholy history of the poor, jovial, old horsy Squire.[1] His sister, who survived him, lapsed into second childishness, but found her chief pleasure, as aforetime, in hoarding up whatever money she could get —amusing herself towards the last by rubbing the coins to keep them bright.

Some time this year FitzGerald invited Fanny Kemble[2] to be his guest, and to give a reading at Woodbridge. Very anxious that the occasion should be a success, and that Woodbridge and neighbourhood should show to advantage, FitzGerald called on his friends and told them their duty. Among these was the Rev.

80. Fanny Kemble at Woodbridge. Miss Maude.

---

[1] There is a stained glass window to him in Hasketon church.

[2] She went to America in 1832, married in 1834 Mr. Pierce Butler, a southern planter, and was divorced from him in 1848, when she resumed her maiden name.

Thomas Maude of Hasketon. 'Mrs. Kemble—the great Fanny Kemble,' said he, 'is coming to Woodbridge. Now, you must put on *all* your finery, *all* your jewels, and come to hear her.' Whereupon Mr. Maude's little daughter Cordelia[1] spoke up promptly: 'I haven't a jewel in the world; but you have a ring' (pointing to a gold ring with a square emerald which he was wearing). 'Lend it to me.'

'Well,' he replied, 'I won't lend you the ring: I'll give it you, as your very own.' Cordelia seized it with an exclamation of delight, and dashed upstairs, fearful lest he should repent of his rashness and want it back again.

The room chosen for the readings was the Lecture-Hall near St. John's Church. There was a crowded audience, and when Mrs. Kemble came on the platform and curtsied, FitzGerald got up and bowed to her.[2] His example being immediately followed by the whole room, she was not a little surprised, amused, and confused. Then—something still more wonderful for so shy a man—he mounted the platform, and in a few graceful words introduced her to the audience. Needless to say, the readings were received with intense delight, and her singing of 'Oh dear! what can the matter be?' was never forgotten.

The next time FitzGerald was at Hasketon he said to Cordelia Maude, 'How about that ring?'

'It's quite safe, thank you,' replied the young lady, showing it on her finger, but not going too near him.

'Don't sell it,' said FitzGerald gravely, 'and don't give it away. But you may pawn it.'

On one occasion at Hasketon he spoke eulogistically of *Vanity Fair*, and asked Mrs. Maude whether she

---

[1] She married Colonel Barlow of Hasketon.
[2] See *Further Records*, by Francis A. Kemble, vol. ii. p. 166.

had read it. 'Oh, no,' she replied, 'I should not care for it.'

'I will send it over, if you like to try it'; then to Cordelia, 'You're much too young to read it.' This excited the young lady's curiosity, and she and her brother set off to Boulge Cottage, found the book, and carried it off. Having discovered his loss, FitzGerald promptly made his way back to Hasketon, and after speaking to the culprit with much severity, and thoroughly frightening her, concluded his remarks with: 'If you had asked me, I would have promised to lend you the book when you were old enough.' To Cordelia Maude, FitzGerald paid what was in his lips a glowing compliment. He said that she never grew to be a woman. Like his friend Browne, she remained ever youthful, with all youth's beautiful characteristics (and a few—a very few—of its faults). Had he written a *Euphranor* for young women, she might have stood in the foreground, not as Phidippus, but Phidippa—a type of beautiful and practical, if impulsive, womanhood.

81. A Visit to Archdeacon Allen, February 1852.

In February 1852 FitzGerald paid a long-promised visit to Prees Vicarage, near Shrewsbury, to see Archdeacon Allen, though he dreaded the journey, and said that Mr. Churchyard's son Tom made less fuss about a prospective journey to New Zealand.[1] Archdeacon Allen was one of those noble-minded men who are at once the pride of the church and the delight of all who come into touch with them. No man feared God more or man less. He lived with God. Sin was sin to him; there was no palliating it. The 'mockery of drunkenness' in Dickens's novels was 'terrible to him.' From his house could be seen most

[1] In the letters FitzGerald by mistake says 'America.' Thomas Churchyard died in New Zealand about ten years ago.

of the nearer Welsh hills in a hood of haze; he knew all their names and would point them out. Beautiful scenery entranced him. Before such he would sometimes stand with uncovered head in silence, 'as if in the presence of God.' He was not blind to his own imperfections, but comforted himself with a saying of his own, 'The road to heaven is made up of resolutions made, broken, and renewed.'

His hair, formerly raven black, was now turning grey; presently it became snowy white, contrasting strangely with his shaggy black eyebrows, which retained their original colour. Folios—he was a folio of a man himself (six feet one in boots)—were still his love. Charles Lamb was not more passionately attached to these 'huge armfuls.' FitzGerald thoroughly enjoyed his visit, becoming quite popular with the children, especially with a mite of six, whom he dubbed 'Little Ticket,' and he adapted a French play (probably one of Molière's) for their performance. When Allen took duty at a neighbouring village FitzGerald presided at the harmonium, not, however, before gravely requesting the Archdeacon's son to tell the congregation that they would that morning have the privilege of listening to the performance of a distinguished foreigner, Signor Geraldino. FitzGerald also amused himself by making a water-colour sketch of Prees church. 'He had a wonderfully delicate artistic touch in brush and pencil, as in everything else.'[1]

Whilst at Prees, FitzGerald heard of the death of his father, and at once hurried home. The poor man had never held up his head after the colliery crash. We spoke of the sale at Boulge, but the treasures of Naseby and Castle Irwell were also dispersed, some going for a song—the clock, for example, with moving figures, that had been so

82. Death of FitzGerald's father, 18th March 1852.

---

[1] Letter from Allen's daughter, Mrs. Grier, to me, 23rd September 1902.

familiar an object to Edward's eyes. However, all was
now over. The 'blundering Irishman' had made his last
blunder. Sheep-stealers, dishonest stewards, collieries,
his own muddling head, were no more to trouble him.
Says Edward: 'Like poor old Sedley in Thackeray's
Vanity Fair, all his coal schemes are at an end. He
died after an illness of three weeks, saying "that engine
works well" (meaning one of the colliery steam engines),
as he lay in the stupor of death.' He was buried at
Boulge.

In June, FitzGerald is at Ham with his mother, revelling
in the cheerful Thames scenery, and visiting Strawberry
Hill with its Horace Walpole memories, and Hampton
Court, the gardens of which pleased him, for he was sure
gardens should be formal, and unlike general nature.

FitzGerald's passion for making commonplace books,
paradises, museum books, or whatever he liked to call
them, was now to bear issue in the shape of
a printed volume, *Polonius: A Collection of
Wise Saws and Modern Instances*, with a choicely written
and delightful, though disjointed, preface, glinting with
reminiscences of saffron mornings spent with dear friends
in Bedfordshire and Northamptonshire, and years packed
in moments. Polonius (fortunate philosopher!) moralises
in glorious October amid the fragrance of the yellow trees
of Sharnbrook, by the old sundial at Bromham, which
bluntly bids him 'Go about your business,' and in the
stately gardens of Castle Ashby. Selden, Bacon, Newman and others are drawn upon for the body of the book,
but it was upon Carlyle (from whom are no fewer than
thirty extracts) that it chiefly battened. FitzGerald's
admiration for Carlyle—though he liked none of Carlyle's
works as a whole—is, indeed, here made very conspicuous.
In the preface he says: 'Carlyle notices, as one of

83. 'Polonius,' 1852.

Goethe's chief gifts, "his emblematic intellect, his never-failing tendency to transform into *shape*, into *life*, the feeling that may dwell in him. Everything has form, has visual existence; the poet's imagination *bodies forth* the forms of things unseen, and his pen turns them into shape." The same,' adds FitzGerald, 'is especially characteristic of Carlyle himself, who to a figurative genius, like Goethe's, adds a passion which Goethe either had not or chose to suppress, which brands the truth double deep.' Among the thirty passages from Carlyle are several of considerable length, for example :—

   (8) Valour and Mercy[1] (Boswell's *Life of Johnson*).
(29) Self-Contemplation[2] (*Varnhagen von Ense's Memoirs*).
(64) Liberty. What is it?[3] (*Past and Present*).
(84) How to write a good book[4] (*Biography*).

Then, too, he quotes from Carlyle's translation of *Wilhelm Meister*.[5] The following are the titles of some of the other extracts :—

(51) *Old Age.*—Goethe is a great instance of a mind growing, growing and putting out fresh leaves to eighty years of life.
(66) *Socrates' Paternoster.*—'O auspicious Pan, . . . grant that I may esteem wisdom the only riches,' etc.
(70) *Imaginary Evils.*—Story from Wesley's Journal of the gentleman and the puff of smoke.
(78) *Choice of a Calling.*—'Whatever a man delights in he will do best.'
(97) *Genius.*—What is Genius but the faculty of seizing things from right and left, here a bit of marble, there a bit of brass, and breathing life into them?

---

[1] That mercy . . . worthy or unworthy.
[2] Finally, we . . . should be avoided.
[3] Liberty? The true . . . new definitions.
[4] A loving heart . . . to light and is.
[5] 'Fun in the old fiddle,' and 'Each man who has . . . powers,' Book II. chapter ii.

(104) '*Love your friend and his foible.*'

(112) *Have at it, and have it*, and other sayings characteristic of the activity and boldness of our forefathers.

(118) *Solitude.*—Be not solitary, be not idle.

(132) *Tossing the thoughts.*—'A man were better relate himself to a picture or a statue than to suffer his thoughts to pass into smother' (Bacon).

The copy of *Polonius* before me is the one presented by FitzGerald to W. Kenworthy Browne. It is beautifully bound in green leather, with the edges gilt and tooled; and, as an additional illustration to 'Nature and Habit' (92), FitzGerald had pencilled in it the line from Horace (*Epistles*, i. 10)—

'Naturam expellas furca, tamen usque recurret.'[1]

84. At Goldington Hall. On Song-Making.

In June 1852 FitzGerald is making his annual visit to Browne at Goldington Hall, and amuses himself by sketching Goldington Green from his bedroom window. 'I never draw now,' he writes to Frederick Tennyson, 'never drew well; but this may serve to give a hint of poor old dewy England.' In an unpublished letter[2] to Sir Henry Bishop (18th June 1852) written from Goldington Hall, after saying that he had not an air called 'The old Horse,' and referring to another called 'The old Hen,'[3] he observes, 'In talking of words to these English tunes, it seems to me a great pity that when the old original words, or something at all equivalent, is available, your clever coadjutor does not avail himself of them. It struck me as a mistake that so many of the songs (meaning the words) in your present edition ran upon what the Germans

---

[1] 'Drive out Nature with a fork, still she will return.'
[2] Now in the British Museum.
[3] 'The cackling old hen she began to collogue,'—a Suffolk song.

call "subjective" feeling, and that, too, of one kind, suited chiefly to mere ladies and gentlemen; and that so few were "objective," such as stories, ballads, scraps of narrative, supposed to be uttered, with a variety of humour, *naïveté*, or pathos, by *other* than ladies and gentlemen—by country people, soldiers, sportsmen, etc.' In respect to the tune of 'The king shall enjoy his own again,' FitzGerald thought that instead of its being linked to a new song by Mackay, unsuitable to the rollicking cavalier tune, 'it would have been much better to have retained the humorous and quaint cavalier words—with perhaps a little amendment.' He then speaks of a song called 'The Forester' with which he had 'scarce anything to do.' The words were written to some old tune, and FitzGerald thought they would suit the tune better than 'some aspiration about an evening star, or evening bell, or evening gun, fitted for a modern young lady at a rosewood pianoforte.' He then quotes Goethe, who said that nothing is so hard to make as a modern ballad; 'just because people *felt* within, instead of simply *seeing without*,' and goes on: 'As to the simplicity—not to say silliness—of some of the old songs, I am sure the last thing a song should be is to be wise. The thought should be as simple as possible; and argument of all kinds avoided. . . . As to polite singers not liking the old words relating to the habits and thoughts of simple people, country people, etc. (to whom the tunes are so natural, and with whom they have survived), who that remembers Miss Stephens and Miss Tree in "Auld Robin Gray"—yes, and even such delicate fooling as "We're a' noddin'"—will not confess that excellent music may be discoursed that way?'

In October, Thackeray sailed for America, but before

leaving sent FitzGerald a letter teeming with kindnesses that touched him to the quick.

FitzGerald, who had steadily persevered with his Spanish studies which had been commenced in the cottage at Bramford, presently found himself attracted by two Spanish authors in particular—Cervantes and Calderon; and by and by he set himself the task of translating six of Calderon's plays into English, namely: *The Painter of his own Dishonour, Keep Your Own Secret, Gil Perez, Three Judgments at a Blow, The Mayor of Zalamea, Beware of Smooth Water*. They were published in 1853. To this work—contrary to his practice — he affixed his name, for the reason 'that there was a rival in the field' (Denis Florence M'Carthy). It was done in the way which we have now come to look upon as peculiarly his own. While faithfully trying to retain 'what was fine and efficient,' he 'sank, reduced, altered, and replaced' much that seemed not; and though he apologised for taking such liberties with the Spaniard, he pleaded that he had not meddled with any of his more famous plays, attempting thus (timid, diffident, and inexperienced man) the impossible feat of appeasing Zoilus.

Calderon, the greatest dramatist of Spain, was born in 1600, just five years before Cervantes set Don Quixote bustling. By 1615, when the second part of *Don Quixote* appeared, Calderon—only a boy—had written his first play, and thenceforward, year after year, he climbed steadily up the steepy slopes of Parnassus. In Philip IV. of Spain he found a generous Mæcenas; the death of Lope de Vega in 1635 left him without a rival; and he lived and wrote right on to his death in 1681, or thereabouts. Those of his plays which FitzGerald translated are bright and pleasant to read—here and there

85. Six Plays of Calderon published, 1853.

a merry passage, and here and there an outburst of splendid poetry, and one feels that the translator is on excellent terms with his author.

Possibly the best of the plays is the *Mayor of Zalamea*. The sturdy old mayor, whose one idea was to see justice done, let captain, general, or king fulminate as he might, wins the heart. His grim reply when the king observed of the villain of the piece, 'At least you might have beheaded him as an officer and a gentleman,' is 'Please your majesty, we have so few Hidalgos here about, that our executioner is out of practice at beheading. And this, after all, depends on the dead gentleman's taste: if he don't complain, I don't think any one else need for him.'

After 'the Mayor' comes *Gil Perez*, the hero being a ubiquitous outlaw of the Rob Roy order—

> 'Flying from him, it was I fled from home
> To Portugal; where the first man I saw
> Was he I thought I'd left at Salvatierra:
> Flying to Andalusia, the first face
> I saw was his I left in Portugal:
> Till, rushing homeward in despair, the man
> I thought I'd left behind in Andalusia,
> Met me at once, and having knocked me down
> Left me for dead.'

The Painter of his own Dishonour is enlivened with funny little anecdotes, of which the following may serve as specimen: 'A man got suddenly deaf, and seeing the people about him moving their lips, quoth he, "What the devil makes you all dumb?" never thinking for a moment the fault might be in himself.' Mayors, generals, hidalgos, alguazils, robbers, ladies, or kings, we are glad to make their acquaintance by means of FitzGerald's pure and lucent English—English drawn from the crispèd streams of Chaucer and the Elizabethans. Calderon's thoughts about books in *Keep Your Own Secret* must have appealed forcibly to the author of *Euphranor*, who thus renders them—

> ' Books, my friend,
> Truly are so seductive company,
> We are apt to sit too long and late with them
> And drowse our minds in their society ' ;

and yet what interests us most of all in this play is another passage which adumbrates the famous opening stanza of the Omar. Apostrophising the sinking sun, Cæsar says—

> ' Another sun shall mount the throne
> When thou art sunk beneath the sea ;
> *From whose effulgence, as thine own,*
> *The affrighted host of stars shall flee.'*

It is intensely interesting to notice how FitzGerald was, unwittingly, mounting towards his masterpiece. His place in life was seeking after him. There is a greatness about these six translations, but they were destined to be eclipsed by two other and finer plays of Calderon, which FitzGerald was by and by to busy himself upon. The sop thrown to the critics was wasted, for Zoilus, in the shape of the *Athenæum*, instead of being appeased, attacked the work with so much severity that FitzGerald endeavoured to withdraw it from circulation. Here the psychologist may take notice of the fact that FitzGerald, like most other men, was a repertory of contradictions. The most original and fearless of critics, a man who in respect to the work of others bows to none, nevertheless tacitly acknowledges the superiority of judgment of an anonymous critic who, whatever his skill as a linguist, had, as his criticisms clearly show, no more taste or power to appreciate the graces of poetry than the rank and file of Woodbridge, whose density their

E. B. COWELL

gifted neighbour has drafted into a proverb. From a FitzGerald one would have expected, 'By God! 'tis good, and if you like 't you may.' But no; directly his own work is at the bar, anybody's judgment is better than his. He confessed as much to Donne. 'I rely,' he says, 'on my appreciation of what others do, not on what I can do myself.'

On 25th July 1853 he speaks of going to one of his great 'treats,' namely the assizes at Ipswich, where, says he, 'I shall see little Voltaire Jervis' (Chief Justice), 'and old Parke' (Baron Parke, afterwards Lord Wensleydale), 'who, I trust, will have the gout — he bears it so Christianly.'

BOOK IV

FARLINGAY

SEVEN YEARS (1853—NOVEMBER 1860)

CHAPTER X

PERSIAN STUDIES

1853—1855

Bibliography
15. *Euphranor.*
16. *Salaman and Absal.*

ABOUT 1853 Mr. Job Smith removed to Farlingay Hall,[1] a farmhouse about half a mile out of Woodbridge, and Boulge Hall became the residence of Fitz-Gerald's brother John. John FitzGerald presently began to make improvements, adding a wing on the east side, dormer windows, and a porch. Like Edward, he had a great dislike to the felling of trees; consequently the various growths round Boulge Hall became in time so luxuriant that the park was all but screened from view, and the house added to itself the chill and gloom of a monastery. To a friend who suggested the axe, he exclaimed with scorn and righteous indignation, suggestive of his old and proud ancestors, the Lords of Kildare, 'Do you take me for a timber-merchant?' These sombre groves, however, were the haunt not of monastics but of merry children, whom John liked to see about him, and who looked upon them as made especially for hide-and-seek. Edward, who was the best of friends with his brother (when

86. Farlingay.

---

[1] Now a picturesque villa, the residence of Mr. W. W. Welton.

they were apart), but who considered residence near him was not to be dreamt of, now gave up his cottage at the Park gates, and, without deciding on any abode, packed up his effects and sent them, by arrangement with Mr. Smith, to Farlingay Hall, which he soon began to regard as his home. But a more correct term would be 'headquarters,' seeing that during most of the seven years of his connection with Farlingay he led a very nomadic life, spending much of his time with relatives and friends. In a letter to Carlyle, 14th October 1854, he says: 'I am at present staying with a farmer in a very pleasant house near Woodbridge, inhabiting such a room as even you, I think, would sleep composedly in. My host is a taciturn, cautious, honest, active man, whom I have known all my life. He and his wife, a capital housewife, and his son, who could carry me on his shoulders to Ipswich, and a maid-servant who, as she curtsies of a morning, lets fall the teapot, etc., constitute the household.'[1] He continued to spend many of his evenings in Crabbe's 'little old dark' cobblery at Bredfield, regularly comforting his soul with a pipe and 'a glass of good hot stuff' which derived its finishing-touch from a 'little silver nutmeg grater,' and he would sometimes stay at Bredfield two months together.

In 1853, influenced by E. B. Cowell, FitzGerald, at the age of forty-four, commenced seriously the study of Persian, and had by the next year, with the help of Sir William Jones's *Grammar*, made sufficient advance to be able to translate some of the extracts from the Persian poets. What a joy it would have been to Sir William Jones,[2] the first and one of the most

87. Persian Studies.

---

[1] *Letters*, vol. i. p. 294. Quoted by permission of Messrs. Macmillan.
[2] Sir William Jones, 1746-1794.

FARLINGAY HALL

enthusiastic of English Oriental students, could he have peered into the succeeding century and seen the rare fruit produced by his book in the most gifted of his pupils. 'From my earliest years,' Jones had written, 'I was charmed with the poetry of the Greeks; nothing, I then thought, could be more sublime than the odes of Pindar, nothing sweeter than Anacreon, nothing more polished or elegant than the golden remains of Sappho and Simonides; but when I had tasted the poetry of the Arabs and Persians . . .' There the letter breaks off; the rest is lost. The 'but' remains, however, and had pages more been preserved a stronger impression of his feelings could not have been left. Probably every one, upon first making the acquaintance of Persian poetry, has felt a similar enthusiasm. It is a new ocean, and we stand looking upon it in amazement—like Cortez, silent upon his peak of Darien.

A word or two must now be said on the subject of Persian history and literature. The earliest myths of Persia are to be found in Firdausi's poem, the *Shahnameh*, which records the deeds of the herculean Rustum and his father Zal, both of whom are referred to in FitzGerald's masterpiece—

'Let Zal and Rustum bluster as they will.'

The long line of kings, which included Xerxes and Longimanus, terminated in B.C. 331, when Darius III. was defeated by Alexander the Great, on whose death (B.C. 323) Persia fell under the rule of the Seleucidae, whose history is that of a perpetual struggle with the Romans. A new era commenced B.C. 226 with the foundation of the illustrious Sassanian dynasty, which included the three mighty monarchs Bahram Gur or

Bahram of the Wild Ass,'[1] so called on account of his love for hunting that animal; Kaikobad the Great, and his son Kaikhosru,[2] and terminated in A.D. 641, when the country was subjugated by the Arabs. About this time the ancient language or idiom of Persia, Pehlevi, died out, making way for Parsi; but though the people forsook the old tongue, the nightingale, according to the pretty fancy of the poet Hafiz, remained faithful to it—a fancy of which FitzGerald made skilful use—

> 'And David's lips are lockt, but in divine
> High-piping Pehlevi, with "Wine! wine! wine!
> Red wine!" the nightingale cries to the rose
> That sallow cheek of hers to incarnadine.'

For many years after the Arab conquest Persia was merely a province of the Baghdad caliphs, and during their supremacy flourished the first great Persian poet—Firdausi (A.D. 950-1020). The year 1028 saw the rise of Mahmud of Guzni,[3] who rapidly hewed out for himself a great empire, of which Persia formed a part, and was succeeded by his son, whom the Persians, however, drove from the throne in favour of a sultan of their own nationality—Togrul-Beg. Togrul-Beg was succeeded in 1063 by his nephew, Alp-Arslan, and Alp-Arslan by his son, the magnificent and prosperous Malik Shah. As early as 815 the influence of the famous sect who called themselves Sufis, and their creed Sufism, had already become noticeable. The Sufis held that God alone exists, all things in Nature being a part of Him, and

---

[1] 'And Bahram, that great Hunter—the Wild Ass
Stamps o'er his grave, but cannot break his sleep.'—*Omar*, q. 18.
[2]   'What have we to do
With Kaikobad the Great, or Kaikhosru?'—*Omar*, q. 10.
[3] 'And peace to Mahmud on his golden throne.'—*Omar*, q. 11.
'The mighty Mahmud, Allah-breathing Lord.'—*Omar*, q. 60.

that the only heaven and hell are those which exist in men's minds—

> 'I sent my soul through the Invisible
> Some letter of that After-life to spell :
> And by and by my soul returned to me,
> And answered, " I myself am Heaven and Hell."'[1]

Broadly, they believed that by strict life, study, and development the Sufi could become actually God, and religion remained no longer necessary to him; while others who failed to win that perfection in this life would attain it in states of transmigration. Thus all would finally be absorbed in the Deity. Sufism gave birth to a whole galaxy of poets, who in allegory and voluptuous verse, the burden of which was wine and women, 'represented the mystery of divine love and the union of the soul with God.' How much was allegory and how much appetite, every reader must decide for himself. Of the so-called Sufi poets, none of whom adhered strictly to the creed, the greatest are Omar Khayyam—though whether he was a Sufi or not will always be a matter of dispute—(born about 1050); Attar (born 1216); Jelaledin, author of the *Mesnavi* (1207-1273); Sadi (1184-1292); Hafiz (?-1388), and Jami[2] (1419-1492).

While FitzGerald was studying Persian with Cowell, Carlyle was constructing that forbidding aërial grave which he called his 'sound-proof room' at the top of his house in Cheyne Row. One elected to work among flowers and bees and country sights and sounds, the other in the chilliness and ugliness of an elevated pit.

Some years previous, as we have seen, E. B. Cowell had translated several of the *Odes* of Hafiz (published in 1854), and to these, to the selections from Hafiz in Sir William Jones's *Grammar*, and to Eastwick's translation

---

[1] *Omar*, q. 66.   [2] Pronounced Jarmy.

of the *Gulistan* of Sadi, which FitzGerald had also carefully studied, may be traced some of the ideas which he subsequently used in his rendering of the *Rubaiyat*. From Hafiz came the presentment of the Deity amusing himself behind the veil by contriving the drama of life; in Hafiz, too, there are parallels to the lines about Kaikobad and Kaikhosru, the morning draught at the door of the tavern, the caravanserai with its two portals, and the 'cypress-slender minister of wine.' The influence of Sadi, too, though less evident, may be traced. Presently FitzGerald was drawn to Jami, and took upon himself to translate the beautiful allegory of *Salaman and Absal*, which he finished under a tree in the garden of Bredfield Vicarage. Jami, who lived chiefly at Herat, is remembered on account of three works: the exquisite *Yussuf and Zuleika* (Joseph and Potiphar's wife),[1] the *Beharistan*, and *Salaman and Absal*—the last a product of his old age. FitzGerald's rendering is beautiful in the extreme. The story is one of a Shah who teased Allah for a son. A shrewd sage tried to dissuade him both from making himself the captive of a woman and from supplicating for what would probably prove a bane. Of woman, indeed, the sage had but a mean opinion. Says he—

88. 'Salaman and Absal' published, 1856.

> 'Deck her with jewel thick as night with star;
> Pamper her appetite with houri fruit
> Of Paradise, and fill her jewelled cup
> From the green-mantled Prophet's well of Life—
> One little twist of temper—all your cost
> Goes all for nothing.'

---

[1] Some idea of this poem can be got from the extracts given in *Persian Love-Songs*, a charming volume of the Bibelot Series, published by Gay and Bird. Jami makes Yussuf, after the lapse of some years, marry Zuleika, admit that he had always loved her, and say exquisitely—

> 'I would not passion's victim be,
> And turned from sin—but not from thee.'

The Shah, however, continued to pester Heaven with his prayers, and at last the child came. As nurse for it they chose a girl—for she was but a girl—named Absal—

> 'So young, the opening roses of her breast
> But just had budded to an infant's lip;
> So beautiful, as from the silver line
> Dividing the musk-harvest of her hair
> Down to her foot that trampled crowns of kings,
> A moon of beauty full.'

She loved the babe, but, alas! when he grew older she loved too the boy and the man, and exhausted every feminine artifice to ensnare his affection—

> 'Thus by innumerable witcheries
> She went about soliciting his eyes.'

And she succeeded—so well, indeed, that when his father discovered their passion, Salaman, rather than be told, fled with her to a lovely island—and Salaman's Isle is surely one of the most seductive spots in faery—the home of green parrot, jewelled peacock, Iran-lovely roses, and mellifluous nightingales. Here, hand in hand, they gathered fruit from loaded trees, drank from limpid fountains, reclined under leafy branches, and 'sang divisions with the nightingale'—

> 'There was the rose without a thorn, and there
> The Treasure, and no serpent to beware—
> Oh think of such a Mistress at your side
> In such a solitude, and none to chide!'

Salaman, much against his will, was ultimately induced to forsake his love by a sage of his father's court; but do what he would, Absal still reigned in his breast, and he fled with her again—this time not to an island, but to the Wilderness of Desolation, where they had determined to die together. Having constructed a pyre of sere wood, he with his torch set it roaring, and the lovers, hand in hand, sprang into the central flame, exulting. But the sage

> 'In secret all had ordered; and the flame
> Directed by his self-fulfilling will
> Devouring her to ashes, left untouched
> Salaman—all the baser metal burn'd,
> And to itself the authentic gold return'd.'

The sage finally made the long-silent voice of reason sound in Salaman's soul, and drew him from dwelling on his lost earthly love by telling him of a celestial love—Zuhrah, who presently

> 'Revealed herself
> In her pure lustre to Salaman's soul,
> And blotting Absal's image from his breast,
> There reigned instead.'

Salaman represents 'The Soul of Man,' Absal 'The sense-adoring body'; the flood on which they sailed to the bewitching island, 'the false paradise of sensual passion'; the return of Salaman, 'the return of the lost soul to its true parentage, and back from carnal error looking up repentant to his intellectual right.' The distraction of the prince, and his second flight, and the pyre on which he sought to immolate himself—

> 'That was the discipline
> To which the living man himself devotes
> Till all his sensual dross be scorched away.'

Zuhrah was the 'Divine Original,' which now that he was divested of the dross of the body, revealed itself in him in all its effulgence. As king and conqueror he mounts the throne, wears the crown of human glory, and finally is absorbed, as the Sufi taught, into the Deity.

The story is interspersed with anecdotes, 'which have their use as well as humour by way of quaint interlude music between the little acts.' *Salaman and Absal* was published anonymously in 1856 by Parker and Son, the printers being Messrs. Childs of Bungay. Recalling, subsequently, the delightful hours spent with the Cowells at the time he was translating it, FitzGerald observes, half-humorously, half-seriously, that he had then *two* to sympathise with him, and that probably his public would be 'nearly as numerous.'

While Edward was translating *Salaman and Absal*, his brother John at Boulge was devoting himself with renewed energy to social questions—writing, for example, against the slave-trade as followed in America, several trenchant pamphlets,[1] in which, among other things, he urged all Christian men to protest actively by refusing to purchase slave-grown products.

In the spring of 1854 FitzGerald spent five weeks, five dulcet weeks, 'at Spiers's,' in Oxford, with the Cowells, where, an old canary-coloured sofa to sit on, cocoa or tea on the table, and Oriel opposite, they studied together Hafiz, Jelaledin, and other delicious Persians. FitzGerald calls Cowell 'a great scholar, . . . such as I have not hitherto seen at all like from the universities. . . . He deals more in Sanscrit and Oriental literature than in the studies of the place. . . . He is most modest, nay shy, with hidden humour.'

89. With the Cowells at Oxford. Death of his mother, 30th January 1855.

In March 1854 England and France declared war against Russia, a condition of affairs which affected FitzGerald, from the fact that W. Kenworthy Browne had to leave Bedford; the Bedfordshire Regiment of Regular Militia, of which Browne was a first-lieutenant, and subsequently a captain, having to do garrison duty at Galway. Whilst in Ireland, Browne wrote a diary,

[1] *Man-Stealing by Proxy*, 1850; *Christian Slaveholders disobedient to Christ*, 1854.

taken up chiefly with observations on farming, which has been preserved; and under January 1856 he speaks of being at the Imperial Hotel, Dublin, at the windows of which, sixteen years previous, he had 'sat with FitzGerald.'

In May (1854) FitzGerald was in the west country again, visiting his sister Mrs. De Soyres, whom he had scarce seen for six years. He stayed at Bath, where he met the aged poet Landor, and ascended 'Vathek's Tower,' erected by Beckford. Back in Suffolk, he sails once more in a newly bought boat on his 'dear old Deben,' in company with Virgil, Juvenal, and Wesley.

On 30th January 1855 he lost his mother, who retained to the last considerable traces of that beauty which had been her greatest gift. She was buried at Boulge church, where there is a large and ornate monumental tablet to her memory, with a smaller one beside it to her husband, illustrating, as has been sagaciously remarked, 'the proportion they bore to each other in life.'[1] John FitzGerald, who succeeded to his mother's estates, resumed a little later,[2] 'by royal licence, the additional surname and arms of Purcell.' Henceforward in his tracts and other publications he signs himself 'J. F. Purcell FitzGerald,' or 'J. F. P. F-G.'—quite an alphabet.

In March 1855 came the news of the death of the Emperor of Russia, and people began to hope that peace was in sight. Captain Addington at Goldington (sitting among his cats) has no doubt that Mrs. W. K. Browne will be glad to see her husband returned from Ireland, and FitzGerald is quite sure that he (FitzGerald) will be equally glad to meet his old friend 'the bloody warrior,' as he now calls him.

In the summer of the next year, Carlyle, who had for

[1] Miss Margaret White in *The Idler*, July 1900.   [2] 1858.

eighteen months been toiling at the *Frederick*, and felt the need of a change, decided to fulfil a promise of many years' standing, and pay a visit to FitzGerald, who just then was continually fluctuating between Bredfield Rectory and Farlingay. On 1st August, Carlyle is told that he will be welcome at either place, and Mrs. Carlyle is begged to say what her husband is to eat, drink, and avoid. Farlingay being decided upon, Mr. Job Smith and FitzGerald made every conceivable preparation for the expected guest, who was promised entire liberty, with room, garden, and time to himself. The 'shrieking, mad,' and to Carlyle 'quite horrible rail operations' terminated at Ipswich, where FitzGerald met him with a trap, and after a look round the town they set out for Farlingay, which they reached late in the afternoon. It was delightful, sunny, autumn weather. When Carlyle got down in a morning he was sure to see 'good Fitz sitting patient on a big block,' a huge tree-stump sown with mignonette. They had walks through pleasant lanes and on quiet country roads. There were drives to Dunwich and the massy ruin of Framlingham Castle. The visit to Aldeburgh, however, pleased Carlyle the best. It took place on a Sunday morning; and the pony and trap with the strange, uncouth pair—FitzGerald in his scare-crow clothes, and Carlyle with the usual long clay pipe in his mouth—passed the church just as the worshippers were leaving it after morning service. The shocked look on the face of conventionality and 'gigmanity' was entirely to their taste, and furnished them with much laughter. Carlyle found Aldeburgh a 'beautiful, quasi-deserted little sea town,' one of the best bathing-places he had ever seen. 'Nothing can excel the sea—a mile of fine, shingly beach, with patches of smooth sand every here and there;

90. Carlyle at Farlingay, 8th to 18th August 1855.

clear water shelving rapidly, deep at all hours; beach solitary beyond wont, whole town rather solitary,' and he thought Mrs. Carlyle might do worse than pay it a visit. With FitzGerald, 'lonely, shy, kind-hearted man,' the best of landlords, 'who discharged the sacred rites with a kind of Irish zeal and piety,' and did everything except leave his guest well alone, which he did not quite do; with Mr. Smith, whose dialect was 'almost equal to Nithsdale'; with Parson Crabbe, pink of genial and good-hearted clergymen, Carlyle 'did not fare intolerably.' The only unpleasant occurrence was an adventure of cows, who being natives of Woodbridge, and therefore not literary, had for the author of the *French Revolution* no more respect than the 'demon fowls' of Cheyne Row. They raged and lowed incessantly for the better part of a night, nobody could imagine why: the result, 'endless sorrow of poor Fitz,' endless apologies from him and Farmer Smith's household, and finally, banishment of the cows.

The fields were golden with wheat, and Carlyle spent most of the day under an elm near the house reading up Voltaire, etc., for the *Frederick*. In the evening he, Fitz-Gerald, Mr. Smith, and Alfred sat indoors and smoked. Carlyle plied Mr. Smith with questions about soils and crops, and he and FitzGerald discussed literature, that 'ass of a column' at Naseby and its proposed rival. Scraps of Carlyle's conversation have been preserved, and among them his declaration that Burns ought to have been King of England, and George III. an exciseman. Unlike Tennyson, he spoke little, as FitzGerald noticed, of his own works, but once referred something to 'about the time men began to talk of me.' Here and there in the *Frederick* we detect the presence of FitzGerald, and reminiscences of the talk under the elm at Farlingay.

COPY OF THE PHOTOGRAPH PRESENTED BY CARLYLE TO
ALFRED SMITH, OCTOBER 1855

PERSIAN STUDIES

Speaking of Friedrich Wilhelm's Potsdam regiment of giants, Carlyle says, 'This also seems to me one of the whims of genius—an exaggerated notion to have his stanza polished to the last punctilio of perfection,[1] and might be paralleled in the history of poets.'[2] And later, when Friedrich Wilhelm gets one hundred and fifty more giants as a present from Peter the Great, 'Invaluable—to a "man of genius" mounted on his hobby! One's "stanza" can be polished at this rate.'[3] The visit terminated on August 18th, when Carlyle, who declined to be shut up in a railway carriage, 'like a great codfish in a hamper,' returned in the Ipswich steamer—'ugly home voyage'—to his horrible room at the top of the house in Cheyne Row, whence later he sent FitzGerald a final inscription for that visionary Naseby pillar, and Alfred Smith a photograph of himself. Said Alfred, 'Carlyle's a big man, no doubt, though I don't know much about him. So I'll put him in a frame'—which he accordingly did.

[1] Precisely FitzGerald's way. No one could have been more fastidious. I am sure Carlyle was thinking of FitzGerald when he wrote these words.
[2] *Frederick*, Book IV. ch. iii.
[3] *Ib.* ch. vii.

CHAPTER XI

OMAR KHAYYAM

IN the meantime FitzGerald had become acquainted with the *Rubaiyat* of Omar Khayyam. While studying in the Bodleian Library at Oxford, E. B. Cowell had stumbled upon a most beautiful Persian manuscript, written on thick yellow paper, with purplish black ink, profusely powdered with gold; and further examination proved it to be an original copy of the *Rubaiyat*[1] of Omar Khayyam, with whose works he had previously been unacquainted. Delighted with his discovery, he brought it under the notice of FitzGerald, for whom he subsequently made a transcript. Thenceforward Omar was FitzGerald's constant companion, and after a time we find him busy on his now famous translation, or rather adaptation, of it.

91. Omar Khayyam.

Omar Khayyam was born at Naishapur, in the middle of the eleventh century, or about the time of the Norman conquest of England, his second name, Khayyam —the tentmaker—being derived from his calling. He was placed for instruction under the Imam Mowaffak, and formed a firm friendship with two fellow-pupils, namely Nizam-ul-Mulk and Hasan Ben Sabbah. The three, believing that as they were pupils of so great a man as Mowaffak, one at fewest would attain to fortune,

[1] Rubaiyat is the plural of Rubai, which signifies a quatrain, or verse of four lines.

made a compact that whoever obtained this prize should share it with the others. Nizam rose to greatness, becoming vizier to the sultan Alp-Arslan, and upon being reminded of the promise of his youth, gave Hasan a snug place in the government, and Omar a handsome yearly pension. Hasan, after meeting this kindness by plotting against his benefactor and raising an insurrection against the Sultan, ensconced himself in the northern mountains, whence he harried all the country round, and put to death, among others, his old friend Nizam. Omar, on the other hand, lived contentedly at Naishapur, applied himself sedulously to his studies, particularly mathematics and astronomy, basked in the favour of Malik Shah, Alp-Arslan's successor, who employed him with seven other scholars to reform the Calendar, and 'became the Sir Isaac Newton of his day.' To Sufism, the prevailing creed, he devoted prolonged study. One day, walking in a garden with a pupil named Nizami, he said, 'My tomb shall be in a spot where the north wind may scatter roses over it.' And so it fell out. Omar died in 1123, and was buried at Naishapur, by a rose garden, and when, years after, Nizami visited the spot, he found that the trees had stretched their boughs over the wall and dropped their blossoms on the tomb.

As to the result of Omar Khayyam's Sufic studies, opinion is divided. There are two principal theories. The first we will call the FitzGerald theory, not because FitzGerald believed absolutely in it, but because he leaned to it; the second the Cowell theory, Professor Cowell having been its chief exponent. According to the FitzGerald theory, Omar Khayyam's Sufic studies had the result of causing him, in the end, to turn with contempt both from the faith and its interpreters, whether ascetic saint or visionary poet. Henceforth he

92. The two Theories.

was the agnostic, the Sufis were his butt, he was their aversion and dread. According to the Cowell theory, Omar always remained true to Sufism, and his great poem is a diatribe not against the tenets of the Sufis, but against the bigotry of the Mahometans. When I visited Cambridge in November 1901, I was able to hear Professor Cowell's opinions from his own lips.

'Are we,' I said, 'to take Omar's words literally, or is there a hidden meaning?'

'The poem,' he replied, 'is mystical. I am convinced of it. When in India I had many conversations with the Moonshees on the subject, and they were all of this opinion. They ridiculed the idea that the poem is not allegorical.'

'Omar's laudation of drunkenness,' said I, 'is difficult to explain away.'

'By drunkenness,' said Professor Cowell, with a smile, 'is meant "Divine Love."'

'Then Omar was a Sufi, and not, as some will have it, heterodoxical?'

'Certainly, Omar was a Sufi.'

'But if his laudation of drunkenness is a difficulty, still more must we regret some of the expressions he uses towards the Deity.'

'They merely illustrate,' observed Professor Cowell, 'Omar's disbelief in the Mahometan heaven and hell. He ridicules the very orthodox Pharisees among the Mahometans with their strict observance of minutiæ.'

'Then,' said I, 'what it all means is this: trouble not your head about the rewards of Heaven or the pains of Hell, as understood by the Mahometans; do not puzzle your brains about anything; but live a right life, and trust, never cease to trust, in the goodness of God?'

'It is so.'

TOMB OF OMAR KHAYYAM AT NAISHAPUR

'But FitzGerald did not agree with you?'

'Sometimes he inclined to this belief, though generally not. He could never quite make up his mind.'

Having outlined the two cardinal theories as to Omar, we will give an account of the *Rubaiyat*, reserving consideration of FitzGerald's rendering or adaptation for a subsequent chapter.

The oldest manuscript of Omar's poem is that in the Bodleian Library at Oxford, which was written by the scribe Mahmud Yerbudaki in A.D. 1460 (some three hundred years after Omar's death), and contains 158 rubaiyat or quatrains. The Calcutta, the Paris, and other manuscripts contain many more quatrains, but it is with the Bodleian MS. that we shall mainly deal, that being the one which inspired FitzGerald's muse. These quatrains, as Mr. Heron-Allen observes, and as a glance at his translation shows, were written not at one time 'as components of a consecutive whole,' but at intervals extending over a great part of Omar's life, and collected into their present form, probably after his death. Every quatrain is complete in itself, and the poem must be regarded as a collection of 158 pithy, poetical sayings, put together without Omar's knowledge by some Persian Boswell. They represent the poet in many moods. He is always poetical, generally reasonable, sometimes altogether unreasonable, and occasionally, if we accept the agnostic theory, even presumptuous and blasphemous. There is considerable repetition, and he is frequently inconsistent.

93. **Omar's Poem.**

One of the most fascinating features of the *Rubaiyat* is the vivid presentment it gives of Omar himself. We seem to know the roistering old sinner as if we had sat and taken a bite and a sup with him on the edge of the wilderness; whereas, in com-

94. **Omar's Personality.**

parison, Hafiz, Jami, Attar, and the rest are only shadows. Like Byron, he appears everywhere through his verse. A compound of Anacreon, Koheleth, Voltaire, and Villon, he is, nevertheless, the milk of human kindness—having 'engrafted,' to use his own expression, 'the leaf of love upon his heart.' 'So far,' he says, 'as in thee lies, cause no pain to any one.' His creed is his goblet, his Koran the text round its brim. We see him, moustached and bearded—he calls himself old—on the drinking-bench of the tavern just outside the town, his outlook a waste relieved only by a ruined furnace; in the potter's workshop moralising among the two thousand pots; or reclined on the edge of the wilderness, with his jug, his loaf, and his book of verses, and 'Heart's Desire' singing to him—the most picturesque figure in the entrancing gallery of literature. We refuse to believe that for his æsthetic mind coarse pleasures had a real attraction. If he is loud in the praise of wine, it must be rose-coloured, musk-scented wine, served by Heart's Desire, who is cypress-slender, beautiful of face and musical of voice. Moreover, the profound scholar, the absorbed philosopher, would scarcely be also the drunken debauchee—the 'Mahometan blackguard.'

But it may be asked, 'Is not "wine, wine, wine" the constant refrain of the *Rubaiyat*?' That is so; nevertheless, we are still disposed to repeat that Omar was no debauchee—that, as Charles Lamb would have said, 'It was only his fun'; though to get oneself into this frame of mind certainly requires some faith, especially after reading the more outrageous of the quatrains as rendered by Mr. Heron-Allen. For example: 'A season of roses, and wine and drunken companions—be happy for a moment, for this is life';[1] 'we have returned to our

[1] Heron-Allen, Q. 36.

wonted debauch; ... wherever the goblet is, there thou mayest see us, our necks stretched out like that of the bottle';[1] 'Khayyam, if thou art drunk with wine, be happy';[2] 'Let me be modest about my knowledge, if I recognise any degree higher than drunkenness';[3] 'Seek me—ye will find me sleeping like a drunkard';[4] 'Though thy life pass sixty years, do not give up: wherever thou directest thy steps, walk not save when drunk.'[5] Take him literally, then, Omar was a drunkard, a companion of drunkards, and a eulogist of drunkenness. And what shall we say to this: 'Drinking and Kalenderism —that is vagabondism—and erring are best'?[6] Or this: 'Drink wine, rob on the highway, and be benevolent'?[7] Numerous have been the pleas put forward in Omar's favour, and it is well to defend him, for, understood literally, he wants defending very badly. Some imagine that irony is intended; and certainly the excessiveness, the deliriousness of his praise of wine does lend colour to the idea. Had Defoe lived in Persia eight hundred years ago, and did we know as little about his personality and familiars as we do of Omar's, it is possible that *The Shortest Way with Dissenters* might to-day be setting as many people by the ears as Omar's 'Shortest Way with the Puzzles of Existence.' Under any circumstances, it is pleasanter to be charitable; nor need we take seriously the random talk about vagabondism.

We have referred to the attractions of 'Heart's Desire,' 'Saki,' 'the cypress-slender minister of wine,' as she is variously called, with whom Omar held dalliance. Indeed, respecting the other sex Omar was much of Gautier's opinion. A woman might be a man, as far as he was concerned, if she was not

95. Heart's Desire.

---

[1] Heron-Allen, Q. 99.   [2] Q. 102.   [3] Q. 121.
[4] Q. 132.   [5] Q. 138.   [6] Q. 133.   [7] Q. 123.

beautiful. 'Heart's Desire,' besides being cypress-slender, was tulip-cheeked; through lips that were a rosebud she gave forth nightingale notes; and she could play delightfully on the lute, with fingers as provoking as her mouth. How dainty are some of the verses in which she figures:—

'This jug was once a plaintive lover like me, and chased a pretty girl; this handle is the arm that encircled her neck.'

Again—

'Arise, give me wine, talk is waste of time. Thy little mouth satisfies my needs. Give me wine the colour of thy cheeks; my penitence is as full of tangles as thy curls.'

Number 43, the quatrain that suggested FitzGerald's 19th, has a deliciousness that FitzGerald did not quite exhaust—

'Wherever there are roses or tulips there has been shed the blood of a king; every violet shoot is a mole that once embellished the cheek of a beauty.'

For the mole on the cheek of the lovely maid of Shiraz —and all Easterns admire moles—the poet Hafiz would have given two cities.

Omar was not averse from society, but he really cared only for a few companions, and liked best to meditate alone, unless a jug be company. For the beauties of Nature he had a poet's passion—the blossoms on the bough, the flowers of the plain. Most pleasing to him was the rosebud 'which gathers its skirts round itself,' and the tulip which every morning raised its chalice for the dew of heaven.

The theory that Omar's quatrains were arranged as we now have them subsequent to his death may explain some of their inconsistencies. In 26 he expresses belief in a future state; in 35 he tells us that we die as the tulips do. In 4 and 91 we are enjoined not to cause pain to any one; in 123 'to turn foot-pad and be benevolent.' In many places he expresses his belief in a sort of predestination, yet by his own showing it lay with himself whether he should or should not kiss the lips of a cup, sun himself on a river bank, or twist his fingers in Saki's curls. In 119 and 125 he praises poverty — under the rag of poverty one is equal to a Sultan—yet he advocates the life bibulous, which poverty would make impossible. In 1 he hopes for God's mercy, yet in the very next quatrain says, 'Burn me an Thou wilt, or cherish me an Thou wilt.' Here God is lauded, there taxed with injustice, as if He were a mere creature.

96. The Inconsistencies of Omar.

As we have seen, Omar had endeavoured to solve the secrets of existence, to understand the Deity and the ordering of things on earth, but unsuccessfully. Despite his learning, everything to him seems in a tangle; so, partly in earnest because he loved wine, partly in despair because a pleasant life was slipping from him and he felt that happiness was to be grasped now if ever, and partly out of contempt for the views of men who, pretending that they understood the working of Providence, knew nothing about it—he tilts the winecup, and (in jest, perhaps) elevates drunkenness to a place above the most esteemed virtues. As FitzGerald remarks, 'The spectacle of the old tentmaker pretending sensual pleasure as the serious purpose of life, and diverting himself with speculative problems of Deity, Destiny, Matter and Spirit, Good and Evil, is more apt to inspire sorrow than anger.' Omar comes to the conclusion, as all must who have pondered these matters,

97. Omar's attitude towards God.

that it is not necessary to understand them; where he is at fault is in expressing distrust of the Deity. He is sarcastic and angry because he cannot understand, whereas the only right attitude is recognition that God has withheld certain knowledge from us for a wise purpose. Instead, however, of acquiescing in the Divine will, the reasons for which no man can fathom, he takes upon himself to lay upon the Deity the blame for everything that is amiss. Even repentance, he asserts, is useless. As an example, he mentions that he once stole a prayer-mat from a mosque; he repented, and then went and stole another mat. In fact, he furnished his house with stolen mats, easing his mind every time by repentance. A twinkle lights his eye, certainly, but he is sincere enough in his conclusion, to wit: 'What is the good of repentance? God made me a man of sin. It is all destiny. If any one is to blame, it is God Himself.' Yet he can acknowledge God's mercy and praise Him for giving the juice of the grape; and occasionally he takes the correct attitude of a creature to a Creator: 'I do not always prevail over my nature. . . . I verily believe that Thou wilt generously pardon me, on account of my shame that Thou hast seen what I have done.'[1]

Hitherto we have considered Omar and his work in the light of the FitzGerald theory, the theory that is generally accepted in England and America—assuming that Omar was an opponent of the Sufis and an agnostic —or, as FitzGerald puts it, 'a philosopher of scientific insight and ability far beyond that of the age and country he lived in,' whose moderate ambition and moderate wants suggest that although the wine he celebrates is the juice of the grape, he bragged more than

[1] Q. 109.

he drank of it. But then, as we pointed out, there is the other theory, and, regarded in the light of that, Omar's poem falls into quite another category, that to which belongs, for example, the Song of Solomon, in which the Bride and Bridegroom are considered to symbolise Christ and His church. Using English eyes, one is apt to be prejudiced, and to look suspiciously on the allegorical interpretation, whether of the Song of Solomon or of Omar; but the Easterns regard it all as very natural. Flinging aside man-made creeds, Omar trusts himself unreservedly to God's goodness—washing down the misery of the world in the wine of Divine Mercy; and, leading a benevolent life, is assured that all will be well. The God of the extreme Mahometans is no God at all, but a mere figment of their own diseased imagination. Moan not for fear of hell, whether in palace, cottage, cell, or synagogue. Be happy. Thou knowest not whence thou camest, thou knowest not whither thou shalt go. Some look for joys of Heaven. I tell you it is Heaven now if you surrender yourself to the loving-kindness of God. God is love; and Divine love, which I am never weary of glorifying—Divine love, except which there is nought under the sun worth men's serious consideration, that under the figure of the wine-cup I sing, that shall be my theme till I die. Nothing else affords me comfort, and I must dwell upon it until my grateful heart fails to find words capable of expressing its emotion. As for death, why should I fear it? To God I owe my life; to Him I will surrender it when He bids me. Such is the Omar Khayyam of Professor Cowell and the Eastern interpreters.

Mr. Heron-Allen is inclined to think that there are wellnigh as many theories respecting Omar as there are students of him, for everybody 'reads into the quatrains his own pet philosophy, and interprets him according to his own religious views.' . . . 'For me,' he continues, 'Omar was at once a transcendental agnostic and an ornamental pessimist, not always supported by the courage of his own opinions, but profoundly imbued with the possible beauty of the present world.' In whatever light we regard him, however, we must treat him as we should any other great author—that is to say, take out of him whatever is beautiful, dainty, inspiring, and cheering, leaving the residuum, and there will be a feast sufficient for any man. As for the remark that readers 'care for but one Omar, and his real name is FitzGerald'—that, if true, says little for the readers' intelligence now that the complete Omar is accessible to all. As well say there is only one Boccaccio that people care for, and his real name is Chaucer.

Peace having been made with Russia (March 1856), Captain W. Kenworthy Browne—'the bloody warrior'—returned from Ireland, 'doffed his warlike habiliments,' to use Captain Addington's flowery expression, and resumed his peaceful occupations at Goldington, where FitzGerald again visited him. The meeting was a happy one, and FitzGerald made much of his friend's little sons, Elliott and Gerald, often accompanying them on their jaunts, particularly to Captain Addington's. Turnpike Cottage had a gate each side the turnpike, and it was the delight of the young Brownes to take advantage of their friendship with the captain by riding their ponies through his garden and so avoiding the gate-man. In June, FitzGerald, Browne, and the Rev. George Crabbe took a trip together to the Rhine, one of the mementoes

98. Goldington Hall and Germany.

'THE BLOODY WARRIOR'

CAPTAIN W. KENWORTHY BROWNE AT ALDERSHOT

of the journey being a *Baedeker's Manual of Conversation*, with the following in Browne's writing, 'W. K. B., Heidelberg, Monday, June 16, 1856. E. F. G., G. C., and W. K. B.' Of this journey I have been unable to find previous record, and in view of what it must have meant to him, it is singular that his writings contain no reference to it.

In the meantime Cowell had been appointed Professor of History at the Presidency College, Calcutta, and was making arrangements for departure. To be separated from his friend was to FitzGerald a good deal of a wrench. 'Your talk of going to India,' he wrote, 'makes my heart hang really heavy at my side.' But Cowell exhorted him to be cheerful, and as a parting gift gave him a book in which he had written the following lines—

<small>99. Cowell goes to India, August 1856. Reminiscences of Bramford.</small>

> 'Thou hidden love of God, whose height,
>   Whose depth unfathomed no man knows,
> I see from far Thy beauteous light;
>   Inly I sigh for Thy repose;
> My soul is sick, nor can it be
>   At rest, till it find rest in Thee.'[1]

11*th July* 1856.

Before Cowell's departure, however, the friends met again at the residence of Cowell's mother, Rushmere, near Ipswich. They strolled together in the hay-field in front of the house, and FitzGerald remembered every incident of the day—the men with their hay cromes, the conversation of his friend, the hum of the bees, the fragrance of the hay, his own husky voice—with a sincere, sad, and affectionate interest. It was as a parting of lovers. Mr. and Mrs. Cowell sailed for India early in August in the *Monarch*, the route taken being,

---

[1] I had this information from Professor Cowell.

of course, that round the Cape, and they arrived, to use Cowell's own words to me, 'just in time for the horrors of the mutiny.' Among the passengers was a Mr. Astell (now Squire Astell of Old House, Ickwell, Biggleswade), with whom they read Hindustani.

'Ah, happy days!' writes FitzGerald plaintively, recalling the joys of the cottage at Bramford; 'when shall we three meet again—when dip in that unreturning tide of time and circumstance? In those meadows far from the world, it seemed, as Salaman's Island—before an iron railway broke the heart of that happy valley where gossip was the mill-wheel, and visitors the summer airs that momentarily ruffled the sleepy stream that turned it as they chased one another over to lose themselves in whispers in the copse beyond. On returning—I suppose you remember whose lines they are—

"When winter skies were tinged with crimson still,"

at such an hour drawing home together for a fireside night of it with Æschylus or Calderon in the cottage, whose walls, modest almost as those of the poor who clustered—and with good reason—round, make to my eyes the Towered Crown of Oxford hanging in the horizon, and with all honour won, but a dingy vapour in comparison.'[1] The expression 'the Towered Crown of Oxford' had, Professor Cowell told me, a double meaning. It refers both to the Magdalen Tower hard by Cowell's rooms at Oxford, and to the first-class obtained by Cowell in the B.A. examination. At Calcutta, Cowell indulged to the full his appetite for work. From 6 A.M. to 8.30 he read with a Pundit. His mornings were spent at the Sanskrit College, his after-

[1] FitzGerald's preface to *Salaman and Absal*.

PROFESSOR COWELL

noons in lecturing on English Literature; in vacations he studied Persian with a Moonshee, whom he used also to consult when FitzGerald, who was reading Nizami, applied to him respecting difficulties.

In matters of art FitzGerald still interested himself, though less than formerly. He speaks with some enthusiasm of a Holy Family on a panel in his possession, which had the inscription, 'Petrus dein gnatis fecit, MDXLVIII.,' on a scroll on the left-hand corner. It is 'admirably painted,' and 'the expression of the figures —Virgin, Child, St. Joseph, St. John, and St. Catherine— is very tender.'[1]

[1] *Notes and Queries.*

CHAPTER XII

SIX MONTHS OF WEDDED LIFE

4TH NOVEMBER 1856—MAY 1857

Bibliography
17. Attar's 'Bird Parliament' adapted.

<small>100. A week at Donne's. George Borrow.</small>

IN October 1856 FitzGerald spent a week at Bury with the good, handsome, and accomplished Donne, the wittiest of his friends ('You don't know Donne's fun yet') — who, however, could never take up pen without putting on the Quaker. Few men have had more virtues attributed to him than 'our Donne,' though through the snowy marble of his character there zigzagged, according to Fanny Kemble, 'a vein of deep and black malignity,'[1] but we may charitably assume that Mrs. Kemble saw him at some exceptional moment, for he was pre-eminently the amiable, the meek, the uncomplaining man.

At Donne's FitzGerald met George Borrow, the elephantine, shaggy-browed, stentorian voiced, mysterious author of *Lavengro*; linguist, gypsy-lorest, pugilist, naturalist, one of the most picturesque of the genii of the pen. He was fifty-three, comfortably settled, after countless wanderings, with a well-lined widow in a

---
[1] *Further Records*, ii. p. 154.

SIX MONTHS OF WEDDED LIFE

Hereward the Wake sort of retreat—very difficult of access—among the sedges and rushes of Oulton, near Lowestoft. He described himself as a Le Sage in water-colours; and, indeed, the adventures of Gil Blas were not more varied. Borrow read FitzGerald a long translation which he had made from the Turkish, and FitzGerald lent Borrow Cowell's MS. of Omar. Later, Borrow presented FitzGerald with a copy of *The Romany Rye*, which FitzGerald liked only in parts, and, *more suo*, told the author so. As to Borrow personally, FitzGerald was repelled by his masterful manner and uncertain temper, and they did not become very intimate.

Of the relations between FitzGerald and Lucy Barton we have already spoken at some length. For several years he seems to have been trying to persuade himself that marriage, and marriage with Lucy Barton, was desirable. For instance, we may notice that in *Polonius* (published in 1852) there are two extracts on the subject of marriage, and both recommendatory to that state—one from Carlyle, the other from Bacon. W. Kenworthy Browne, who tried his utmost to prevent the union, declared that FitzGerald was veering towards a precipice, and that nothing could come of such a union but unhappiness. In reply, FitzGerald said that he had given the matter long and serious consideration, and that, moreover, he had pledged his word to take care of Miss Barton. 'Give her,' said Browne, 'whatever you like, except your hand. Make her an allowance.'

'I would cheerfully do so,' replied FitzGerald, 'but then people would talk.'

'That from *you*!' followed Browne; '*you*, who do not care a straw what anybody says about anything!'

'Nor should I care,' exclaimed FitzGerald; 'but Miss

101. FitzGerald's marriage, 4th November 1856.

VOL. I. O

Barton would care a very great deal. It would be cruel.'

FitzGerald, who very well understood Miss Barton's character, had himself the gravest doubts whether they would be happy together, but he hoped against hope. He admired certain of her qualities, he honoured the memory of her father, he sympathised with her poverty; he had promised, and she had interpreted that promise in one and only one way, to provide for her. He was not in love; there was no courting or growing 'amorously lean' on his part. Both were fifty, and Miss Barton was tall, gaunt, and plain. He looked forward simply to the quiet settling down together of two elderly persons who had hitherto been very good friends, and would, he fervently hoped, in spite of appearances, continue so. He used to say that he never rejected the advice of a friend without regretting it, and the course he now followed, contrary to Browne's urging, was to furnish his dictum with an additional and the most melancholy illustration. The marriage ceremony took place at All Saints' Church, Chichester, where Miss Barton had friends, on 4th November 1856. The newly married couple resided first at Brighton, and afterwards at 31 Great Portland Street, London; but a very few days sufficed to reveal that they were totally unfitted for each other. Mrs. FitzGerald's prim, methodical, fussy, masterful nature, and her fondness for society ways—fostered by her residence with the Gurneys (she could see no enjoyment in a dinner unless one dressed for it)—soon discovered themselves. To FitzGerald, careless, disorderly, unconventional, who had for so long followed his own sweet will, punctilious etiquette and fastidious neatness in attire were, above all things, hateful. It was the 'stupid dulness' of the formal dinner, he used to say, which contributed more than anything else to drive him out of Society. He once said to a friend, alluding to his disagreement with his wife: 'I could not be bothered with all those whims—dressing for this and dressing for the other. I couldn't put up with it.' Then their differences of opinion on the food question did not tend to diminish friction. While FitzGerald was practically a vegetarian, and liked the little meat he did eat 'home done,'[1] his wife not only liked meat, but (to his horror) liked it underdone—a feature, in his opinion, almost as bad as cannibalism. That difficulty, however, might have been got over, seeing that meat-eating was not in respect to others regarded as a *casus belli*; but to exchange the plaid-shawl in which he loved to envelop himself for an evening coat, a stiff collar, and cravat, was not even to be dreamt of. Many women, with a little tact, a little forbearance, and quiet instead of rasping words, could have wound FitzGerald round their finger. A fine opportunity of making a happy marriage was here lost. He was enticeable; but no woman on earth, or man either, could force him. By considering *him* more, and *outsiders* less—outsiders, too, who counted for nothing—she would have come to her kingdom. Then, too, since his mother's death FitzGerald had been a man of means, and this fact, considering that Mrs. FitzGerald herself had been practically penniless, should have had some weight with her. She, poor woman, could not see things in this light, however. Strong as was her will-power, FitzGerald's was stronger, and, as he once said, he could, had he chosen, have borne down all opposition and made her a slave, but he declined to exercise his power. On the other hand, to give up the hours of his life which was fast ebbing away—and who more conscious than he

[1] Done thoroughly.

of the resistless march of time?—to give up the precious hours of his life to formality, conventionality, and fashion, was to him out of all question. His imperious temper often caused him to use wounding words, which, it is but justice to him to observe, he subsequently lamented; and if she suffered, he also suffered acutely. The early months of a married life are rarely altogether cloudless. There is always a certain amount of disillusion. These months, which so many mistake for paradise, are only the portal of paradise.

With FitzGerald, all was now sable and sad. His life, despite its tinge of melancholy, had hitherto been a pleasant poem, and it was the charm of his own character in great measure that made it so. The scenes at Tenby, at Bedford, at Boulge Cottage, at Bramford, are as idyllic as anything in Theocritus, and they succeed each other like the changes in a kaleidoscope. Suddenly there is an end to the beautiful phantasmagoria. The spiteful fairy, whom some one had affronted at FitzGerald's birth, interposes her hand between the picture and the light, and life suddenly becomes haggard, dark, and lugubrious. How strange that everybody could love FitzGerald, put up with his peevishness and eccentricities, nay, love him the more for them, except one person—his wife! Blame neither very much, for Mrs. FitzGerald in her way was kindly. She simply failed to chime with her husband. Instead of attracting, they repelled each other, found each other absolutely unendurable.

In the middle of December—they had been married only a fortnight—Mrs. FitzGerald went by herself into Norfolk, where she spent five weeks, partly at Mr. Hudson Gurney's, and partly at Geldestone, where her husband joined her, and they looked about for a home. At first they thought of Norwich. 'I want my wife,' FitzGerald had written on January 1st, 'to learn all she can of housekeeping, and employ herself in it: I think she is given to profusion, and her hand is out of practice, of course.' Finally they returned to London and took apartments at Portland Terrace, Regent's Park. Recalling old and pleasant days with the Cowells, FitzGerald wrote (January 22), 'I believe there are new channels fretted in my cheeks with many unmanly tears since then.' Indeed, he had become utterly miserable. Mrs. FitzGerald either had not the tact or would not take the trouble to make his home agreeable to him, and he pined for his old solitary life. Whilst in London he saw Carlyle once, and Donne, Thackeray, Tennyson, and Spedding, whose first volume of Bacon was out. He showed Tennyson some touching lines written by a poor sailor lad who died at sea—

> 'The sullen waves close o'er him : but there's not
> A stone to mark the burial of the brave ;
> A single bubble bursting marks the spot
> Where rests the sailor in his sailor's grave,'

and Tennyson paused 'to murmur over that single bursting bubble.' Thackeray, who was also present, 'thought there must have been a hundred bubbles rather than one.'[1]

FitzGerald's studies continued to be mainly Persian : he goes through Hafiz, Jami, Nizami, and Attar's *Mantik*, the last especially interesting him. The letter of January 22nd lately referred to closes with a pathetic passage hinting at the sad home trouble : 'Till I see better how we get on, I dare fix on no place to live or die in. Direct to me at Crabbe's, Bredfield, till you hear further.' Next comes the news of the death of 'Anglo-Saxon Kemble' (26th March 1857). 'Poor John!' writes his sister

[1] *Sea Words and Phrases*, No. 2.

Fanny, 'his devotion to his studies was very deep.' His life was not much more successful than the Torrijos expedition.[1] A brilliant scholar, given over, to his own hurt, to intense study and 'deep philosophising.'

In the midst of his troubles FitzGerald occupied himself in studying the Persian poet Attar, a manuscript of whose *Mantik-ut-Tair*, or Bird Parliament—an exposition of the doctrines of Sufism—he had obtained from Mr. Napoleon Newton of Hertford; and presently, by the help of the publications of Garcin de Tassy, he set about the translation, or rather the adaptation, of that poem, for he followed his usual method. By March 20th (1857) he had got twenty pages done, and said, 'It is an amusement to me to take what liberties I like with these Persians.'

<small>102. The Birds' 'Pilgrim's Progress.'</small>

The *Mantik*—like Jami's *Salaman*—is a story interspersed with anecdotes, in the best of which figures Shah Mahmud—'the mighty Mahmud' of the *Rubaiyat* who scattered before him the misbelieving, black horde of India.[2] It has a number of passages containing thoughts which come up again in FitzGerald's Omar. The story of the poem is briefly as follows: The bird world had assembled on a no less solemn business than to choose a Khalif. The first to speak was Tajidar, the lapwing, who declared that they had a Khalif already, that he knew this Khalif, his whereabouts, and how to reach him, and that they would know him too, but for the curse of their self-exile, seeing that he is everywhere—among them indeed at the moment. Would they reach their king they must repent of their misdeeds and go on pilgrimage by a long, dangerous, and dismal road, up to the mighty mountain Kaf. Some of the audience express a desire to make

---

[1] *Records of a Later Life*, vol. iii. p. 150.
[2] FitzGerald's Omar, q. 60.

this journey, but others object—the pheasant, the nightingale, and the parrot in particular. The last, a very Omar Khayyam among birds, says—

> '" Some "—and upon the nightingale one eye
> He leered—" for nothing but the blossom sigh :
> But I am for the luscious pulp that grows
> Where, and for which, the blossom only blows :
> And which so long as the green tree provides
> What better grows along Kaf's dreary sides?"'

In short, 'take the cash and let the credit go.' But Tajidar tells him that this life, which he finds so nectareous, is daily slipping away; and to every other objection he has a suitable answer, the result being that the birds choose him for their king, and resolve to follow him to the mountain. When, however, it comes to starting, the thought of the terrors of the track makes many faint-hearted, and they slink away; while others, having spent what little strength they had in preparation, cannot muster up enough courage to do anything further. Finally, however, a goodly host start on this avian 'Pilgrim's Progress,' but more than half turn tail at the first cold snap. Many sit as if stupefied, and some fall behind. The more brave and strong, however, push forward—

> 'Yet league by league the road was thicklier spread
> By the fast falling foliage of the dead.'

Scorched, frozen, famished, poisoned, slain by beast or reptile, thirty only 'desperate draggled things, half-dead, with scarce a feather on their wings,' reach the mountain. 'Who are you?' asks the Guardian Angel. And Tajidar replies—

> 'We are
> Those fractions of the Sum of Being, far
> Disspent and foul disfigured, that once more
> Strike for admission at the Treasury Door.'

The Angel then flings open the portal—

'They were *within*—they were before the *Throne*,'

in a wellnigh insufferable blaze of glory, and in the centre of it is the likeness of *Themselves*—as it were transfigured, looking to Themselves. They had returned to the Being of whom they originally formed part. Then a voice is heard—

> 'All you have been, and seen, and done, and thought,
> Not *you* but *I*, have seen and been and wrought:
> I was the sin that from Myself rebelled,
> I the remorse that towards Myself compelled.
> I was the Tajidar who led the track:
> I was the little briar that pulled you back:
> Sin and contrition—retribution owed,
> And cancelled—pilgrim, pilgrimage, and road,
> Was but Myself toward Myself; and your
> Arrival but Myself at my own door.'

Such is Sufism according to Attar. Whilst holding that Attar had less imagination than Jami, and less depth than Jelaledin, FitzGerald considered his touch lighter than either. Of his stories—which pleased FitzGerald better than Jami's—the best are that of the Shah who rode unmoved through his huzzaing capital, but promptly expressed gratification when the heads of criminals were tossed out of the prison to him; of Mahmud and the lad fishing, which ends with the couplet—

> 'This is the luck that follows every cast
> Since o'er my net the Sultan's shadow pass'd';

and that of Mahmud and the Stoker; but not less memorable are those of the man

> 'Who to an idol bowed—as best he knew—
> Under that false god worshipping the true';

and of Mahmud who, hesitating to fulfil a vow, referred the matter to a dervise—

> 'Who, having listened, said, "The thing is plain:
> If thou and God should never have again
> To deal together, rob Him of His share,
> But if perchance you should—why then, beware!"'

In one of the stories the Prophet, dipping his lips into a stream, found the water sweet, but the same stream drunk from an earthen pot left by a traveller tasted bitter. To the Prophet's surprised look

> 'The vessel's earthen lips with answer ran,
> The clay that I am made of once was man'—

a thought that drifted into FitzGerald's Omar. It was a passage in the *Mantik* which suggested the lovely lines—

> 'Earth could not answer, nor the seas that mourn
> In flowing purple, of their Lord forlorn'—

founded on the Eastern belief that the sea and all its denizens are of an inferior nature, bereft of God. It was the *Mantik*, too, that suggested to FitzGerald the lines about the drum beaten at the Sultan's door, David's song, the False Dawn, and the Eternal Saki. FitzGerald's version of the *Mantik* was finished in 1859, but not published till after his death.

In the meantime, the home trouble had gone on from bad to worse. That FitzGerald recognised that he too was blamable is evident from his remark: 'How often I think with sorrow of my many harshnesses and impatiences! which are yet more of manner than intention.' He longed to see again his friends the Cowells. To E. B. Cowell he writes, 'My wife is sick of hearing me sing in a doleful voice the old glee of " When

103. The Paddock at Goldington Hall. Baldock 'Black Horse.' The Separation.

shall we three meet again?"' He looked back with regret and soft melancholy to the vanished delights of the cottage at Bramford; recalled the walks with his friends, the monkey-tree, the old mill, the willows by the river, all sacred; and often sang to himself a verse—a verse with one word altered—from Miss Williams's song 'Evan Banks'—

> 'Oh banks to me for ever dear,
> Oh stream whose murmur meets my ear,
> Oh, all my hopes of bliss abide
> Where *Orwell* mingles with the tide.'

Winter passed, and FitzGerald and his wife were still in London. Men went by with great baskets of primroses, crocuses, and other spring flowers, calling as they passed—

> 'Growing, growing, growing,
> All their glory going!'

—'some old street cry,' as FitzGerald thought. In April he spent a few days with his brother John at Twickenham, where he copied out Omar and sent it to Garcin de Tassy in return for courtesy. On the 21st, as he sat 'on the sunshine of the little balcony' outside the windows of his house, letters from Professor and Mrs. Cowell were placed in his hands. Says he in replying to Cowell, 'My wife cried a good deal over your wife's letter, I think, I think so. Ah, me! I would not as yet read it, for I was already sad.' Later, FitzGerald and his wife took a house at Gorleston, near Yarmouth, but amity between them still seemed quite unattainable. On the 18th of May he went down to Bedford, that is to say Goldington, to try and forget his troubles in the company of his devoted friend Captain W. Kenworthy Browne, and we now get that charming picture of him lying in the pightle or paddock at the back of Goldington Hall

GOLDINGTON HALL FROM 'THE PADDOCK'

reading Omar Khayyam. Says he: 'When in Bedfordshire I put away almost all books except Omar Khayyam which I could not help looking over, in a paddock covered with buttercups and brushed by a delicious breeze, while a dainty racing filly of W. Browne's came startling up to wonder and snuff about me.'[1] Stirred by the delights of springtide, he turned into monkish Latin the Omar stanza—

> 'Now the New Year reviving old desires,
> The thoughtful soul to solitude retires,
>   Where the White Hand of Moses on the Bough
> Puts out, and Jesus from the Ground suspires.'

So he lies there in 'the jolly spring weather, in the jolly springtime, when the poplar and lime dishevel their tresses together,'[2] forgetting for the moment the ache at his heart, and revelling in the perfume of Omar. On Oak Apple Day (May 29) he made a journey, probably with Browne, to Baldock, just over the Herts border, in order to see 'The Black Horse,' both mill and hostelry, famous on account of the old song written by a nameless curate about Mary FitzJohn, the Beauty, who lived there—

> 'Who has e'er been at Baldock, must needs know the mill,
> With the sign of the Horse, at the foot of the hill.'

It was especially interesting to FitzGerald (whom you could draw all round the country with an old song) on account of the description of a visit to Baldock, which included a sight of the 'rustic Diana' and a taste of her sugared lip, made by one Percival Stockdale,[3] Dr. Johnson's 'Poor Stockey,' a hundred years previous. FitzGerald finds the mill with its scanty stream a little way out of Baldock, but without the sign of the Black

---

[1] *Letters* (Macmillan).   [2] *Euphranor.*
[3] Who in 1809 published two volumes of autobiography.

Horse; makes his way to the church, on the steeple of which had been hoisted a large oak apple bough, and discovers the tomb of the famous Mary of the song, who, after Stockdale's visit, had married one Henry Leonard. The stone is inscribed: 'In Memory of Mary, the wife of Henry Leonard, who died April 26, 1769, aged 43 years'—'about twelve years,' comments FitzGerald, 'after Stockdale saw and saluted her, rightly guessing that she was then "perhaps above thirty, but yet lovely, fair, and blooming." A little further westward lies her husband, Henry Leonard, "who died April 28, 1802, aged 78 years," buried not by her side, but by that of a second wife, who may have been as good, but whom we will not believe to have been such a beauty, as his first.' 'There are two aquatint engravings of Baldock still extant to attest that she was its most celebrated ornament. One represents the town and the fields adjoining, and "Mr. FitzJohn" on his horse looking at the country people making hay; the other print is of the mill itself, with its Black Horse over the gable, and genteel company in hoop and ruffle and cocked hat, politely conversing along the road or fishing in the mill-stream.' So Fitz-Gerald did his little bit of antiquarian research, and on getting back to Goldington wrote a paper on it which was to slumber in his desk twenty-two years before finally getting to press.[1]

On 5th June he is back at Gorleston watching the vessels going in and out of the river, and sailors walking about with fur caps and their hands in their pockets. Everything that he does reveals an aching heart. A letter of his to Borrow, from whom he was now distant only a few miles, contains some sad lines from the

[1] *Temple Bar*, January 1880: 'Percival Stockdale and Baldock Black Horse.'

SIX MONTHS OF WEDDED LIFE

Persian, in which regret is expressed for a wasted life, 'unfulfilled commands' and 'unlawful deeds.' Night after night he walked about on the hills—now built on—behind Gorleston, utterly miserable. He was in a labyrinth from which no one could extricate him; never in his life had he been so lonely. His heart yearned for some one to administer comfort. He longed for some one to whom he could confide his troubles, but no one came. Years after, he bitterly reproached Fate for producing no friend at this moment; and yet, what could any additional friend have done except express sympathy? There was but one way to escape from the labyrinth, namely, to burst in a straight line, heedless of the thorns, through the thickset intervening hedges; and this he finally decided to do. He resolved upon a separation, and Mrs. FitzGerald (though not without spirited remonstrance) concurred. 'FitzGerald,' observed Mr. Alfred Smith to me, 'acted as he thought in the kindest and most honourable manner, and the separation was carried out with the greatest regard to the happiness of both, and with much liberality.' Mrs. FitzGerald received an ample allowance by deed placed in the hands of trustees, and the ill-sorted pair parted for ever. FitzGerald had broken through his labyrinth, but he was covered with wounds; the thorns had entered deeply into his flesh. How great a trouble this marriage failure was to him, only those who were in his company at the time (and I have talked with several) could really understand. For long he was thoroughly broken down, absolutely and hopelessly wretched; but after a time, as we shall see, grief gave place to indifference, the sad to the mildly satirical.

Mrs. FitzGerald resided first at Hastings, and afterwards at Croydon. Once or twice she attempted to see her husband again, but the gates of his heart were barricaded against her. Some—nay, considerable—affection for him she continued to preserve, for she liked to have his portrait in a little red leather case always near her, and right until his death clung to the hope that they would be reunited. So ends the pitiful story of FitzGerald's six months of married life. For his conduct in separating from his wife he was attacked, by persons who understood neither him nor the circumstances of the case, with viperous virulence; but though their remarks necessarily pained him he made no retort, but quietly and with dignity went his own way. Surely it was better for them to separate than to live together wretchedly—to live, for example, a Colonel and Mrs. Short sort of life. Among those who strongly disapproved of FitzGerald's conduct at this crisis was one of his nearest friends whose affection for him, formerly so marked, from that time perceptibly cooled. Kind letters, indeed, sometimes passed between them, but the old fervour was gone, and they never afterwards met.

FitzGerald's married life—those six sable months—passed from him like a troubled dream. He fell back into his old pensive ways and solaced himself again with his books at Farlingay, Lowestoft, and Bedford, and his eight good, simple, well-bred, industrious, melancholy-flecked nieces at Geldestone, and compiled for his own amusement a Glossary of Suffolk Words and Phrases.

104. The 'Far niente' life again.

It was about this time that he made the acquaintance of Bernard Quaritch, the well-known bookseller. Quaritch, who had often seen FitzGerald in his shop, somehow found out his customer's surname, and maladroitly asked him point-blank whether he was Edward Marlborough FitzGerald (the man with the tarnished reputation). FitzGerald, with acerbity, promptly replied that he was not, giving his correct name; nevertheless the acquaintance which commenced so inauspiciously was renewed, and in time ripened into a sort of friendship.

In the meantime, Edward's brother John was busy enlarging, mutilating, and adorning (as he called it) Boulge church — building an aisle on the south side, and putting in a new east window. He had often fulminated against the 'remnants of Romanism' in Woodbridge church, and he now removed what he considered objectionable features in his own — namely, the wooden angels that formed part of the roof (the church is dedicated to St. Michael and All Angels), and made a ceiling which he covered with unmistakably Protestant dark blue and gold stars. John FitzGerald's extreme Evangelicalism, indeed, sometimes led him into ridiculous absurdities. To denude his church (bare enough before) of the few ornaments left it by the Reformation, to tear down its architectural angels and to hide its fine roof with a ceiling daubed with blue, was foolish enough; but still more foolish was an argument which he had with the Archbishop of Canterbury relative to the Apocrypha, the whole of which he hated with all the hatred of his narrow-minded nature. Surely, in the light of the jewels scattered up and down its pages, and especially in Ecclesiasticus, the attitude of the Church towards these books as expressed in the sixth article of the Church should satisfy any reasonable man. But John was not satisfied, and the following dialogue took place :—

J. F. If I were a clergyman and had daily service, could I omit the reading of these books?

ARCHBISHOP. No, sir.

J. F. Could I from the pulpit explain to the people

the falsehoods and unsound doctrine contained in these writings?

ARCHBISHOP. No, sir.[1]

J. F. Then I cannot read in the desk what I cannot endorse from the pulpit.

If John was in an anti-Apocryphal and polemical mood, it was of no avail even to agree with him before he began. He would assume that you were an antagonist for the sake of argument, and pour upon your dissimulation all the vials of his wrath — with much sissing, many an amazing action, and an occasional whistle. His virtues, however, more than palliated his weaknesses. Indeed, as his brother said, he was a man one could really love two and three-quarter miles off.

---

[1] A better answer would have been, 'It would be a waste of time, sir, in the light of the sixth article.'

CHAPTER XIII

GOLDINGTON

MAY 1857—30TH MARCH 1859.

Bibliography

18. *Gentleman's Magazine*, Death of George Crabbe.
19. Omar Khayyam, 1st edition, 15th February 1859.

IN September 1857, just after he had arrived at Goldington, FitzGerald heard of the death of his old friend, the Rev. George Crabbe, vicar of Bredfield; and in his letter to Crabbe's son, George Crabbe the third, he says: 'I feel your father's loss more than any I have felt, except Major Moor's, perhaps.' Then follows a pathetic reference to Mrs. FitzGerald: 'I want your sisters so much to go to my wife at Gorleston when they can,' Mrs. FitzGerald being anxious to return to them in that way some of the sympathy they had shown to her during her trouble early in the year. 'I am convinced,' continues FitzGerald feelingly, 'that their going to her would be the very thing for herself, poor soul; taking her out of herself, and giving her the very thing she is pining for, namely, some one to devote herself to.'[1]
FitzGerald reached Bredfield in time to be present at the funeral. Melancholy enough the house seemed with its smell of crape and bombazine, while the friend with whom he had spent so many happy hours lay there still and

105. Death of George Crabbe the Second.

[1] *More Letters* (Macmillan).

silent, the 'Radiator' never more to emit rays; with the people coming in and going out with black about them, 'were it no bigger than that about the soldier's arm,' and vying with each other to do honour to the man who had loved them all, and had believed good of them all, 'except Mary Ann Cuthbert.' Next to the family and FitzGerald, nobody, however, felt the blow more sensibly than the Rev. H. S. Drew.[1] The last argument on Infant Baptism had been held, and victory, as at the first, had been claimed by both parties. It was very mournful to pass the battlefields, and visions of poor Crabbe's animated face and revolving hat seemed very real. In the 'cobblery,' the stuffy, smoke-impregnated, little dark study where FitzGerald and Crabbe had so often sat with their pipes, talked and drunk 'something warm,' a partially consumed cheroot which Crabbe, as it seemed, might any moment come and finish, lay in its china ash-pan. The burial took place in a simple manner on the south side of the churchyard, and the descending September sun of one of the finest summers remembered, broke out to fling a farewell beam on the closing grave.[2] The respect in which Crabbe was held by his parishioners is shown by the fact that they 'all' (including Mary Ann Cuthbert, apparently) subscribed for the purpose of placing to his memory a tablet in the church; and by the warmth of affection towards him displayed in some anonymous verses[3] (grovelling though the language, with its reference to the 'higher classes') written by one of his humbler admirers. After the death of her father, Miss Caroline Crabbe resided at Stockton, in Wiltshire, or stayed with

---

[1] The Rev. Heriot Standbanks Drew died at Pettistree, near Woodbridge, 31st December 1893, aged eighty-five years.
[2] See notice of Crabbe in the *Gentleman's Magazine* for November 1857, furnished by FitzGerald.
[3] Nine in number.

GOLDINGTON BURY

GOLDINGTON

friends at Bradford-on-Avon, where FitzGerald sometimes visited her. A letter lies before me written by her to Emma Cone of Boulge—who afterwards became wife of William Marjoram, of whom we shall speak later—on 11th February 1858. It is in reference to the death of Mr. Robert Knipe Cobbold, of the 'White House,' Bredfield.[1] Not only does it throw light on the character of one of the most interesting persons of the FitzGerald drama, but it shows how near the welfare of the people of Bredfield was to the hearts of all the Crabbe family. She says: 'I am very sorry he is taken away, both for the Bredfield people and for himself. When people have had a long and painful illness, or are very old, they are glad to leave the world, but he seemed to be in health and to enjoy life. Besides, his life was such a useful one. . . . I do believe he thought of others before himself. What pleasure it gave him to see the children enjoy their treats, and we were so glad to think some one was left in the place who took an interest in his neighbours and was able to help them. But we do not know what is really best. He was a God-fearing man, and I trust, with you, he is gone to a kind and merciful Father and to a Heavenly home.'[2]

As we have seen, Mr. Robert Elliott of Goldington left two children, Robert, and Elizabeth, who was married to Mr. W. Kenworthy Browne. Robert, who had two children, Harriet and Florence Hannah Maria (now Lady Power), died in 1853, his wife in 1854; and the children, who became wards in Chancery, were handed over to W. Kenworthy Browne, who educated them with his own family under a governess, the Miss Thompson of Fitz-

106. Goldington Bury, 23rd September 1858.

---

[1] Son of the author of *Margaret Catchpole*.
[2] Unpublished letter in the possession of Mrs. William Marjoram.

Gerald's letters. On 23rd September 1858 Browne removed from Goldington Hall to Goldington Bury, a larger house in the Queen Anne style, situated a little to the north-east and nearer the church.

The Bedford Conservatives now wanted Browne to stand for the borough as the second Conservative candidate, and he agreed to the proposal, though, as the Whigs, led by Mr. George Hurst, presented a formidable front, the fight was expected to be a stout one. In the meantime, he devoted himself with unflagging zeal to his magisterial and other duties. For one thing, he was warmly interested in promoting an alteration of the law relating to the imprisonment of debtors under orders from the county court, a law which had been 'cruelly turned to the oppression of the poor.'

In January, FitzGerald is at his old lodgings, 88 (to which the number had been changed from 31) Great Portland Street. He had given up his studies, for there was no one (Cowell being in India) to prick the sides of his intent, 'vaulting ambition having long failed to do so.'

In the Middle Ages superstition regarded any unusual celestial appearance not only with awe, but as an omen of ill, and nothing visited it with greater concern than a glorious comet. We are all tinctured with the credulity of our forefathers, and FitzGerald, gazing up at the comet of 1858,[1] a transplendent object in the shape of a noble falcon swooping downward with arched neck and lowered head, or a magnificent rocket just burst and on the point of falling, may pardonably have wondered whether the sight portended anything to him—a thought to be no sooner conceived than dismissed as unworthy of even the momentary credence of an intelligent being.

107. Death of W. Kenworthy Browne, 30th March 1859.

[1] Donati's.

W. KENWORTHY BROWNE

Yet scarce had the radiance of the celestial visitor vanished before there fell upon him the most crushing blow of his life, namely, the loss of his devoted friend, mentor, and hero, W. Kenworthy Browne. It was the 28th of January 1859, and the Elstow Harriers were returning after a day's sport at an easy pace along the road leading from Great Barford to Bedford. Browne, aglow after the exercise — the picture of health — was chatting with a friend as they rode side by side. Dusk was falling, the air nipped, and Ouse, seen through the naked limbs of the trees and its fringe of bleached reeds, crept as leisurely towards the sea as the horsemen in green paced towards Bedford. The dogs were mostly some distance ahead, but some of them having fallen behind, a horseman in front of Browne, turning in his saddle, struck at one of the laggers with his hunting-whip. By accident, the lash flicked the head of Browne's horse, which, without even a moment's warning, reared on its haunches and fell backwards on its rider, crushing him beyond the hope of recovery. At first, indeed, he was thought to be dead. They carried him home to Goldington Bury, and managed to get him to his bedroom, that on the first-floor with three windows, on the right as you face the house. Here, 'broken in half, almost,' he lingered in dreadful agony for nearly nine weeks, though death was daily expected. The sorrow in the home we pass over. FitzGerald, torn with grief, hastened to Goldington, but for long could not be permitted to enter the chamber of suffering. 'Then,' says FitzGerald, 'Browne tried to write a line to me, like a child's! and I went and saw no longer the gay lad, nor the healthy man I had known, but a wreck of all that; a face like Charles I. (after decapitation, almost) above the clothes, and the poor shattered body underneath, lying as it had lain eight weeks.' Tears that he could not wipe away came to his eyes. 'Instead of the light utterance of other days came the slow, painful syllables in a far lower key; and when the old familiar words, Old fellow, Fitz, etc., came forth, so spoken, I broke down too in spite of foregone resolution.'[1] The sufferer, looking at FitzGerald 'with his old discrimination,' said one day, 'I suppose you have scarce ever been with a dying person before?'

It was now Sunday morning, March 27th. Seated in the parlour at Goldington Bury, FitzGerald noticed two books which had been presents from himself. One was the copy, in grey-coloured boards, of *Godefridus*. He opened it. There was the familiar picture of the two naked horsemen, the first of whom was turning round and flourishing a whip. FitzGerald must have shuddered, for had the figures been clad in hunting-clothes, the picture might have been taken for a delineation of Browne's accident. He read the inscription: 'W. Browne from E. F. G. *Sed tu noli deficere: quod ille quaerit, tu esto.*' Then taking a pen, he wrote under it, whilst his poor friend lay dying in the room above, 'This book I gave my dear W. K. B. about twenty years ago; when then believing it, and believing it *now*, to contain a character of himself (especially at pp. 89, etc.), though he might be the last to negotiate it as his own likeness. I now think his son [Gerald] cannot do better than read it, with the light his father's example sheds upon it.—EDWARD FITZGERALD, Goldington Bury, Sunday morning, March 27, 1859.'[2] The other book was a copy of his own *Euphranor*, presented by him

---

[1] *Letters*, vol. ii. p. 3. Quoted by permission of Messrs. Macmillan.
[2] This book is now in the possession of Captain Gerald Kenworthy Browne, to whom I am indebted for the use of it.

GOLDINGTON CHURCH

to Browne, and in it he wrote: 'This little book would never have been written, had I not known my dear friend William Browne, who, unconsciously, supplied the moral.—E. F. G., Goldington, March 27, 1859.'[1]

On the night of 29th March, Browne spoke of FitzGerald, and the next day 'gave up his honest ghost.' FitzGerald's comment on an event that had so deeply affected him is characteristic. 'Well, this is so; and there is no more to be said about it. It is one of the things that reconcile me to my own stupid decline of life, to the crazy state of the world. Well, no more about it. . . . Poor old Omar has *his* kind of consolation for all these things.'[2] Captain Browne was buried in Goldington churchyard, the service being read by the Rev. William Airy—'All very quiet and solemn.' A stone with his initials marks his resting-place, and there is a tablet of white marble to his memory in the church. Thus closed one of the most remarkable and picturesque friendships in the history of literature.

To his dying day FitzGerald treasured in his heart of hearts the recollection of his splendid friend, and the epithet we have used indicates perhaps better than any other the feeling with which he regarded him. The happy days they had spent together at Tenby, Bedford, Goldington, Lowestoft, in Ireland, and in Germany, often recurred to his mind. Browne—Phidippus—my master —was his ideal man, his ideal friend; and he felt the blow in proportion to his affection and admiration for him. Never again did FitzGerald have the heart to visit Bedford. No more Ouse with doddered willows and sky-parting poplars; no more fishing, with *Sartor*

---

[1] See chapter ix., section 76. This book now belongs to the Rev. E. Kenworthy Browne, who furnished me with most of the information in chapter xiii.
[2] *Letters.*

Resartus or Selden instead of bait, and a paint-brush instead of rod. Bletsoe, Turvey, Keysoe, Elstow, Goldington—adieu! The music of their names had all departed. They were nothing without Browne. 'Samarcand shall see my face no more!' Writing to Mrs. W. K. Browne, 25th April 1859,[1] FitzGerald says that he takes it for granted that she would not wish him to visit Goldington for some time, and he begs her not to ask him for compliment's sake. He would go, however, if she really desired it. As mementoes, Mrs. Browne sent him her husband's snuff-box, bought seven years previous by FitzGerald in Langham Place, 'the little stick that used to come on visits to London,' and the picture of the Spanish pointer by Stubbs. In memory of Browne, he had the picture put in a very broad black frame. The death of Browne not only spoilt Bedford for FitzGerald, it spoilt London too; he lost all curiosity about what London had to show. Browne was too much connected with his old taverns and streets not to fling a gloom over all.

[1] Unpublished letter.

END OF VOL. I.